A World of Equals

A Textbook on Gender

A World of Equals

A Textbook on Gender

Edited by

Susie Tharu

A. Suneetha

Uma Maheswari Bhrugubanda

Orient BlackSwan

A WORLD OF EQUALS: A TEXTBOOK ON GENDER

ORIENT BLACKSWAN PRIVATE LIMITED

Registered Office
3-6-752 Himayatnagar, Hyderabad 500 029, Telangana, India
Email: centraloffice@orientblackswan.com

Other Offices
Bengaluru, Chennai, Guwahati, Hyderabad, Kolkata,
Mumbai, New Delhi, Noida, Patna, Visakhapatnam

© Orient Blackswan Private Limited 2022
First published 2022

ISBN 978-93-5442-096-2

Typeset in Adobe Garamond Pro 11/13 *by*
Shine Graphics, Delhi 110 094

Printed at
Akash Press, New Delhi 110 020

Published by
Orient Blackswan Private Limited
3-6-752, Himayatnagar, Hyderabad 500 029, Telangana, India
Email: info@orientblackswan.com

Contributors

Asma Rasheed teaches at The EFL University, Hyderabad and is associated with Anveshi, Research Centre for Women's Studies. She teaches and researches critical pedagogy, ELT, gender studies, and translates from Urdu to English.

Deepa Sreenivas teaches at the Centre for Women's Studies, University of Hyderabad. She has published in the areas of popular visual culture, feminist pedagogy and childhood studies.

Rama Melkote is a retired professor of Political Science from Osmania University. She is a founder-member of Anveshi and has been an important public figure in Telangana for several decades.

Gogu Shyamala is a writer and scholar. She is the editor of *Nallapoddu*, a historical anthology of Dalit women's writing. She is associated with Anveshi and was Resident Fellow at the IAS-Nantes, France for the year 2020–21.

A. Suneetha is Senior Fellow at Anveshi, Hyderabad. Her research interests include gender and minority, violence against women and Muslim politics in the Deccan. She is on the editorial team for Anveshi Broadsheet on Contemporary Politics.

A long time student of Literary and Cultural Studies, Susie Tharu is best known perhaps for the two-volume anthology co-edited with K Lalita: *Women Writing in India: 600 B.C. to the Present*. She is a founder-member of Anveshi, Hyderabad.

Duggirala Vasanta is a retired professor, Department of Linguistics, Osmania University. She has been associated with Anveshi since 1986.

Vasudha Nagaraj is an advocate. She defends women in cases of domestic and sexual violence in trial courts. She also litigates on behalf of Dalits, tribals, human rights and environmental groups in the High Court.

Uma Maheswari Bhrugubanda teaches at The EFL University, Hyderabad and is associated with Anveshi. She teaches, researches and publishes in the areas of cinema, gender and sexuality, feminist theory, religion and secularism, and translation.

When you see this symbol in the book, it means there is accompanying content (such as links to useful information, videos, songs, illustrations, etc.) which you can access on the Orient BlackSwan Smart App. Look at the inside page of the front cover for more information on how to access this content on the Orient BlackSwan Smart App.

Contents

UNIT 13 Becoming Man

UNIT 14 Just Relationships: Being Together as Equals

UNIT 15 Our Bodies, Our Health

Acknowledgements

The editors would like to begin by thanking all the authors and translators. Without their enthusiasm and continued support this book would not have been possible.

Several other people too have been part of this book's journey and have helped shape it in its present form.

Many thanks are due to Smt. Shailaja Ramaiyyer and Dr K. Padmavathi for initiating this project back in 2015 and to Dr Parvathy of JNTU (H) for her commitment and support. Thanks to all the teachers of JNTU (H) and its affiliated colleges who taught the gender sensitisation course and gave us very useful feedback. We would like to name Dr Fatima Mary Sidotam in particular.

As we began revising and expanding the scope of the book to address an all-India readership as well as to include new chapters on masculinity, we were fortunate to have had the support of a number of people.

K. Lalita and Veena Shatrugna read initial drafts and gave us valuable suggestions for improvement.

Nikhila H. and Sherin B. S. contributed to the discussions on popular cinema in the book.

Torsa Saha enlivened the book with her illustrations.

Many other friends, colleagues and collectives helped in a number of different ways. Our deep gratitude to:

Achuth A., Laxman Aelay, Ashala Srinivas, A. Vijaya, Baidurya Chakrabarti, Bhangya Bhukya, Bhimrao Sawatkar, Chinna, Kavita Datir, Krishna Kumar, Pranoo Deshraju, Sujatha Devarapalli, Leila Gautham, Mohana Krishna Indraganti, Tejaswini Madabhushi, K. Satyanarayana, G. K. Mohan, Maya Pandit, M. A. Moid, M. Ravinder, M. Swathy, M. Madhava Prasad, Muralikrishna Mallepaku, Prabha Nagaraja, Shankar Pamarthy, Rahul Roy, Sajjad Shahid, Singaraju Ramadevi, Prasanna Shashidhar, Madhumeeta Sinha, Shugufta Shaheen, R. Srivatsan, Amit Sonawane, Pradeep Sunkari, Sabbanda Venkanna, Santhosh Raut, Shabnam Virmani, Shad Naved, Shankar Melkote, Srinivas Avasarala, Shital Morjaria, Srilakshmi Tadepally, Gita Ramaswamy, Vasudha Katju, T. Muraleedharan, Tashi Choedup, Swathy Margaret and to the Aravani Art Project, TARSHI, Tanishq and Turquoise Tales.

Finally we would like to thank Bikram Sharma for his meticulousness and patience. We are also grateful to all the other members of the Orient BlackSwan team—James Kanjamala and Satish Valla for their association with the project in its initial stages, and to Veenu Luthria, Padmaja Anant and Uday Rao for their enthusiastic and consistent support over the last five years.

Publisher's Acknowledgements

TEXTS

Amandeepa Sandhu, 'Rinku's Hair' in *Being Boys,* edited by Deeya Nayar and Radhika Menon, Tulika Books, 2015. Reproduced with permission of Tulika Books.

Jamaica Kincaid, 'Girl'. Copyright © 1978, Jamaica Kincaid, used by permission of The Wylie Agency (UK) Limited.

Krishna Kumar, 'Growing up Male' in *What is Worth Teaching?* by Krishna Kumar, Orient Blackswan Private Limited, 2009. Reproduced with permission of the author.

M. Muralikrishna, excerpt from *Autobiography as a Resource for Educational Theory: A Dalit Life Story.* Reproduced with permission of the author.

Uma Maheswari Bhrugubanda, *'How I Upstaged the "Clevers" of my Class',* translation of *'Ma Iskoolu Yaanivasariki Dummu Lepesina'* in *Dargamitta Kathalu* by Mohammed Khadeer Babu. Kavali: Kavali Prachuranalu, 3rd ed., 2006. Reprinted with permission of Mohammed Khadeer Babu.

M. Madhava Prasad, 'The Runaways', translation of 'Odi hodavaru' in *Jaguva Mattu Itaru* (Jaguva and Others) by K. V. Tirumalesh, Bangalore: Kalyani Prakashana, 1990. Reproduced with permission of the translator.

Gogu Shyamala, 'Obstacle Race' in *Father May be an Elephant and Mother Only a Small Basket, But...* by Gogu Shyamala, Navayana, 2012. Reproduced with permission of Navayana Publishing Pvt Limited and the author.

Vikram Seth, 'Founder's Day Speech' in *The Great Speeches of Modern India* edited by Rudrangshu Mukherjee, Random House India, 2011. Reprinted with permission of Penguin Random House, India.

Ritty A. Lukose, 'On Being Chethu: A Conversation with Devan', extract from 'Fashioning Gender and Consumption' in *Liberalization's Children* by Ritty A. Lukose, pp. 54–95. Copyright, 2009, Duke University Press. All rights reserved. Republished by permission of the copyright holder. www.dukeupress.edu.

Vimala, 'Vantillu' ('The Kitchen') in *Women Writing in India: 600 BC to the Present.* vol. 2, edited by Susie Tharu and K. Lalita. New Delhi: Oxford University Press, 1993. Reprinted with permission from Vimala Morthala.

Judy Brady, 'I Want a Wife', first published in *Ms* magazine 1970. Reproduced with permission of Maia Syfers.

Bhikkhunni Mutta, untitled poem, translated by Uma Chakravarti and Kumkum Roy, in *Women Writing in India: 600 BC to the Present,* vol. 1, edited by Susie Tharu and K. Lalita. New Delhi: Oxford University Press, 1991. Reprinted with permission of Susie Tharu.

Siddalingaiah, 'The Dalits Are Here' in *Steel Nibs are Sprouting: New Dalit Writing from South India. Dossier II: Kannada and Telugu,* edited by K. Satyanarayana and Susie Tharu. New Delhi: HarperCollins, 2013. Reproduced with permission of Susie Tharu.

B. N. Uniyal, 'In Search of a Dalit Journalist', *The Pioneer,* 16 November 1996. Reproduced with permission of the author.

Anveshi-Research Centre for Women's Studies. 'A "Conversation" between a Daughter and a Mother', adapted from an interview, http://www.anveshi.org.in/a-conversation-between-a-daughter-and-a-mother/, with permission of Gita Ramaswamy.

Jayaprabha, '*Chupulu*' ('Stares'), in *Women Writing in India: 600 BC to the Present,* vol. 2, edited by Susie Tharu and K. Lalita. New Delhi: Oxford University Press, 1993. Reprinted with permission of the author.

Natasha Choudhary, Asuthosh Tripathy and Beena George, extract adapted from '*Women's Economic Contribution through Their Unpaid Household Work: The Case of India.*' Report prepared by Evangelical Social Action Forum and HealthBridge. Used with permission of HealthBridge.

Suresh P. Thomas, excerpt from '*They Sat Down for Their Rights*', 5 May 2015, https://fountainink.in/reportage/they-sat-down-for-their-rights. Reprinted with permission of Suresh P. Thomas.

Flavia Agnes, 'The Search for a Good Marriage Counsellor' in *My Story… Our Story of Re-building Broken Lives,* 3rd edition, pp. 17–22. Mumbai: Majlis, 1990. Reprinted with permission of Flavia Agnes.

C. S. Lakshmi, poem in *Agents of Change,* Different Registers, *Literary Review, The Hindu,* 3 October 2004. Reprinted with permission of C. S. Lakshmi and The Hindu Group.

'Chityala Ailamma', extract from *We Were Making History: Life Stories of Women in the Telangana People's Struggle* by K. Lalita and Vasantha Kannabiran. Reprinted with permission of K. Lalita.

Interview with C. K. Janu, extract from *No Alphabet in Sight: New Dalit Writing from South Asia. Dossier 1: Tamil and Malayalam,* edited by K. Satyanarayana and Susie Tharu. New Delhi: Penguin Books, 2011. Reprinted with permission of Susie Tharu.

Review of *My Brother … Nikhil* by Dr Shad Naved. Reprinted with permission of Dr Shad Naved.

Sohaila Abdulali, 'I Fought for My Life … and Won', extract from an article first published in *Manushi: A Journal about Women and Society*, 1983. Reproduced with permission of Sohaila Abdulali.

M. Madhava Prasad, 'The Step Cut'. Reprinted with permission of M. Madhava Prasad.

Singaraju Ramadevi, account of masculinity in Telugu cinema. Reprinted with permission of Singaraju Ramadevi.

Love letters from Savitribai Phule to Jotiba Phule in *A Forgotten Liberator: The Life and Struggle of Savitribai Phule*, edited by Braj Ranjan Mani and Pamela Sardar. New Delhi: Mountain Peak, 2008, pp. 39–47. Reprinted with permission of Braj Ranjan Mani.

TARSHI, material from *The Blue Book* by TARSHI, Copyright © TARSHI, 1999, http://www.tarshi.net/downloads/blue-book.pdf. Reproduced with permission of TARSHI.

IMAGES AND ILLUSTRATIONS

Poster in Unit 5.1 on sex selection by the Ministry of Health and Family Welfare GOI.

The Burkini–Bikini cartoon in Unit 6.1 illustrated by Malcolm Evans. Reproduced with permission of Malcolm Evans of Evanscartoons.com.

Ismat Chughtai in Unit 6.2 by cartoonist Shankar Pamarthy. Reproduced with permission of Shankar Pamarthy.

Chindu Yellamma in Unit 6.4 from the book *Chindula Yellamma Yaadi*. Photo Courtesy: Bharat Bhushan, Dr K. Muthyam and Sabbanda Venkanna.

Rupa Bai Furdoonji in Unit 6.4 from Wikimedia Commons. Miss Rupa Bai with Surgeon major Edward Lawrie and Sir Thomas Lauder Brunton, F.R.S. 31 December 1891. https://commons.wikimedia.org/wiki/File:Rupa_Bai_Firdounji_(World_First_lady_anaesthetist),_Hyderabad_India.jpg.

'When They Sat Down for Their Rights' in Unit 8.4 illustrated by Shubhangi Singh. Reproduced with permission of Shubhangi Singh.

Drawings of moustaches in Unit 10.1 from the book '*A Little Book on Men*' by Rahul Roy. Illustrated by Anupama Chatterjee and Sherna Dastur. Reprinted with permission of Yoda Press.

Photograph of Regalla Acchamamba in Unit 10.2 by K. Lalita from *We Were Making History*.

Photograph of Chityala Ailamma in Unit 10.3 by K. Lalita from *We Were Making History*.

Dutee Chand in Unit 11.2 from Wikimedia Commons. Dutee Chand, Odisha Games, 9 July 2017. https://commons.wikimedia.org/wiki/File:Dutee_Chand_4x100m_Relay_Bronze_Medalist_-_Indian_Team_2017_(cropped).jpg. Licensed under CC BY-SA 4.0.

A collage of men's hairstyles in Unit 13.2 from the book '*A Little Book on Men*' by Rahul Roy. Illustrated by Anupama Chatterjee and Sherna Dastur. Reprinted with permission of Yoda press.

Rosa Parks in Unit 14.6 from Wikimedia Commons. Rosa Parks being fingerprinted by Deputy Sheriff D.H. Lackey after being arrested on February 22, 1956, during the Montgomery bus boycott, 22 February 1956. https://commons.wikimedia.org/wiki/File:Rosa_Parks_being_fingerprinted_by_Deputy_Sheriff_D.H._Lackey_after_being_arrested_on_February_22,_1956,_during_the_Montgomery_bus_boycott.png.

Images in Unit 15.1 (the menstrual cycle), 15.2 (a pregnant woman and her partner), 15.3 (how to use a condom), 15.5 (an upset woman), 15.5 (an upset man), 15.6 (men harassing a woman) and 15.6 (a group of friends) from *The Blue Book* by TARSHI, Copyright © TARSHI, 1999. http://www.tarshi.net/downloads/blue-book.pdf. Reproduced with permission of TARSHI.

Human body features in Unit 15.1 from Wikimedia Commons. Human body features, 2 May 2009, https://commons.wikimedia.org/wiki/File:Human_body_features_EN.svg. Licensed under CC BY-SA 3.0 Unported license.

Male Urethra in Unit 15.1 from Wikimedia Commons. Male Urethra N from OpenStax Anatomy and Physiology, 18 May 2016. https://commons.wikimedia.org/wiki/File:2603_Male_Urethra_N.jpg. Licensed under CC BY-SA 4.0.

External female genital organs in Unit 15.1 from Wikimedia Commons. External female genital organs in Handbook of Obstetric Nursing, 1902, by Francis W. N. Haultain and James Haig Ferguson, https://commons.wikimedia.org/wiki/File:Haultain_and_Ferguson_-_external_female_genital_organs.svg.

Human Fertilization in Unit 15.2 from Wikimedia Commons. Human Fertilization, 31 May 2012, https://commons.wikimedia.org/wiki/File:Human_Fertilization.png. Licensed under CC BY-SA 3.0 Unported license.

Pregnancy in Unit 15.2 from Wikimedia Commons. Pregnancy, Blausen.com staff (2014). 'Medical gallery of Blausen Medical 2014'. *WikiJournal of Medicine* 1 (2). DOI:10.15347/wjm/2014.010. ISSN 2002-4436. Licensed under CC BY-SA 3.0 Unported license.

Illustrations at the start of each chapter by Torsa Saha. Illustrations for 'Rinku's Hair' in Unit 1.4, 'How I Upstaged the "Clevers" of My Class' in Unit 2.5, 'Obstacle Race' in Unit 3.2, 'On Being Chethu' in Unit 3.4 and '#MeToo' in Unit 7.1 by Torsa Saha. Reproduced with permission of Torsa Saha.

Hand Graving Smartphone free icon, made by Freepik from www.flaticon.com.

VIDEOS

Ammayi, a short film inspired by Jamaica Kincaid's story 'Girl'. Reproduced with permission of writer and director Mohana Krishna Indraganti.

Babai, a Marathi short film. Reproduced with permission of writer and director Kavita Datir.

Bol/Speak, a production by the International Centre for Research on Women. Reproduced with permission of Shabnam Virmani.

When Women Unite, short film by Shabnam Virmani. Reproduced with permission of Shabnam Virmani.

Preface

This textbook grew out of a course designed for undergraduate engineering students in Hyderabad. Public figures, educationists, journalists, parents and ordinary citizens (like our present publisher) who learnt about the initiative invariably responded by saying 'this is the need of the hour.' The warmth and enthusiasm with which the course was received by students, teachers and, the press, no less, far exceeded our expectations. And the sentiment was shared across genders! We were thrilled to see students take home copies of the course material to share with their parents. Obviously, discussions that had started in class were continued over dinner. NGOs used the lessons in gender training sessions and realised that the material was also useful for stimulating discussion among older adults. Readers particularly appreciated the variety of writers and texts they encountered during the course of their discussions. Why is a book like this, which provides a deeper and more informed discussion of gender issues, the 'need of the hour?'

Uppermost in the minds of those who welcomed and supported this initiative was perhaps the disturbing degree of violence against women that is being reported now. The horrifying rape and murder of 'Nirbhaya' in December 2012 and other such incidents that followed, brought to the forefront the vulnerability of young women in public life and the urgent necessity of addressing the reasons and contexts that lead to such violence. But violence against women is not the only reason why a nuanced discussion of gender issues is urgent and imperative.

In recent months there have been several instances of public figures, industry leaders and well-known academics and scientists who have been charged with sexual harassment or who have roused public anger because of statements they made about women. Some of these statements and actions might have been 'innocent' in the sense that these people may not have thought what they were saying or doing was illegal or unacceptable; maybe they thought they could make verbal or physical advances to a colleague and get away with it. A better education in gender issues could have helped them avoid behaviour that not only causes hurt to others but also injures their reputation and standing. No serious professional today can afford to remain 'innocent' about gender issues.

As more and more women join the workforce and public life it becomes ever more important that men and women are comfortable working with each other. The Vice Chancellor of a university shared the information that foreign companies and institutions frequently complained that their Indian employees often lacked this level of comfort. She hoped the course and this book would go some distance in changing things.

Another reason why we all need an education in the various axes of inequality is that the analyses of inequality and the aspirations for equality have become more complex. And this is true whether those inequalities relate to race, religious affiliation, class, caste, disability, or the sexual spectrum. The worldwide 'Black Lives Matter' upsurges in the aftermath of the killing of George Floyd in the USA in June 2020 brought up issues ranging from violence against black people, bias in police training, to the invisibility of black people in public institutions and the myriad subtle and minute ways in which people of colour are disadvantaged. It is shocking to learn that oximeters, standardised for 'white' skins can give life-threatening erroneous readings when used on darker-skinned people. Young people would surely relate to the fact that all 'fashion' and 'style' assumes a slim, white (and in India, fair and upper caste) body. Dalit students have been driven to suicide by the corrosive everyday prejudice in universities. Scholars and activists worldwide are examining the parallels between the workings of race and caste discrimination. 'One person one vote' only marks the beginning of the journey of democracy.

We should note that there is both a bright and a dark side to these aspirations for equality. The bright side relates to the movements that have emerged and the possibilities that have opened up over the last few decades for marginalised people. As we write this in 2021 in the midst of the COVID-19 pandemic we note that women prime ministers in Germany and New Zealand have been exceptionally successful in steering their countries through the challenge. Kerala's woman health minister proved herself a model leader, and women epidemiologists in India and across the world are providing direction to governments and industries. India's star tennis and badminton players are women; women head our largest and most important banks; women scientists, artists, writers and industrialists have won international acclaim. All this would have been unimaginable even at the beginning of the twenty-first century.

However—and this is the dark side—the fact that a few have 'made it' to the top, does not indicate that bias, prejudice and violence no longer exist. On the contrary, the world has become all the more aware of the multifaceted modes in which these inequalities are produced and maintained. Beyond the constitutional guarantees of equality which we all so easily affirm, there are myriad hidden, everyday scenarios in which power and prejudice operate to devalue, exclude, humiliate, discriminate and suppress.

Over the past three or four decades, social movements of different kinds (for example, the women's movement, the dalit movement, movements against racial and sexual discrimination) have systematically investigated and exposed such everyday as well as structural discrimination. They have also developed concepts and practices to engage with it. An education in the many dimensions of inequality is imperative, both for those seeking to realise their civil and human rights and those who may be, knowingly or unknowingly, guilty of denying these rights to others—or even of breaking the law. Sexual discrimination and violence, is an offence and liable to prosecution under the law.

In brief, a more informed and analytical awareness of a) different dimensions in the understanding of gender, b) the connections between gender and other forms of inequality, and c) existing laws, will help create happier and more productive workplaces, better friendships across social divides and genders, and more egalitarian and fulfilling relationships. A book like this is a small step in this direction.

Although questions of gender and sexuality are central to human experience, they are among the least open to rational study or discussion. This is all the more so with young adults who are often poorly informed (or misinformed) about these questions, even as they are preoccupied with them. This book offers students an opportunity to learn more about these issues, reflect on them in relation to their own lives and to discuss them openly and rationally.

As a first principle, we have avoided both admonition and preaching. The stress is on information about studies/research in the field, recent analyses of gender issues and the arguments around them. We should emphasise here that the course is equally interested in the sphere of the subjective. So, it creates opportunities for students to reflect on their own experience, learn from the experiences of others who are like them as well as others who come from very different walks of life. Through stories, poems, autobiographical accounts and analyses of popular culture, the textbook offers insight into themes and experiences that have been overlooked by the mainstream (a woman's life in the kitchen, a boy learning to cope with caste discrimination at school, the experience of an 81-year-old handcart puller in Pune market, a woman describing the misery of her married life, a famous couple whose relationship is centred on their shared work). Each of these 'texts' is treated as a basis for discussion and further exploration.

While it is very unlikely that students will actually speak about their own experiences in class, especially if these experiences are in any way traumatic, these readings will help them reflect on those experiences, maybe talk about them with close friends, and hopefully also begin to deal with them in their own ways.

We have designed this book in the belief that knowledge and discussion will enable students to think more rationally and justly about gender issues in their personal lives and in society. While information about laws and restrictions is provided where relevant, the emphasis is on *understanding* issues and on the promise of better social and personal relations.

EDITORS

What is Gender, and Why Should We Study It?

1.1 INTRODUCTION

What is *gender*, and why should we study it? Simply defined, gender is the social, cultural and physical condition of being male or female. The interesting thing about gender is that different societies and cultures have different ideas about what it means to be a man or a woman, masculine or feminine. What is more, even within the same society these ideas change over time. Your idea of masculinity or femininity may be different from that of your parents. Family upbringing, education, cultural traditions and practices, the toys children play with, the stories they are told, films, advertising, places like beauty parlours or *akharas*—they all contribute to the idea of gender. Boys are not born aggressive or violent, just as girls are not born naturally gifted with housekeeping skills.

Why should we study gender? The most important reason may be that the experience of gender is emotionally charged for everyone, and especially so for young adults. Being a woman or being a man is a source of different kinds of pleasure and positive emotions. But the experience can also be painful, confusing and a source of many anxieties. We all know that relationships between men and women are also shadowed by violence, both physical and psychological.

However, these aspects of life and the emotions related to them are veiled in secrecy and rarely talked about. Only recently have we begun to actually study them. In the next unit, which is about growing up as male or female, a well-known educationist recalls how, when he was growing up, girls and boys were kept segregated when outside. He constantly pondered over gender-related questions but received no help in thinking them through. We hope this book will be of some help when you think about such topics.

Are There No Problems?

In 2012, the song 'Why This Kolaveri Di?' by film star Dhanush went viral. In a humorous mixture of broken English and street Tamil ('Tanglish!'), a young man asks a young woman why she is so angry.[1] The singer's point seems to be that we live in a modern world; why can't men and women just be friends now? The word 'just' suggests there are no real problems that stand in the way of such friendship.

So the first question is: Are there no problems? In the song, the young man touches on the question of class-caste relations. (He discusses it in terms of being fair- or dark-skinned.) 'Should such things matter?' the singer asks. He is right; they should not matter. But the problem is that they do! What is more, class-caste power is not something in the mind. It is structured into society, and we encounter it every day and in most of the different contexts we move in. Indeed, popular film songs often allow us to feel the pulse of both conservative ideas of romance and changing attitudes towards relationships between men and women. Have you heard 'The Breakup Song' from the 2016 Hindi film *Ae Dil Hai Mushkil*? Unlike many Bollywood songs, this song presents us with the girl's point of view and her decision to break up with her partner. You may also want to learn more about a project called Gaana Rewrite, which was initiated by the not-for-profit women's organisation Akshana Centre. The Gaana Rewrite Competition asked participants to rewrite popular Bollywood songs that were sexist and degrading to women.[2]

Like class and caste, gender is considered a key axis of inequality. Women have had to fight against bias, discrimination and violence in many spheres of life. In the process, they have opened up questions that have enriched our understanding of personal relations, psychology, social formations, culture, politics, law, sports and even science. In recent times, the discussion has also turned to the upbringing of boys, the assumptions society holds about men, the pressure to be 'masculine', and the need to reshape these practices and ideas. In this unit, the story 'Rinku's Hair' delicately explores a young Sikh boy's worry about keeping his hair long. If you search on the internet for 'TED Talks masculinity', you will get an idea of the scope of this discussion. However, we should also note that people benefitting from social or cultural hierarchies are often happy to keep things the way they are. Men are therefore more likely to be happy with existing gender arrangements, just as white people are with race hierarchies, wealthy people with existing economic structures, and upper castes with the caste system. They find it difficult to understand what the *'kolaveri'* is all about! What is more, they are quick to complain if they sense any change that questions their position or displaces their authority.

We suggest that both women and men stand to gain from a world in which they are equal. What is more, society too stands to gain from this equality. In 2015, a worldwide study titled 'State of the World's Fathers' showed why fathers need to be more involved with raising children, as 'an involved father would yield a multitude of benefits, at both the family and the national levels'.

Gender Studies: Three Phases

In this book, you will be introduced to what can be described as the third phase in gender studies. The first phase can be traced back to the 1970s and 80s, when the women's movement first raised the question of gender as an axis of inequality, power and domination. Before that, it was generally assumed that all human beings, or all citizens, were equal. It was believed that some sections of society (such as women and 'lower' castes) needed a little extra help because of prejudices in the past that had held them back—but the fact that gender, class or caste privileges were structured into society, economy and culture was not recognised. The women's movement pointed out that the inequality of women was created and perpetrated by society. A new interdisciplinary field called 'Women's Studies' emerged to study this form of inequality. This was a key moment in gender studies and the process of addressing inequalities women face in all aspects of life.

The second phase stressed the need to understand gender as relational. This meant understanding that different societies had different ideas about what it meant to be a woman or a man, and that even those ideas changed over time. In other words, the idea of gender allowed us to move beyond biological categories to seriously study social and historical dimensions of inequality. Additionally, in this phase, people began talking of gender as involving male, female and those in a gender spectrum that goes beyond the binary.

Today, we realise that it is important to understand gender as also affected by caste, class, region and the many other forms of inequality, difference and heterogeneity in our society. So, as you will see, we need to carefully study specific contexts in which an issue or a question comes up. For instance, to usefully understand the experience of a female homeworker who rolls *beedis* in Srikakulam, we have to understand gender in the context of the restriction of women to the home, the global rise of informal labour, the relative invisibility of home-based work, poor pay for domestic workers and the sensitivity of trade unions to specific issues. The experience of an educated, middle-class, dalit man looking for work or housing in Bangalore will be markedly different from that of an upper-caste Hindu or young Muslim man in the same situation.

This book also introduces you to some of the many issues that come in the way of gender equality and mutually respectful relationships. If you look at the table of contents, you will get a sense of these issues. You will also see that Unit 14 is about 'just friendships', by which we mean friendships that are 'just' or connected to justice and equality. Truly 'just' relationships are between equals.

Democratic Nations, Rights and the Promise of Equality

One of the main reasons for studying gender is that we are interested in equality in the broadest and most inclusive sense of the term. Most modern nations describe themselves as democratic and committed to equality. They also seek to promote 'brotherhood' among their citizens, and aspire towards liberty from bondage of all kinds. Governments endorse the rule of law, as opposed to the rule of strength or use of violence. They protect the rights of the individual. As a political unit, the nation aims to provide a good life—in particular, security and happiness—for all its citizens.[3] In other words, attention to the gender question expands our understanding of equality and therefore also the scope of our nationalism.

A well-known slogan from the 1970s is 'women hold up half the sky'. Men hold up only one half—even if they sometimes think they hold up the entire sky.

Both halves of the sky need to be held up. And finally, in a democracy, equals come together to study and discuss matters that concern them. This is what we also aim to do through this book.

> ***Points to discuss:***
>
> 1. Can you think of a reason why we have placed the word 'brotherhood' within single quotation marks?
> 2. Can you think of a famous slogan from history that expresses the ideas that underlie nationalism? [Hint: the French Revolution.] If not, can you make up a slogan?
> 3. Many people feel that the important ideal of equality is too easily forgotten in the focus on a single national culture. What do you think? For example, can the nation be equally proud of the Gond culture of central India, the stories and songs of fisherfolk of Odisha, the Christian culture of Nagaland or Mizoram, the architecture and gardens of the Mughals, Carnatic music, the narratives of the Mahabharata and the songs by Akka Mahadevi or Lal Ded?

1.2 GENDER EQUALITY MILESTONES

It should give you some pleasure to note that in India we have had an important history of government initiatives and laws directed at ensuring gender equality. Although it is true that laws are not the whole story, they are very important. It is also important to know the kinds of behaviour that are criminal and can invite legal punishment. What follows is a brief account of the most important milestones in gender equality.

In 1935, women received limited voting rights along with men. In 1950, independent India was among the very first countries in the world to have universal suffrage, or the right to vote in elections. In many countries, including some European countries, this happened much later. Article 14 of the Indian Constitution guarantees the equality of all citizens. This includes men, women and children, the poor and the rich, dalits, tribals, Other Backward Classes (OBCs) and members of all religions.

1975 was an important turning point. The United Nations (UN) declared it the International Year of Women. The Government of India set up a committee to study and report on what was happening to women in the country. The report of the Committee on the Status of Women in India, titled *Towards Equality* (1974–75), came as a shock since it demonstrated that, on many counts, the condition of the vast majority of women had actually deteriorated since Independence. What was more, the pace at which the deterioration was taking place had accelerated over the years. The sex ratio was declining. Women were excluded from the new jobs that had been created with the arrival of industrialisation and modernisation. The number of women in all elected bodies was declining. Girls in rural areas did not attend school or dropped out.

For scholars and administrators, the questions were: How did this happen? How did belief in constitutional guarantees and modernisation turn out to be so deceptive? How did the development process overlook women? Did their education make scholars and administrators blind to the continuing marginalisation of women?

The report came out at a time when other questions were also being raised: about violence in the family (from abuse and assault to dowry deaths); about sexual violence and custodial rape (rape by the police or by other authority figures such as hostel wardens); and about wages and property rights. Academics began to ask why the humanities and social sciences had remained blind to these concerns, and women's groups all over the country took up these issues. One of the very first groups of this kind was the Progressive Organisation of Women (POW), formed by women students of Osmania University in Hyderabad in 1974. Other such organisations that emerged in the late 1970s and 80s include the Forum Against Oppression of Women (FAOW) in Mumbai, and Saheli and Jagori in Delhi.

Another disturbing fact was that it was very difficult for women to get justice in the courts. Patriarchal attitudes present in the law and in the functioning of courts worked against women. There was a call for law reform and for the passing of new laws. In Unit 7 on sexual harassment, Unit 9 on domestic violence and Unit 12 on sexual violence, you will find information on the special laws that have been introduced to support women in their fight against violence. These special laws have been framed keeping in mind the unique form of violence experienced by women—the kind which is often invisible and considered by many to be 'natural'. Not only new laws, but also changes in infrastructure (such as all-women police stations and family courts) have been introduced to enable women to make use of the law.

The 73rd amendment to the Indian Constitution, passed in 1992, provides for the reservation of a third of the seats in village *panchayats* for women. This major legislation was aimed at correcting the imbalance in the political representation of men and women, and ensuring more attention to issues that concern women.

That said, we need to remember that gender issues extend beyond law and government policy. Much of what we understand as gender oppression or injustice takes place in the complex social and cultural sphere of everyday life. The discussions in the units that follow will introduce you to some of these issues. We have tried to do this through autobiographical accounts, stories, films and, of course, informative lessons and discussions.

We are frequently bombarded with messages about being men or being women in our everyday lives. These come in the form of explicit instructions (dress like this, don't cross your legs, wear Brand X jeans, or use Brand Y whitening cream) as well as subtle, unspoken messages. There is a widespread feeling today that this 'education' which takes place in our homes, schools, streets, in the media, and which even affects our dreams and desires, is at best inappropriate and outdated, and at worst, dangerous. We need to rethink and revise our ideas and assumptions about gender and other issues of inequality in the contemporary context. Only open discussion and a rational and informed approach can help us grapple with these questions in our own lives and in the world around us.

1.3 THE CONTEXT TODAY

We turn to some key aspects of the current context in India that have a bearing on our study of gender.

Today, there are more women in colleges and universities, and more women working in different kinds of jobs, than there were even a decade ago. We therefore encounter more women in public life than before. Just less than half (42%) of the students studying in institutes of higher education today are female. Women have aspirations for success and their parents are supporting them—often with great difficulty. Commentators have called this a quiet revolution.

As Unit 8 on women's work shows in greater detail, women are found (often, in substantial numbers) in almost every sphere of employment. What this means is that in cities as well as in smaller towns, men and women are interacting with one another in colleges, workplaces, public transport, public places such as streets, shopping areas and cinemas, in the field of sport and in numerous other areas.

At the same time, student populations have become more inclusive and heterogeneous. Young people from different classes and castes, and students from regions that used to be regarded as 'backward', are now in college. There are many first-generation learners. This is a result of the success of Indian democracy. The desire for equality in every group has become stronger and more complex. Campuses have become places where students must develop the skills to engage with different people, shed outdated attitudes and learn how to deal with conflict productively in a diverse society.

Employers are acutely conscious of the need to attract and retain a skilled workforce. Since a larger proportion of employees are now women, there is a new acceptance of women's needs. For example, government institutions and some companies allow paternity leave for fathers to help with childcare, longer periods of childcare leave for mothers and sometimes also for fathers, flexible schedules for women with young children, crèches for the care of young children and workspaces that are free of prejudice.

Institutions and companies have become aware that diversity in their teams—be it sales, production or management—leads to wider reach and greater profits. Global companies especially stress the need for people who can work in a 'flat' company culture, among equals. Nowadays, there is also a deep concern about sexual bias, harassment and violence in public life. Much that might have remained hidden earlier is now becoming public. Big names have been indicted. There is significant awareness that men and boys need to be informed about the legal and social implications of their behaviour.

1.4 FURTHER READING

Now read and enjoy this story by Amandeep Sandhu. You can take turns to read it out loud, section by section in class, or read it at home. Have you ever experienced anything similar?

Rinku's Hair

'GIRL! GIRL! GIRL! You're a girl,' Rajan taunted Rinku in the school playground. 'We don't play with girls—go!'

Eleven-year-old Rinku and his elder-by-two-years sister, Pinku, were the only Sikh children in the school they'd joined after moving to Bengaluru some months ago. Pinku was happy there and had made friends, but Rinku hated it. Almost every day, the boys in his class would pull at the topknot his hair was tied in, covered with a small white handkerchief. His hair would tumble out and the teasing would begin: 'Girlie, girlie!'

He hated them. He hated Bengaluru. And he hated his long hair. 'Why can't I just cut it?' he asked Ma angrily, as she washed his hair one Sunday.

'*Beta*, we are Sikhs. We grow our hair long.'

'Why does Daddy not have long hair then?'

Now Ma went silent. After a while she said, 'Daddy does not listen to me.'

'I want to be like Daddy.'

'You don't want to listen to me?'

The next Sunday, after breakfast, Daddy left to get a haircut. Rinku was jealous. He admired his father's guts. He wanted to grow up quickly so he too could cut his hair. It was hair-wash day again, and again he fought with Ma. This time she scolded him into silence.

At school, Rajan and the others now had nicknames for him: Candy, Babe, Chica … The teasing tore him up. He felt like beating up those teasers but the school had very strict rules about physical fights. He couldn't complain either, for then he would be called a snitch.

It started right from assembly. Rajan would push him from the boy rows to the girl rows. The girls would push him back. Though he was not tall, Rinku started standing at the back of the boy rows so no one could push him around. But he got scolded by his class teacher for not standing according to his height, and was hauled up front. Everyone sniggered.

One day, returning home from school, Pinku said, 'Look, Daddy's haircutting place has a new signboard!' Rinku looked up and gaped at the big, shining scissors above Chamku Hair Style Saloon. After that, each day, on his way to school and back, Rinku would slow down in front of the barber shop, look at the signboard for a while, and then go home.

❖ ❖ ❖

Even Rinku did not know when he started looking for a big pair of scissors at home. It became his obsession till he finally found one in the kitchen. He moved the blades and listened to the scraping sound they made. Now he had to wait for the right time to use it. He stopped fighting with Ma and kept away from Pinku. One day, while Daddy was in office, Ma asked Rinku if he wanted to go with Pinku and her to the mall. He said he would stay at home. It was his big chance.

Rinku smuggled the big scissors from the kitchen to the bathroom, opened out his hair and brought the scissors to it. Then he panicked. Frozen in front of the mirror, his hair falling over his shoulders, scissors in hand, Rinku was paralysed with fear. No, he couldn't do it. Ma would get to know. She would be furious. Recovering, he tied his hair back loosely and replaced the scissors in the kitchen. For many days after that he felt ashamed, and cursed himself for chickening out when he'd got his chance.

When the next opportunity came, Rinku grabbed it. Pinku was away playing with her friends and Ma had gone to her kitty party. He rushed to the bathroom with the scissors, opened his hair, and wasted no time in snipping off a bit at the ends. The hair fell on the floor and then panic gripped him again. This time he tied his knot tighter before picking up the cut strands and the scissors and running out of the bathroom.

❖ ❖ ❖

But what was he to do with the hair? The dustbin was too obvious. Ma might see it.

He was thinking of dashing out of the house to throw it in the garbage mound outside, when he heard Ma return. Where would he hide it? With Pinku's things! He ran to her bed, and lifted her mattress to shove the hair under it. There, on the wooden plank, he was surprised to see Ma's underclothes. He dropped the mattress and picked up the other end. This side was clear and he quickly placed his cut hair there.

That night, after Ma and Daddy went to sleep, he whispered, 'Pinku, I want to tell you something.'

'I'm sleeping,' Pinku grumbled.

'I cut my hair!'

'What?' Pinku sat up wide awake.

'Yes, a bit. Just a bit.'

'You're crazy, you idiot! But where? Your hair looks the same.'

'You can't tell,' said a disappointed Rinku. 'But once I cut it more, I'll become a boy! I don't look like one. I have long hair, like you, like a girl.'

'As if! Long hair doesn't make you a boy or a girl!'

They fell silent. Then Rinku asked, 'You'll do me a favour?'

'What?'

'I have hidden my hair under your mattress. You'll throw it out for me?'

'Under my mattress? Yuckkk! How dare you! No, I won't. I'm going to tell Ma!' Pinku jumped up to put on the light.

'Wait,' whispered Rinku forcefully. 'I saw Ma's things under your mattress. If you tell her about my hair, I'll tell her that you steal her clothes.'

'I ... I ...' Pinku fumbled. How could she tell Rinku that she had only taken Ma's bra to see how it felt to wear it? She'd meant to quietly put it back, but now this irritating Rinku had caught her.

Pinku pulled out her torch and looked under the mattress. Then she tore a piece of paper from her notebook, made Rinku pick up the hair and put it on the paper, folded it neatly and put it into her schoolbag. 'Ugh! You are so yuck!'

'Thank you, Pinku!'

Next week Rinku cut his hair some more. Again he asked Pinku to throw it out and she had to agree. In about three weeks he lost a good six inches of hair and was thrilled! 'Wait and watch,' he thought to himself when Rajan and the others troubled him in school. The summer holidays were starting in a month and he decided he would cut his hair bit by bit, so that by the next school term he would become a boy like other boys. He didn't let himself think about what Ma would say.

Dadaji came to stay with them as he always did in summer. For the first time, Rinku watched curiously as his grandfather brushed his moustache, applied Simco on his beard and tucked it in with pins, how he made a knot of his hair and tied his turban neatly, pleat on pleat. Dadaji would ask Rinku to hold the long cloth and stand in one corner of the room, and then he would slowly walk towards Rinku layering the turban on his head. Sometimes Dadaji would remove his turban and put it on Rinku's head.

Rinku helped Dadaji wash his turban. They stood on the roof with the cloth open between them, holding its ends, so it dried in the wind. The cloth bulged out like the sails of a ship, and they went on a ride together in the sea, talking about dolphins and sharks and whales. When they went for a walk in the park, Dadaji told him stories about the Sikh gurus and about Punjab. He made *sarson ka saag* for Rinku and the others, and Rinku helped him all through the cooking. Ma got a holiday.

In Dadaji, Rinku had found a friend. Someone he could talk to, who would relate to his anxieties. He started discussing more adult topics, such as what other boys in the class talked about, the latest movies, and even football. One day, Rinku came back from school on a high and blurted out to Dadaji, 'Rajan did not tease me today. He's started teasing that new boy, Karim, who wears a white *topi* on his head.'

Dadaji was surprised. 'But why does Rajan tease you?'

'Because I have long hair. He and the others call me a girl.'

'Do you know why you have long hair?'

'Ma forces me to keep long hair.' Rinku got his chance to complain.

'I don't think anyone can force you. When you grow up you can keep your hair whichever way you want.'

'I can cut my hair?' A pang of guilt arose in Rinku for having cut some already in secret. He wouldn't any more, he quickly decided.

'Yes, you are free to do that, even though our tradition is different. Like it is Karim's tradition to wear a cap.'

'Why doesn't Daddy keep his hair long?'

'*Beta*, I think I am responsible for that. When Daddy was small like you, I had a travelling job. I never spent enough time with him, to talk ...'

'Daddy also doesn't spend any time with me.'

'Yes, I can see that. I was also like that. So I never got to talk to him about anything. Even about why it is a tradition for Sikhs not to cut their hair or to tell him all the stories I tell you. That is why I come over to be with you and Pinku. I don't want to neglect you.

About your hair, what do your friends say?'

'That I am a girl. That only girls have long hair.'

'Now that is sad. Have you ever faced up to them when they tease you?'

'No. They open my hair. I hate it. I hate this school.' Rinku was on the verge of tears.

'When someone teases you, you must face up to them. It shuts them up.'

'No one wants to talk to me or play with me.'

'The bullies will never accept you, *beta*. A bully will find ways to harass you. If not about your hair, then about how you look, or how many cars you have ... anything.'

'That means ...'

'That means, if you don't let it bother you, what the bully says or does, he will stop. Not immediately maybe, but slowly.'

Rinku didn't look convinced.

'Okay, I will show you what you can do with your hair. You need not wear a handkerchief,' Dadaji said.

'Then?'

Dadaji asked him to wait till the next day, and that evening he disappeared for an hour or so.

Next morning, when Rinku was getting ready for school, Dadaji brought out a square piece of cloth, eighteen inches by eighteen inches, with laces at its ends. He first covered Rinku's head with it, starting at the forehead and tying one set of laces tightly behind his head. Then he deftly wound the rest of the cloth around the topknot and secured it in place with the other laces. It was firmer than the small handkerchief, which felt loose even when it had just been tied. This would be much more difficult for bullies to remove. Dadaji said,

'Now go to school in your new *patka*. And because you are secure, it becomes your job to protect Karim from losing his *topi* which can't be tied to his head.'

Rinku looked at himself in the mirror and grinned. His whole head was covered now. He touched his topknot and it was hard and set, like a rock. The maroon *patka* also matched his shorts and tie. He suddenly felt mature, older than he had been just the previous day. His eyes gleamed with pride.

It was Rinku's eyes that kept Rajan away from him. No one touched him at assembly either. There was something about Rinku that had changed overnight. It was not just his *patka* but the way he walked, the way he looked. Karim stood next to him and no one said anything even to him. Rinku's friends came to admire his new look and wanted to take selfies with him on their mobile phones.

And at lunchtime, he shared his tiffin with Karim, who was thankful for finding a first friend in school.

NOTES

1. A century ago, Rokeya Sakhawat Hossain wrote 'Sultana's Dream', a story that has a humorous take on how women see men! The story can be found on the internet here: https://digital.library.upenn.edu/women/sultana/dream/dream.html.

2. You can find a report on the initiative and sample rewritten songs here: http://www.firstpost.com/entertainment/gaana-rewrite-reimagines-sexist-bollywood-lyrics-in-a-feminst-manner-to-promote-safety-in-public-places-3358482.html.

3. In political theory, nationalism is associated with the rise of modern, democratic states where liberty, equality and fraternity are important ideals. This is all the more so in post-colonial nation states such as India. Nationalism, here, does not refer to anti-minority chauvinism.

Socialisation: Making Women, Making Men

2.1 INTRODUCTION

Before we leave for college or go to work, most of us look into a mirror. We see our reflection. But things get a little complicated if we ask, 'Who exactly is looking at this reflection?' It is true that the eyes that actually see the reflection belong to the person who is looking. But at another level—and this is more interesting—she (or he) is looking through the eyes of others who will see her (or him). She checks her reflection carefully, worrying about what they will think. She combs her hair and arranges it to look good to those people she wants to please (and sometimes maybe to shock those people she wants to shock!). She adjusts that image of herself to leave a good impression on her teachers, on someone who may be interviewing her for a job, on a boy or girl she likes, on her special group of friends. Finally, she leaves the house with a face that

is acceptable to society and one that she is happy with (mostly!). It is her own face—but it is also a social face.

This is an illustration of the process through which society shapes and trains people to become social individuals. Social scientists call this process *socialisation*.

From a young age, boys and girls are taught to be the kind of people their society wants. The process begins early—in the family. It begins with the clothes children are made to wear, the games they play and the toys they are given. They learn about the parts of their bodies that should be hidden, bodily functions that should not be talked about and questions they should not ask. This 'training' continues in school through teachers, textbooks, games and other activities. Boys, especially, learn a great deal about 'being a man'. Songs, films, advertisements and stories contribute to this process. Children are also socialised into appropriate or 'correct' behaviour for their class, caste, religion, place in the family and so on. For example, everyday statements or advice which we never think about too much, such as, 'Never speak back to the *dora*'s family', 'meat smells bad', 'a good girl does not look at men', all add up to tell us how to behave and how to act with others. In the process of growing up and becoming adults, children are expected to absorb that training and make it their own. Sometimes the training is subtle, sometimes it is overt. Young people from elite families learn to expect that others should respect and serve them, while others are taught that they should be subservient. Girls learn how to do housework. They might become shy, soft, and afraid; they are taught to remain silent even when insulted or attacked (this is often regarded as preparation for marriage). Boys may feel that it is manly to be aggressive and unmanly to express emotions. They may feel ashamed to help with the housework.

The experience of being trained to become a woman can be difficult for girls who enjoy playing games or wearing clothes that are supposedly only for boys. Likewise, the experience of being trained to become a man can be difficult for boys who enjoy performing activities or wearing clothes that are supposedly only for girls. It is truly painful and confusing for those whose gender is not clearly male or female (for more on this, read Unit 11 on the gender spectrum).

As children approach puberty—when girls begin to have periods, and both boys and girls change physically—a new wave of instructions hit them about being careful, or not spending too much time with the other sex. Since these instructions and warnings often come without any information about what is happening to them physically and what it all means, it can leave them embarrassed and confused. We

hope you will find the information in this book about the body and sexuality useful.

You may have heard a famous saying by the French philosopher, Simone de Beauvoir: 'One is not born, but rather becomes, a woman.' In other words, gender is not natural—it is socially shaped. The important thing to understand is that babies are not born with femininity or masculinity. They are shaped into socially acceptable women and men. As children grow, they learn the many unwritten and often unspoken rules about being a good girl or a smart boy.

In this unit, we will read and discuss five accounts of growing up. Each directs our attention to a different aspect of what is involved in becoming a man or a woman. Each also explores some of the problems associated with traditional socialisation. You will see the short film *Ammayi* (*Life of a Girl*, 2016) made by Mohana Krishna Indraganti. His film, and the short story 'Girl' (written by the famous Caribbean writer Jamaica Kincaid), capture the process through which a girl is socialised. Both highlight the relentlessness, irrationality and violence of this process. The girl in *Ammayi* manages to rebel a little more easily than the girl in Kincaid's story. Notice also that it is primarily the responsibility of mothers to ensure that both girls and boys are trained to be what society wants them to be. We need to understand that society has different messages and requirements for women from different groups—these different groups may cover caste, class, religious affiliation or any other form of difference. A dalit girl growing up in a village learns what it means to be a woman in ways that are quite different from a middle-class girl in a city.

In comparison to girls, boys are expected to be strong, rough, dominating; they are not supposed to feel fear, express emotion or cry.

They worry a great deal about **performance**. This is related to a successful career, sexual prowess or capability, and the notion that they have to lead and control—even if this is done through violence. Such ideas of masculinity make it difficult for men to behave naturally around women or to have happy, intimate relationships with them. There is a compulsion for girls to look pretty and for boys to look strong and healthy. What is more, boys must excel at school—even stand first—as we learn from many popular advertisements, such as those made by Complan.[1] Indeed, most advertisements for 'health' drinks for children promise to better prepare them for a competitive world, with more recent ones including girls. All this can exert huge pressure on girls and boys.

The extract from the essay 'Growing up Male', by Krishna Kumar, further explores these issues from the perspective of a boy growing up in a small town in India. He goes to a boys' school and is deprived of ordinary everyday interactions with girls. Since the girls and boys behave so differently (boys loiter in the streets on the way home; girls rush back home in groups), he begins to think of them as somehow not quite human and grows afraid of what a relationship with a woman might involve.

Caste differences also play a role in the experiences that young boys and girls face in their growing years. Many families are particular about who may enter the kitchen and eat or drink from the plates or glasses that family members use. We know that in some schools, upper-caste children refuse to eat the midday meal if the cook is a dalit. Not all boys enjoy male privilege equally. If you are a child from a dalit caste or speak a marginalised language or belong to a minority group, then the experiences you face may be very different from those of other children. In 'The Story of My Silence', M. Muralikrishna reflects on his school life as a dalit student, giving us new insights into why some students are 'active' in class while others are 'dull'.

The last piece, by Mohammed Khadeer Babu, is a delightful story about a boy who is poor and, what is more, though he lives in Andhra Pradesh, doesn't speak Telugu at home. He is laughed at and dismissed by his teachers and by the elite girls who are the teachers' favourites and generally considered to be the 'clever' ones. Schools should be places where all children are treated equally, but often they actually reinforce social divisions and can demoralise children from poor or otherwise marginalised families. In this case, the protagonist is from a poor Muslim family and does not speak the 'good' Telugu of the upper-caste teachers and students. The story is about how he battles the humiliation he faces at school, and his heart-warming fight for self-respect. It is interesting that in the story, the dialogue the boy recites at a school event, to the delight of the audience, is that of the dacoit Gabbar Singh, a character from one of the biggest blockbusters of Indian cinema—the 1975 Hindi film, *Sholay*. Played by actor Amjad Khan, Gabbar Singh was the anti-hero outlaw of the film whose mannerisms and lines were immensely popular across the country. Gabbar's Hindustani dialogues, which the boy listened to many times on his father's tape recorder at home, obviously appealed to him and were easier to remember and recite than the classical Telugu of his textbooks. In comparison, what the 'clevers' of the class reproduce is classical religious music which is less accessible and more the culture of a smaller percentage of people.

One of the reasons for an interest in gender socialisation is that socialisation is producing unacceptable results. Scholars and activists are asking: Is the violence in our society connected to the socialisation of men? Is it right to treat the environment of harassment that girls have to endure, and the anxieties that boys experience, as 'normal'? Can it not be changed to enable women and men to enjoy happy and meaningful relationships? And finally, not all girls want to be soft—they also want to be strong, play games, take risks or climb mountains. Similarly, boys need to express emotion and should be allowed to do so freely; they can be afraid, sympathise with people, care for others or write poetry. Imagine a society where both boys and girls are socialised into being sensitive, kind and strong.

2.2 PREPARING FOR WOMANHOOD

'Girl' by Jamaica Kincaid was first published in *The New Yorker* in 1978. The story reads like a waterfall of instructions from a mother to her daughter, a young girl who is probably around twelve or thirteen years old. You will notice that there are no full stops in the piece, only semicolons! The girl receives instructions about housework—from washing clothes to cleaning the house, from cooking to sewing and mending. What is interesting is that the mother not only wants to teach the girl housework, but is also anxious to teach her something else; she wants to teach her to be a good girl, or, to put it more accurately, she wants to train her in such a manner that everyone in society will recognise her as a good and respectable girl. There are instructions on how to walk, how to eat, what to sing where, whom to talk to and whom to avoid. You may have heard such instructions in your own house too. Twice, the girl tries to respond, but without much success. In this piece, we feel that the girl is unhappy,

confused, angry and even ready to rebel. Most of the time, however, both boys and girls absorb instructions and obey them, even when they are not forced to. In other words, they internalise their socialisation. Read the slightly abridged version we have given below.

Girl

Wash the white clothes on Monday and put them on the stone heap; wash the colour clothes on Tuesday and put them on the clothesline to dry; don't walk bare-head in the hot sun; cook pumpkin fritters in very hot sweet oil; soak your little cloths right after you take them off; when buying cotton to make yourself a nice blouse, be sure that it doesn't have gum in it, because that way it won't hold up well after a wash; soak salt fish overnight before you cook it; is it true that you sing benna in Sunday school?; always eat your food in such a way that it won't turn someone else's stomach; on Sundays try to walk like a lady and not like the slut you are so bent on becoming; don't sing benna in Sunday school; you mustn't speak to wharf-rat boys, not even to give directions; don't eat fruits on the street—flies will follow you; *but I don't sing benna on Sundays at all and never in Sunday school*; this is how to sew on a button; this is how to make a button-hole for the button you have just sewed on; this is how to hem a dress when you see the hem coming down and so to prevent yourself from looking like the slut I know you are so bent on becoming; this is how you iron your father's khaki shirt so that it doesn't have a crease; this is how you iron your father's khaki pants so that they don't have a crease; this is how you grow okra—far from the house, because okra tree harbours red ants; when you are growing dasheen,[2] make sure it gets plenty of water or else it makes your throat itch when you are eating it; this is how you sweep a corner; this is how you sweep a whole house; this is how you sweep a yard; this is how you smile to someone you don't like too much; this is how you smile to someone you don't like at all; this is how you smile to someone you like completely; this is how you set a table for tea; this is how you set a table for dinner; this is how you set a table for dinner with an important guest; this is how you set a table for lunch; this is how you set a table for breakfast; this is how to behave in the presence of men who don't know you very well, and this way they won't recognise immediately the slut I have warned you against becoming; be sure to wash every day … don't squat down to play marbles—you are not a boy, you know; don't pick people's flowers—you might catch something; … this is how to make a bread pudding; this is how to make doukona;[3] this is how to make pepper pot; this is how to make a good medicine for a cold; … this is how to catch a fish; this is how to throw back a fish you don't like, and that way something bad won't fall on you; this is how to bully a man; … this is how to love a man; and if this doesn't work there are other ways … this is how to make ends meet; always squeeze bread to make sure it's fresh; *but what if the baker won't let me feel the bread?*; you mean to say that after all you are really going to be the kind of woman who the baker won't let near the bread?

> **Points to discuss:**
>
> 1. Look up 'benna' on the internet. Why would the mother think it wrong to sing benna at Sunday school?
> 2. Are boys taught housework while growing up? Discuss your experiences at home.
> 3. Do you think both boys and girls should learn how to cook, clean and wash? Give reasons for your answer.

> 4. Do mothers alone give instructions like those listed in 'Girl'? Who else in the family gives similar instructions?
> 5. List the consequences of such socialisation on girls.
> 6. What message about her sexuality does the girl in Kincaid's story receive?
> 7. What are boys taught as they grow up? Who are their teachers?

Ammayi

Watch the film *Ammayi* by Mohana Krishna Indraganti.[4]

> **Points to discuss:**
>
> 1. In what way is the experience of the girl in *Ammayi* similar to that of the girl in 'Girl'? In what way is it different?
> 2. Are there differences between the mothers of the two stories? Describe the differences.
> 3. Is being 'good' the same for boys and girls?
> 4. Make a list of the qualities that supposedly make for 'a good girl' and 'a good boy'. Compare the two lists. Are they the same?
> 5. With reference to the above question, if the listed qualities qualities are not the same, discuss the differences with your classmates.
> 6. Have you heard the words 'chastity' and 'virginity'? What do they mean? Are they considered important qualities for both boys and girls?

2.3 PREPARING FOR MANHOOD

In the following excerpt from the essay 'Growing up Male', the eminent educationist

Krishna Kumar looks back on his experiences as a boy. He does this in order to better understand some of the emotional stress of being a man in our society, and how schools today can help improve the way girls and boys, men and women, relate to each other. Segregation, in society as well as in schools, is a major problem. Girls are restricted to protected spaces. They are not encouraged to play or move around with ease in public places. Boys play in the open, occupying the streets. Without ordinary, everyday interactions with girls, boys stop thinking of them as individuals. Girls become a great mystery that boys have to painfully solve without help from adults. Hence, as men, they end up fearing or misunderstanding women, and feel that the only way to relate to them is by dominating or controlling them.

Towards the end of the excerpt, the author suggests that since conventional socialisation gives rise to so many problems, schools should be places of **counter-socialisation**. By which he means education should try and change the way society socialises girls and boys, women and men. You may find the idea of counter-socialisation useful in thinking about the issues of inequality raised in M. Muralikrishna's account of his childhood experiences and in Mohammed Khadeer Babu's story about a school's anniversary celebrations.

Think about the following questions as you read: Boys—does this description fit your experience of growing up male? If not, how is it different? Girls—does this description help you better understand boys?

Growing Up Male

In my boyhood, the most significant event that shaped my map of men's and women's positions in the world was my entry into a state-run all-boys' secondary school after finishing the primary grades.... One got so used to being with girls and to seeing them as ordinary children that it proved almost traumatic to move up to a secondary school where all children were boys and even the teachers were all men. This sudden separation from girls made no sense at first; a little later it led us to see girls as enigmas; and finally, we accepted it as a protection that society had offered us against the danger of coming in contact with a female human before we were ready for such contact. This rationalising took years; it was a tedious process, demanding tremendous amounts of psychic energy and, of course, we never had access to an adult to ask any questions about the great mystery of girls and their separation from us.

The Great Mystery of Girls

Girls went to a school that was designed in a conspicuously different way from the boys' school. In the centre of the girls' school was a courtyard where they played in total seclusion and safety from the outside world. After all these years since my childhood, I can still hear the shouts of girls playing games in that courtyard—shouts that we heard from our side of a broken wall we often toyed with the idea of climbing. Enclosed by a ring of classrooms, Ashoka trees and the wall, the girls' school was legally accessible through a twenty-foot-high iron gate that was opened only twice a day—to let the girls in and to let them out. The boys' school had no such courtyard or major entrance. Our playground was an annexe—just a big space attached to the school, devoid of any symbolism of confinement. This architectural difference between boys' and girls' schools is an important aspect of our school culture and it has persisted to this day.

Every evening we watched those hundreds of schoolgirls in their blue skirts walking home in silent clusters of six or seven, crowding the narrow streets of the small town in a compact, neat style. As they walked, they looked impossibly purposeful. We boys used the street for so many different things—as a place to stand around watching, to run around and play, to try out the manoeuvrability of our bicycles. Not so for girls. As we noticed all the time, for girls the street was simply a means to get straight home from school. And even for this limited use of the street they always went in clusters, perhaps because behind their purposeful demeanour they carried the worst fears of being assaulted. Watching those silent clusters for years eroded my basic sense of endowing individuality to every human being. I got used to believing that girls are not individuals. . . .

Domination

Aggressive behaviour and the desire to look ferocious, combined with and arising from a deep fear of women, were common among us by the time we came to the final years of secondary school. Some of the boys who were older talked about marriage as an event that involved tremendous risk and adventure. We had learnt from textbooks, songs, dramas and lectures about the great celibate saints and poets of the Bhakti period. In the lives and personal development of some of them, we thought freedom from women had played an important role. We had also read some verses written during the Riti period, and some of these, especially the ones we were supposed to read during undergraduate classes of Hindi literature, gave such precise descriptions of the female body that even our teachers felt too embarrassed to read them aloud.

To us it appeared that marriage was the only sure means to get close to a woman, and we found it very ironical and cruel that this one means was fraught with an impossible challenge and personal risk. No one seemed to know precisely what the challenge or risk was, but it was unquestioned knowledge that if you did not want to be defeated by a girl you must dominate her. Boasting about one's strength was extremely common. Some of the older boys were devout worshippers of Hanuman and Shiva—in that order—and they firmly believed that these gods were especially meant for men. . . .

In the first part of his autobiography, *Kya Bhooloon Kya Yaad Karoon* (1969), the Hindi poet Harivansh Rai Bachchan describes in great detail the tremendous anxiety he experienced in the months preceding his marriage. . . .

The crucial part of growing up male was to learn to see girls as objects. I say 'learn' because I still remember my perception of girls before I had begun to see them as objects and that my perception then was very different from what it became later. The sources of learning were many, the most important among them being other boys. Our contact with girls was minimal, in the sense that we hardly ever talked to any girl who was not a relative. And, of course, a sister did not count as a girl. On the other hand, we saw hundreds of girls each day of our lives—girls we could never hope to talk to. We saw cinema posters and sometimes films, which mostly veered around cardboard female characters. Some of us read books that verged on pornography, where the treatment of the woman was like that of a lifeless object that has no capacity to either suffer or enjoy. The conversations we overheard around us often consisted of references to women as a problem, and some of these conversations were among women themselves. I can recall several conversations among old women referring to girls as temporary property.

Equally profound was the influence of abusive terms that many boys used all the time, even in the presence of adults, including teachers. These terms were metaphors for sexual intercourse, and the terms mostly referred to different categories of men. So, one learnt to see men as belonging to different types and levels of mettle or perdition, depending on who they had subjected to intercourse. In brief, as a boy I was surrounded by a powerful discourse that delineated girls and women as sex objects, with little or nothing of their own in life in terms of sensation or demand.

Counter-socialisation

This kind of discussion leads one to wonder whether socialisation is a closed process. Such a thought finds fertile ground in the commonly held view that the school and community should be complementary to each other in socialising the young. If one accepts this principle of complementariness, then there is no hope for changing the prevailing code of sex typing through education, which means that there is no hope that education can intervene in the cultural reproduction of entrenched sex roles. Yet educationists never tire of telling the world that education is an agency of change. How does one get out of this contradiction? I think the way out is to propose counter-socialisation as the school's domain. That is, we need not see the school as an institution working in harmony with the community or the larger society in the matter of sex-role socialisation. On the contrary, we need to perceive the school in conflict with the community's code of socialisation.

This line of thought would lead us to reflect on the ways and means by which the school can act as a counter-socialiser in sex-role learning. If the community believes in segregating the sexes during adolescence, the school must set an alternative example by mixing the sexes. Similarly, while the larger social ethos offers stereotyped models of men's and women's roles, the school must insist that the adults working in it will not act in stereotyped and stereotyping ways. In the world outside of the school, knowledge about sex is taboo; in the school, such knowledge must be accessible.

Cinema and television cash in on conservative images of women and men; the school's media—that is, textbooks and other materials—should offer images and symbols that motivate the reader to look at human beings in terms of their own struggle for an identity, rather than reciting prefabricated conversations. And finally, if acceptance of the prevailing order and its norms is what society demands, then the school should demand the spirit of inquiry and offer opportunities to practise it. If all this sounds like an idealistic tall order, then one must remember that the agenda of changing women's place and role in society is no different.

Points to discuss:

1. Did you study in a school that was only for boys or only for girls? Can you recall your experience and share it with the class?
2. How did single-sex/co-educational schooling affect your relationship with the other sex?
3. Ask your teacher to share his or her experience of co-educational or segregated schooling.
4. Do you agree with Krishna Kumar that such segregation comes in the way of boys and girls interacting comfortably in different situations?
5. Krishna Kumar suggests that lack of interaction leads to a fear of women,

and that this is connected to the violence against them. Think carefully about his statement. Do you agree or disagree with him?

6. What were the fears Krishna Kumar had as a boy? What were the fears about women and marriage that his seniors and friends talked about?

7. Krishna Kumar talks about 'counter-socialisation'. Do you see it happening around you anywhere? (This course is one attempt at counter-socialisation!)

2.4 FIRST LESSONS IN CASTE

The following excerpt is taken from M. Muralikrishna's thesis titled 'Autobiography as a Resource for Educational Theory: A Dalit Life Story'. The thesis was the first of its kind to focus on the schooling and higher education of working-class first-generation dalits, and poses many challenging questions for educational theory. In the excerpt, the author recounts his school days, the different schools he studied in, and the various experiences of being ignored and marginalised which led to his 'silence' in the classroom and to him gradually being labelled a 'dull' student. When there was a positive atmosphere in school, he was an enthusiastic and eager learner, but when the classroom ceased to be a welcoming space and he received little to no attention or appreciation from the teachers, he became withdrawn and lost all motivation for learning. Read this thought-provoking account about how caste shapes the experience of schooling for a young boy.[5]

The Story of My Silence

As a child, I was never silent at home or on the streets or among my friends. But through much of my schooling I was silent both in the classroom and school compound. I did not like to be silent. No child likes to be silent. In fact, that silence burnt like a hot coal into my personality. It left me feeling diffident, inferior and subservient. It made me 'dull' (not confident enough to think on my own or feel that was a good thing to do) and disoriented (not motivated to work really hard since my hard work was rarely recognised or rewarded in school). Even though the school was indifferent to my desire to learn, it did not stop me from attending classes. My parents worked hard doing a lot of physical labour to earn money to keep me in school. With those earnings they bought me textbooks, notebooks, pens and pencils. A school bag and good clothes, however, were too expensive. There was a wide gap between what the school expected and what my parents could provide. This sense of inadequacy was one among many things that led to me falling silent in class.

But I was not silent at the small neighbourhood primary school I first attended. This school had only two classes and the children were mostly dalits. My class-two teacher encouraged me to join class three in a new primary school that had come up in the village. This school was next to a temple in the upper-caste neighbourhood. There I began to receive harsh punishments because I did not fit into the school culture or its academic discipline. Even then, I did not lose my spirit. I struggled to cope with the new academic standards but still made much progress.

The story of my silence really begins in class five. My aunt had got a job as an *anganwadi* worker, and my grandparents sent me and my younger brother to live with her in her new place. She had me admitted into class five in a private school. This was a double promotion, but my aunt felt I could manage. Saving a year at school was very important because of what it meant in terms of money saved. However, after I joined the private school, I began to slowly lose interest in maths and grew silent in class. As I look back, I realise that it was because the teacher neglected me. He just assumed that I should do as well as all the other students who had been in the school and were accustomed to its ways. Furthermore, it was not to his liking that I had joined class five without studying in class four. I was always lagging behind in maths as I could not cope with the pace, despite my consistent effort, and he offered no help. Other students went for private tuitions to the same teacher whereas I could not afford to do so. I felt dejected and rejected in maths and science classes.

It is important to know that the teachers belonged to reddy and toddy tapper castes. In fact, the majority of girls and boys too belonged to dominant castes. Some of them owned big grocery shops, cloth stores, steel and cement shops, photo studios and hotels in the town market. These children used to sit in their shops during weekends and attend special tuitions during weekdays.

It was the first time that I was studying in a private school, and that too away from home. Everything looked new, and I felt quite out of place. So, it took a lot of time to get used to that atmosphere. Moreover, I was scared of those teachers and students. Some teachers looked very harsh and cruel to me. I did not find any love or affection in their approach. A teacher's care is very important, particularly for students at that age. I was new but looked ordinary. Nobody showed any interest in talking to me, making friends with me or helping me acclimatise. By and large, the experience of this maths class followed me into other classes and gradually I just fell silent in all of my classes. Today I know that

I am not 'dull' and that I have a good mind and can think for myself, but during those years in school, there was no mirror I could look into that told me I was smart or made me feel good about myself.

Interestingly, though my academic performance was not great, it was in that new place that I learnt, at the age of nine, to buy things from the market and to cook meals. I also grew brave and independent. My younger brother and I often had to walk alone through the forest and hills to get to the *anganwadi* school where my aunt worked. It was a remote village, four kilometres away from town with no bus facility. The walk through the hills was scary and tough but we learnt to cope with our fears and the dangers of such walks. But … we also enjoyed the privilege and respect that village children and adults gave us as a teacher's nephews. Even though my private school experience was not so rewarding, those little privileges and self-recognition were a source of joy for me!

My grandfather died when I was nearing the end of class five, and I left the private school because we could no longer afford the fees. My education had been mostly funded by my grandfather, who was a skilled cobbler and maintained a tiny footwear shop in the market. After his death, my brother and I were brought back to our home to stay with my grandmother, and we were admitted to the government-aided upper-primary school. Luckily, this turned out to be a good move. Since I had come from a private school, and scored very good marks in the first monthly class test in English, the teachers as well as the students gave me quite a bit of attention. I was in the teachers' good books (a very important factor in learning and in a child's happiness). For the first time in my school life, I was recognised and appreciated by teachers.

The headmaster of this school was a Christian who gave special attention to children who scored good marks in English. I also became an inspiration for some of the students. Given this little momentum, I studied hard and with much determination. I was also inspired by my dalit Christian and Muslim friends whom I used to compete with in studies. I wanted to please the teachers through my performances in the class and in exams, and for a brief period, mainly because of an accident of circumstances, I kept my position as one of the three top-scoring students in the class. So, in classes six and seven, I was an 'intelligent' student. I used to participate very actively in the class. I also became quite popular among my classmates and teachers. It made me feel proud that two of my classmates used to come to my house to study with me! Since I was doing well in English, I was sent to tuition classes in the evening to further improve my English. Girls from a girls' high school too attended this tuition. My knowledge of English was found to be more advanced than theirs so sometimes they used to ask me for help!

But this happy period soon ended. I had to move out of this school and the tuition class. I was selected for admission into class eight in a Social Welfare Residential High School. The selection was based on the written test performance in which I stood one among the top five students. It was considered a great achievement. Many people, including my previous school teachers, congratulated me. Even though I stayed there for only a week, I wrote all my class notes and studied the lessons that I had missed since classes had already started. But I did not like the atmosphere there—harsh punishments, senior students' domination over juniors, bad food and so on. So, I came back to my home permanently. Since I could not stay in the residential school, I had to face a lot of criticism from everyone and I felt really discouraged and insulted.

Eventually I joined the Government Junior College which simultaneously ran a high school wing within the compound. But here my performance fell again. As an older child, I had a lot of responsibilities at home—such as fetching water for the household from a hand pump some distance away, fetching and chopping firewood, sweeping and washing, as well as fetching groceries and vegetables. I also did odd jobs for police families to keep their goodwill. Moreover, it was a half-day school since there were not enough teachers. And the teachers did not pay much attention to the needs of the students. Part of the reason for this was that the class strength was above forty. But the real reason was that the teachers did not care to motivate students to maintain standards and improve their zeal for education. They did not want or expect much participation in the class. The majority of children who attended this school came from SC, ST, BC welfare hostels and neighbourhoods of lower castes and Muslim communities. It is possible that the teachers did not feel much accountability to these communities. They did not seem bothered much about the high school results. I gradually became a passive listener in class. All in all, my journey in this academic year was very discouraging. So, I decided to move.

I joined the Zilla Praja Parishad Boys High School, which was famous for its excellent results. But here I was considered a dull student because I came from the high school wing of the Government Junior College. Teachers treated me as a nonentity. Students did not care to make friends with me. There was a silent branding of me as a dumb-head. I continued being passive in the class. There was no helping hand for me as I tried to cope with the new, unfriendly situation.

The same students whom I used to compete with during my class seven days now mingled with the 'intelligent students' and ignored me, as I had been identified as a 'dull' student. I could not participate much in the classroom as the teachers always posed questions only to the 'intelligent' students and ignored the 'dull' students, taking for granted that they would not answer the questions. I experienced a lot of anxiety and frustration since I was not able to perform as well as I had done in class seven. It was a humiliating experience for me to remain silent and feel dull in the class while other students performed well. I sometimes felt like I was an alien in a new world and I hated it. Some teachers did not even bother to find out my name and talk to me. There were a good number of male and female teachers in this school, but all were from dominant castes. The majority of local children and children from surrounding villages who attended this school were from the dominant castes. Their names announced everything about their social status and reputation. Another segment of children came from SC, ST, BC welfare hostels in the town. Teachers generally ignored them in class. They were regarded as weak in academics but good for sports. I didn't know where teachers placed me in their social binary.

The culture of the school made it quite clear to me that I did not deserve to be there. It was bad enough that they had to put up with my presence. Why should they listen to me speak? I never felt that I could open my mouth in class and soon I had nothing to say. The teacher paid no attention to me. I might have been invisible. There was no question of his helping me with my difficulties. My classmate, a non-dalit, Narendar, whose brother held a first rank in the batch ahead of us, gave a speech in which he pointed out mistakes committed by the teachers, whereas I could never even think of standing up before all of the teachers and students and *talking*.

But while I sat silent in class, a great deal was happening inside me. I was not silent out of choice. I did not like to be silent. In fact, I resented it. It was the school that forced me into silence. I felt inferior to the children that the teachers liked and interacted with. I compared myself to the non-dalit students and felt so inferior that it became difficult for me to believe that I had any intellectual qualities. The silence burnt into me like a hot coal and left me hurt and scarred. I felt I was someone who could be ignored and taken for granted, and that I did not deserve any attention. Teachers showed interest in non-dalit students; they even held personal conversations with them, chatting about their families and their lives outside of school. These students had a certain social familiarity with the teachers. While I was scared of even talking to the teachers, non-dalit students had the courage to pass comments about the teachers since they had access to the teachers' houses and families. The teachers even went to the extent of addressing the non-dalit students by their respective upper-caste names, such as Patel, Reddy Garu, Chary Garu, Shetty Garu, Ayyagaru. I was never included in these interactions with teachers. Most of my teachers belonged to these castes too. I had no such identity. No social recognition.

I was a student in class but a labourer outside, an oil-mill worker in the summer and during festival vacations, and a daily-wage construction worker over the weekends. It was by accident that I passed my class ten and class twelve exams and went on to higher studies and towns and cities further away. Incidentally, Narendar and I became good friends and roommates during our undergraduate studies in the district headquarters, Mahabubnagar. I was pursuing a BA and my friend was pursuing a teacher education programme called TTC, a pre-service training for primary school teachers.

Points to discuss:

1. The author says that he was not silent at home, but in class he gradually became silent. Why?
2. Does remaining quiet in class mean that someone is a 'dull' student? Does this excerpt make you think in new ways about what being 'dull' means? Elaborate on your answer.
3. Are you more 'active' in some classes than in others? Does the excerpt offer any clues as to why this might be so?
4. How are friendships formed in school or college? Do most of us (perhaps unconsciously) make friends with those who are more or less like us? What happens to those who do not belong to the same background as the majority of the students?
5. Do you think dalit students are isolated in schools or colleges even today? What are some of the ways in which this happens?

2.5 DIFFERENT MASCULINITIES

The story in this section, written by Mohammed Khadeer Babu and translated by Uma Maheswari Bhrugubanda, is a light-hearted yet thought-provoking account of prejudices that a young boy faces in his village school.

How I Upstaged the 'Clevers' of My Class

Goda Lakshmi and that shorty Arcot Kalavani would preen no end as they led the daily prayer.

And all for what? It was just a four-line verse on Vinayaka! With voices really thin and high-pitched, they would pout stylishly as if pure gold was tumbling out of their mouths by the kilo. They'd sing each line, prolong the tune at the end, and then glance coyly at the rest of us who were to pick it up and sing it in chorus. With their smug smiles, they seemed to say, 'Look at us, we are the "clevers" of the class!' This was their daily drama.

I burned with resentment and envy watching their antics. Each day I'd brood bitterly—wasn't I fully and equally capable of leading the prayer song? Hasn't God given me an equally good voice? But who would listen to me?

The school headmistress, Rama Devi, and the English teacher were both very displeased with me because I was so irregular. As for the maths teacher, Malayadri Sir, the only time he ever touched me or came near me was to do additions and subtractions with his cane on my bare back. The social studies teacher, Rukmini, was kind to me and I could always wangle a favour from her, but sadly she didn't have the 'authority' to decide who led the prayer at assembly.

So, all I could do was hide my pain and send out a silent threat to those clevers: 'Just you wait, you smarty-pants, I am going to lead the prayer one day! Come what may!'

That day, we sat in the classroom after the morning assembly, as usual, when Rama Devi Teacher walked in five minutes late, her *chappals* flip-flopping, and announced, 'No class today, I'm busy with the preparations for the anniversary day.' She added, 'All those who are interested in acting, stand up.' Even before she finished the sentence, Kanduri Murali, Kandula Malakonda Rao, Goda Lakshmi, Parvati and N. Manasa all shot up from their seats. These were the clevers of the class; Rama

Devi Teacher was convinced that they were capable of doing everything under the sun!

My heart beat rapidly. I realised that this was my chance to display my true prowess, so I stood up slowly.

But Rama Devi smiled as soon as she saw me. 'What will you do? With your atrocious "*maaki, meeki*" Telugu! Never regular to school, but "*saar*" is interested in drama now,' she sneered. (Ever since the last Independence Day, when I had asked her if I should 'shatter' the thread I was using to tie something up, she always sniggered at my Telugu.)

I sat down crushed while the entire class laughed with their teeth on full display. Utter humiliation! It was just like last year when I was in the fourth class. The clevers would be allowed to bunk two classes in the morning and two in the afternoon session just so that they could rehearse for the plays and other events; dumbos like us would be chained to the class and asked to repeat our lessons endlessly. However, most of the dumbos were better off than me; I was the lowliest among them. The clevers, of course, never talked to me, but even half of the dull buggers in class hardly said a word to me. They treated me with utter contempt.

They always looked down upon me because my uniform was invariably crumpled and soiled. (I felt that my father deserved the worst punishment for not getting me a new uniform despite the fact that I pestered him valiantly for three months. Well, it was true there was never enough money, but still, he could have done something.) The class also looked down on me because I wore my school shorts torn at the back with a safety pin holding it together from the inside. (My grandma made this temporary arrangement with the pin because there was no thread to sew it.) I was the boy who didn't finish his homework, the one who wouldn't have his lunch box ready on time (that was because lunch wasn't cooked sometimes). So they teased me and poked fun at me all the time. 'The dimwit who skips school', 'The dumbo who cannot study', they'd sing. I put up daily with their ragging but Rama Devi Teacher's laugh today really infuriated me.

Am I to blame if I don't know Telugu? We don't speak the language at home. No one speaks it in Kasab Galli. In spite of this, I've been trying my best to speak Telugu and also learning to read and write in English and Telugu. And here was Rama Devi Teacher, not showing the least bit of sympathy, laughing at me. My blood boiled.

That night I slept next to Grandma and poured my heart out to her, sobbing all the while. Grandma got really angry: 'Does this teacher know our language? How dare she scold you for being poor at Telugu.' She hugged me tight and cursed Rama Devi Teacher roundly.

But I couldn't sleep the whole night. My head was abuzz. I was thinking hard, 'How to avenge my humiliation?' And then suddenly I remembered Gabbar Singh!

I didn't really know much about this fellow Gabbar and I couldn't understand a word he said. And yet, I knew everything he said by heart. Whenever my father could spare the cassette player from work, he brought it home and listened to Gabbar Singh's dialogues again and again. What if I recited those dialogues for the anniversary day? The idea seemed fantastic to me!

The next day, when all the clevers went for rehearsals, I slipped out of class and slowly approached the thatched hall where rehearsals were being held. Rama Devi Teacher was all set to shoo me away with her cane when Moustache Subbaraju Sir, who had arrived just then, spotted me. He called out, 'Hello there! You are Karim's son, aren't you? Why aren't you in class?'

'I do have class, Sir, but I want to act,' I replied timidly.

'Oh, I see! And who do you want to act as?' He laughed warmly, his moustache quivering.

'It's Gabbar Singh, Sir! Shall I show you?' And worried he might say no, I launched off in a most fearsome voice, '*Kitne aadmi the?* And starting from there I went through the entire monologue—I recited the '*Goli khaa*' bit; and sailed through the loud guffawing 'Ha ha ha . . .' until tears sprung to my eyes, just as they had come to Gabbar's eyes; and carried on until I finally came to a halt with '*Kab hai holi? . . . holi kab hai?!*' This breathless delivery left everyone including Rama Devi Teacher staring at me wide-eyed and open-mouthed.

As for Subbaraju Sir, he was thrilled to bits.

'Bravo, son of Karim! You should definitely do this act for the anniversary.' Rama Devi Teacher stared speechlessly at him and me by turn.

And thus it was that all the skits and plays and dance performances that the clevers put up paled in comparison to my Gabbar Singh act. I raised a storm on the stage and walked away with all the accolades. And do I really need to add that from then onwards, whenever Goda Lakshmi from the sixth class was absent, or whenever Kalavani came late, it was I who was called upon to lead the prayer at assembly?

Points to discuss:

1. Have you ever felt angry about favouritism shown by teachers, parents or others towards those assumed to be the 'clevers'? Or were you one of the 'clevers' yourself?

2. The above story is also about competition and evaluation in our educational system, as well as a subtle reflection on merit. What does it have to say about these much-debated concepts?

3. The story implies that what is seen as merit is connected with privilege. Since the hero is not one of the privileged students, his talents and capabilities remain unappreciated. How does he deal with this discrimination?

4. Those who grow up speaking the standard form of a region's dominant language (be it Hindi, English, Telugu, etc.) in their home, and therefore speak it fluently, are usually also taken to be intelligent. Meanwhile, those who grow up speaking a dialect of the region's dominant language, and therefore do not speak the dominant language so fluently, are considered unintelligent. What is wrong with this way of thinking?

5. The girls in this story are more vocal and confident than the young boy. Why do you think this is so?

NOTES

1. Watch the Complan advertisement here: https://www.youtube.com/watch?v=zRmvw1ry8IY.
2. Taro; a starchy, edible plant
3. A kind of pudding.
4. Watch the film *Ammayi* by Mohana Krishna Indraganti here: https://www.youtube.com/watch?v=VCEiL2W5a64.
5. Some of you might be interested in reading a piece written by B. R. Ambedkar called 'A Childhood Journey to Koregaon Becomes a Nightmare'. Ambedkar was a very important national leader and architect of the Indian constitution. When he was nine years old, he travelled with other children of his family to spend the summer vacation with his father. During the journey, he faced some experiences which made him realise, for the very first time, that in society's eyes he was an untouchable. Read about this life-changing journey, in his own words, by visiting the following link: http://www.columbia.edu/itc/mealac/pritchett/00ambedkar/txt_ambedkar_waiting.html#one.

Being Boy

3.1 INTRODUCTION

Girls are nagged, controlled, frequently reminded that they are a burden and constantly told that they have to be seen as 'good' girls (in other words, docile, self-sacrificing and obedient). Contrastingly, the birth of a boy is celebrated. Class and caste affect this experience, but in general, early boyhood is bathed in warmth and freedom. Boys are indulged and brought up to be tough and competitive. Their mischief is tolerated; after all, 'boys will be boys'. They play outdoors—running, climbing rocks and trees, cycling, swimming in tanks and rivers—and have 'masculine' toys like cars, trains, catapults, stick-swords and even guns. Aggressive behaviour is overlooked and sometimes even admired.

This is also the time when children encounter class and caste divides. As we read in 'The Story of My Silence', and will read in the story 'Obstacle Race' in this unit, when a dalit boy leaves the safety of his home, he learns what caste discrimination means and faces humiliation. In fact, it is common to humiliate men from 'lower' social groups by ridiculing their masculinity. Remember that in Mohammed Khadeer Babu's story, being a boy brings no special advantages if you are poor or don't speak 'good' Telugu at home.

Parents (especially fathers) may be sterner with boys and discipline them more harshly, even physically. This is partly because they feel boys are more likely to stray, but also because boys are expected to work hard, be successful, find good jobs and assume responsibility for their families. This involves taking responsibility for their sisters and aging parents as well as their own wives and children. Towards their final years in school, there is heavy pressure on them to perform well and find good jobs. Boys soon learn (often with shock) that it is their responsibility to be breadwinners.

They have to be tough, suppress emotions and be wary of women.

There are other pulls and demands. There is the pressure (and also desire) to join male groups or gangs. As the culture of ragging shows, inclusion demands that you accept the authority of the group and obey its rules, even if it is painful or humiliating to do so. Once you are 'in', the gang offers support and the authority to attack others. Boys in gangs practise manliness in different ways. They do rebellious things like driving recklessly, smoking or drinking and even harassing women. The following excerpt from K. V. Tirumalesh's story, 'The Runaways', gives us a look at this process.

'I took the cigarette he offered me. He scratched the match and, cupping his hands, lit it. He lit one for himself with the same light and, in a more grown-up way than myself, inhaled and let out the smoke. It was he who had taught me the bad habit of smoking. During break time at school we would buy cigarettes from the shop nearby, climb a cashew tree and sit on its convenient branches, smoking and chatting. Although I found no pleasure in smoking like this, I would give in to Damu's pressure when he urged, "Smoke, Dembanna, smoke." I would get angry with myself for succumbing to Damu's bad influence and resolve every morning to resist, but when he called out to me, "Come, Dembanna, come," I did not have the courage to say no. Sometimes we would see the maths teacher walking on the road under the cashew tree. From our secure spot we would make fun of him quietly. In truth it was Damu, not I, who made fun of him. I would only grin in response.'

Gangs and youth cults often require certain forms of dress and behaviour. Style can be all-important. Anthropologist Ritty A. Lukose provides a fascinating account of how young boys in Kerala began to flaunt an elaborate style known as *chethu*, which started in the 1990s with the arrival of global goods and advertising in the Indian market. As her interview with a young Malayali man called Devan shows, buying and wearing the right clothes, being seen at the right 'hang-out' places with the right girls, speaking in a particular sharp-edged or *chethu* way and roaming around town can become so important that a boy can forget why he came to college in the first place.

Boys who are quiet, short, studious, artistic, 'feminine', or different in any other way are often teased, sidelined and made to feel wretched. In his Founder's Day speech, Vikram Seth spoke of the **culture of masculinity** in his school and the pressure to conform to that model. He was so miserable that he often went to sleep at night hoping he would not have to wake up in the morning and face another day. R. S.'s reflections on masculinity in Unit 13 on becoming a man tell a story of giving in to pressure and becoming like others, but being unhappy about it.

For a growing boy, sexuality and desire are confusing new experiences. Studies show that in our country, shame continues to loom large over all things sexual, and we get an indication of this from the story we cited earlier. Dembanna from 'The Runaways' recalls:

'First my father discovered that I smoked. Then he found out that I had stolen a 100-rupee note from the box instead of the 10 rupees that I was to take for the market. The third issue was more serious than these. Damu had discovered the place where Madivala Sanjeeva's daughter Sevanthi had her bath and took me along saying he would show me a secret. We climbed a tree and stealthily enjoyed the sight of Sevanthi bathing. Not that we could see anything. You could say that what we imagined was more vivid than what our eyes could see. It is still a mystery to me how this news reached the ears of Sevanthi's parents. Like there are spies behind spies, someone who didn't like us must have been following us. The shame of smoking or stealing was not hard to bear. But how to endure the shame of this third thing? Even mother wouldn't have forgiven it. Even though Damu was the inspiration behind all three sins, I had made up my mind to run away with him!'

As Krishna Kumar observed, there are few places where feelings and doubts about sex can be expressed or discussed. This is why the account in 'Ek Ladki Ko Dekha Toh' in this unit is so brave and beautiful at the same time.

3.2 A VILLAGE BOYHOOD

Gogu Shyamala's story 'Obstacle Race' is about boyhood being structured as a series of challenges that Adivi, a dalit boy growing up in a contemporary Telangana village, must face and overcome. Adivi's experiences (stealing mangoes, managing life in school, studying and so on) are both similar to those of other boys and dissimilar because of his poverty and caste. Read the following excerpt, translated by Uma Maheswari Bhrugubanda, from the story.

Obstacle Race

The overflowing stream wound itself around the village like a snake winds itself around a man. All around the village lay the stream. And hedging the banks of the stream were mango trees. The mangoes had very interesting names. Corn Mango, the insides of which looked like corn pearls; Juicy Mango; Round Mango; Coconut Mango; Blue Mango; Spicy Mango; Goat's Udder Mango, because they always came in pairs like goats' udders; Crooked Mango and so on. The Spicy Mango is extremely sour and tangy when raw, but when it is ripe it is sweeter than words can tell.

All the trees were now bare, with almost no fruit at all. Only the remotest of branches had some fruit left on them. The trees had actually been in full bloom and had borne lots of fruit but they were all leased to the Tandur folks. They came, plucked all the fruit and took them away. Those that remained were on the farthest branches hidden well by leaves.

It was for these mangoes that the gang of children was searching frantically. Adivi was leading them from the front. His full name was Adivaiah. His mother gave birth to him when she went weeding in the green gram fields. Since he was born in the forest, *adivi*, he was called Adivaiah. He was carrying a long stick made from the *thevayili* tree branch. The stick was taller than him and he used it to move the branches and thick foliage that densely covered the paths. He cowered low as he made his way through it all. The others followed his lead.

It seemed as if the mango season was coming to an end no sooner than it had started. The children spent the entire season on the mango trees. At the crack of dawn, as soon as he had rinsed his mouth with water, Adivi would disappear from his home and appear on the mango trees.

That day too he was up on the trees. He was searching for the leftover fruit. Standing beneath him were the Patel Reddi boy and Madiga Narasimha. Adivaiah was plucking the fruits and throwing them down. He had chosen a nice, tasty fruit on the tree and eaten it.

As he reached out for another mango, the branch beneath his feet cracked and broke. The branch he was holding broke too. As the other boys looked on, he slipped and fell, hitting several branches as he fell down. The ground was covered with the thorny shrubs of the *mogali* flower and rows of hemp. He slid along these and finally landed in the stream. He was dazed and hurt. Adivi's friends raced to the spot and crowded round him.

'*Orey* Adivi! Please get up, get up! You will drown in these waves . . . get up!' they shouted and started crying.

But Adivi was not able to get up. He could not even move. He just lay there unconscious and still. His frightened friends felt helpless and started wailing even more. Crying, they dragged Adivi to the shore. They examined his legs and hands closely to see if he was hurt. They held his chin and shook his face to wake him up. Adivi opened his eyes and rose to his feet slowly. His whole body was aching. '*Amma!*' he groaned. His head was bleeding. His mouth was dry. His friends helped him sit up and brought him water in leaf cups from the nearby freshwater ditch. They wiped the blood slowly and, holding him carefully by the shoulders, they took him back into the village.

Even as they were reaching the cattle-feed barn, they heard a voice say, 'O Adivi!' That very instant, the friends holding Adivi dropped him and fled with great speed along different paths. They all knew that the voice belonged to Adivi's father. Even Adivi himself, who had been weak, scared and drained of all energy, gathered strength from god-knows-where to dive into the paddy stacks heaped on the left. He was afraid his father would scold him for climbing trees. As he hid in the stacks, his eyelids drooped again and he fell asleep hiding there.

Calling out, 'Adivi! O Adivi!' his father searched the entire village. Someone must have told him that his son had hurt himself and that he was now sleeping in the paddy stacks, so he went to the stacks and began pleading with Adivi. 'I won't beat you, son. Come, let's go home.' With that, he carried his son

home. He wiped the boy's body with warm water, fed him some *rotte*, and gave him water to drink. He spread out the mat and a sheet and asked Adivi to lie down. Then he rubbed some fresh butter on the wounds.

'With Ellamma's blessings you managed the obstacle of the tree! That's one obstacle successfully overcome. But don't ever climb trees again or you'll hurt yourself like today,' he said to his son as he sat beside him, gently patting his back to put him to sleep.

❖ ❖ ❖

Not long after Adivi joined school, the school teacher was transferred to another village and his place was taken by a new teacher called Siddappa Sir. He belonged to the balija caste. Adivi had progressed from *Aa, Aaa* to *Ru, Ruu* in the Telugu alphabet. The new teacher taught him *E, Ee, Aai* and *O, Oo, Ow*, and Adivi mastered them in a single day. The teacher moved on to the set of consonants like *Ka, Kha*. He was very pleased with the speed with which Adivi picked up the alphabets.

He said to Adivi, 'I'm very happy with your writing—I think you should move to a higher grade.'

At first, Adivi felt very strange going to the high school. All the kapu, brahmin, reddy and Muslim children sat on the benches; only Adivaiah and Madiga Narasimha sat on the floor. Two years passed by. The classrooms changed, but while all the other students sat on benches, these two continued to sit on the floor.

One day, the Deputy Education Officer came into the third class for an inspection. He asked the students many questions. Most of the children were able to answer simple questions but couldn't tackle the more difficult ones. Adivi was the only one to answer the difficult questions. For example, the officer tested them on the multiplication tables. He also asked them questions from a lesson, 'The Letter', in their Telugu reader. No one in the class except Adivi could answer the question. Adivi even answered addition and subtraction sums on the blackboard when the officer asked him to. The officer was full of praise for him.

But when Adivi walked back from the blackboard to take his place on the floor at the end of the classroom, the officer noticed this. He told the teacher sternly, 'Why did you make those boys sit on the floor? Let them sit on the benches along with all the others.'

The teacher promptly moved Adivi and Narasimha from the floor onto the benches. After the inspection, Adivi acquired a new status in the eyes of the students and the teachers. They began to appreciate him better. Adivi now sat on a bench, equal with all the other children. There was no need to lift up his head to see the children sitting high on the benches—he only had to move his head sideways and he could see everyone.

Points to discuss:

1. Most boys (and many girls) have stolen guavas or mangoes from other people's gardens. Knowing that they might get caught adds to the excitement. Is there a difference (for example, in the reasons for doing it, the consequences if they get caught, etc.) between well-to-do children stealing fruit and poor children doing it?

2. There may not be many schools today where dalit children are made to sit on the floor while others sit at desks. But are there other ways in which dalit students are sidelined or ignored? List three ways in which this happens, based on your experiences and observations. Share your list with the class.

3. Adivi can recognise at least eight different kinds of mangoes. In general, children like him often know a lot about the geography of the village, plant and animal life, farming activities and the care of animals, weather and even the art and science of many traditional crafts. Is this knowledge valued in schools? Why, or why not? Would such children make good scientists and engineers?

3.3 SCHOOL DAYS

At the age of six, the writer Vikram Seth was sent to a prestigious boarding school in Dehradun, Uttarakhand. Decades later, he was invited to speak on the occasion of the school's Founder's Day celebrations. The passage below contains excerpts from his speech. Contradicting the general saying, 'school days are the best days of one's life', Seth recalls that he was bullied and felt miserable; he often went to sleep with a terrible feeling of loneliness and isolation, hoping he would never wake up. 'For years after I left, I thought of school as a kind of jungle and looked back on it with a shudder.'

Seth speaks about the pressure to conform to dominant ideas of masculinity and to join boy gangs and groups. He describes the misery of those who are different, and dwells on the importance of families, sisters and parents for a growing boy. He concludes with a moving call to young boys to not give in to pressure and to think for themselves.

Founder's Day Speech, 1992

A few years ago, after a gap of about sixteen years, I returned to Doon.... I remember thinking how beautiful the school was after all and rebuked myself for not visiting it for so many years and not having kept up with it at all.

The fact of the matter is that I had been pretty unhappy during my school days.... My brother Shantum, who followed me five years later, had a good time in school.... I for my part just wanted to forget all about school once I had left.

Now it is strange to say that I was unhappy at Doon. After all, I did well here academically, joined a number of societies, edited the *Weekly*, and took part in debates and plays. Since my reports were good, my parents thought I was fine—and I said nothing to the contrary. I was kept well occupied from morning to night. And yet I had a terrible feeling of loneliness and isolation during my six years here....

Now, part of this was of course simply the general stress and strain of adolescence, but part of it was also the ethos, the atmosphere of the place. It was a place where sports were almost the only thing that mattered as far as the boys were concerned. I was teased and bullied by my classmates and my seniors because of my interest in studies and reading, because of my lack of interest at that time in games, because of my unwillingness to join gangs and groups,

because of my height ... and most importantly of all, because I would get furious when I was bullied....

Given all this, I had serious doubts about whether I should in all conscience stand on this stage and so ungratefully talk about my miserable time here. After a bit of thought and some struggle I decided I should. For one thing, I learnt a lot at Doon. A very great deal indeed, and I am very grateful for that. For another, I thought it would be interesting for you (and by 'you' I mean particularly the boys) to hear someone who has a somewhat different view of things from the usual 'school days were the best days of my life' litany; it might give you heart when you are feeling low or perplexed.

One of the hardest and most harmful things about school—not just Doon but any boarding school—is that boys are deprived of the love and day-to-day company of their fathers and mothers for two-thirds of the year—and possibly for longer, because when they do go back home for the holidays, parents are often so unused to spending time with their children that they do not quite know what to do with them even when they share the same roof. The boys, while growing up, hardly know what it is like to have a sister. The result of this lack of family life, of affection, is very difficult to assess, but I think it has a serious effect on the minds and hearts of boys. It forces them to be independent of their parents, certainly, but it also makes them emotionally insecure, and as a result, more eager, even desperate to conform to their peer group, to seek popularity among companions, and to appear as tough and cool as possible, and as brutal as possible to those who are outside the group or younger than themselves....

Both now and later, and whether or not your environment encourages you to do so, try and think things out independently. Just because a group or someone in authority says something, does not mean you should believe it. Think it out. Think it through. Don't take important matters on trust … If there is something deep within you, whether personal or professional, that pulls you one way, and you have discussed the matter with yourself and come to a clear conclusion, don't let the wish to be thought of as a 'good chap' force you in the opposite direction. You may not be successful or popular in the eyes of the world—or you may be successful only incidentally—but you will have lived your own life, the only one that is to a fair extent under your control, the only one that you have.

Points to discuss:

1. Vikram Seth says that he had 'a terrible feeling of loneliness and isolation' at school. He suggests that it was because he was different—he did not like sports, he was short, he liked reading. But even boys who seem happy in gangs report that, despite all the joking and activity, they feel lonely and unable to express their real feelings. Is this true? Sometimes? Often? Always? Why do you think this happens?

2. Which of the following strikes you as important in this account? Provide reasons for your choice(s).
   a. Despite being unhappy, Vikram Seth did well and learnt a lot at school.
   b. Seth found the culture of masculinity in the school oppressive.
   c. His story provides support and encouragement to boys like him who may be different in some way.
   d. Seth's story encourages all boys to think more critically about school culture.
   e. Seth's is an uncommon experience. The school does not need to worry about this exception since the majority of the boys were happy.

3.4 COLLEGE STYLES

The following passage contains excerpts from a conversation that took place in the late 1990s between Ritty Lukose, a cultural anthropologist studying new youth cultures, and Devan, a young man from a lower-middle-class family in southern Kerala. In school, he studied hard and did well. In college, however, he focussed his time and energy on being *chethu*—the literal meaning of the word is 'to cut', and is often used to describe the cutting and tapping of toddy palm, though the meaning has evolved and is now Malayalam youth slang for 'cool' or 'hip', reflecting a particular type of 'cutting edge' masculine style. The conversation between Lukose and Devan provides insight into the meaning of such style. A young boy in branded jeans and sneakers, sporting a new motorbike, would be admiringly referred to as *chethu*. The term combines ideas of youth, fashion, masculinity, an attitude of nonchalance and the use of public spaces (wandering aimlessly in streets and frequenting malls, movie theatres, coffee shops and ice cream or beer parlours). The word for similarly fashionable girls was *gema*. But while *chethu* had a positive connotation, a *gema* girl was not admired in the same way. She would be regarded as an arrogant show-off who considered herself superior.

On Being Chethu

Devan explains: 'In order to matter in college, it was important to be *chethu*. [For a] *chethu* style [you need to have] jeans, a Yamaha bike. … You need to have six or seven jeans, Killer jeans. You need four or five cotton shirts, three to four t-shirts. … A bike. You must have a bike. … You enjoy life. … A Yamaha bike, money in the hand, a line [slang for 'girlfriend'], that's it … you go to a beer parlour and you sip two beers, you have plenty of friends, you enjoy life. You enjoy the life. You have to speak in a *chethu* style and you have to have *chethu* relations. You are good company for everyone. Then, you study well. If you have all this, then you can say that you have a positive *chethu* style. . . . You don't care about what has happened yesterday. You don't care about what will happen tomorrow. You don't have aims, but you are always happy. That is *chethu*. My idea of the good life is that you must have a lot of money. Per month, you must get ten to fifteen thousand rupees. . . . Living is not just eating. I do like travelling. Prices are skyrocketing. For example, all want to have one car. . . . Then there is food, housing, social gatherings. . . . You see, lots of modern things are coming into our lives. . . . Life is too short. . . . Then, [you must have] a good woman. If you have money, naturally, all other things will come.'

Devan is clearly anxious about the future and knows that being *chethu* can be problematic. There is, he reflects, a negative side to being *chethu*.

'There is a negative side. You throw away work and you become *chethu*. What I mean is you will walk in a *chethu* style. But you degrade yourself sometimes. The positive side of *chethu* is that you should know about what you should do—work. But then you use life as if it's sand. You don't care how much sand came here or how much is there. You don't care what will come in the future and what has come in the past. You will just think about how the sands are flowing now. You only care about the present thing.'

Points to discuss:

1. Devan says that in order to matter in college, it is important to be *chethu*. Do students who 'matter' in your college have a particular style?
2. Devan associates being *chethu* with material possessions (branded jeans, sneakers, bikes and so on). Discuss how the rising awareness of fashion and style among the youth is related to global markets, advertising and marketing.

3.5 EK LADKI KO DEKHA TOH

A girl likes a boy because he has never behaved indecently with her. The boy respects her apprehensions about sex and is not pushy. And yet, he longs to touch her and is intoxicated by that longing. Listen to the podcast from Agents of Ishq (courtesy Parodevi Pictures)[1] in which a boy, Satya, talks about a girl he cannot stop thinking of, the eroticism of her every move, and the fantasy of the moment when they will become more intimate.

NOTE

1. Listen to the Agents of Ishq podcast here: http://agentsofishq.com/ek-ladki-ko-dekha-toh/.

Housework: Invisible Labour

4.1 DO MOTHERS HAVE SUNDAYS?

Have you ever wondered about the women in television advertisements and films? They all seem fresh, smiling and beautifully dressed. They keep their houses miraculously clean. They worry about the health of their children and families and hence they buy only healthy and nutritious products. They lovingly feed smiling sons and other members of the family with unquestionable dedication. Taking care of the emotional, mental and physical well-being of their families seems to come naturally to them. What is more, they seem to do it effortlessly.

But what we do not see on TV is this: women working in the house from early in the morning to late in the night. They fetch and store water, clean the house and the outdoors area, wash everyone's clothes, cook, take care of the children and the elderly and attend to those who may be sick. Even when they fall ill, women are on their feet, taking care of the family. These daily, routine, time-consuming and back-breaking tasks are together known as ***housework***.

We all know that housework is essential to the daily functioning of our families and lives. If mothers and wives did not do this work, we would all be going to college or to work hungry and in unwashed clothes, wouldn't we? It is also equally important for the economy. Schools, colleges, farms, factories, construction sites and offices would fail to run efficiently if mothers, wives and daughters stopped washing clothes, cooking and packing food for us, and looking after us when we are sick. In fact, according to a 2009 estimate, if the 34 crore working-age Indian women were paid for their housework, the total amount would be 29 trillion rupees. This is the equivalent of 61% of India's gross domestic product!

It is easy to understand that housework differs from household to household. Rural women have to deal with a lack of assured water supply, ready fuel, roads and other facilities. Urban households fare better due to the availability of these facilities. In middle-class households that employ domestic workers, women are freed from housework to an extent, but the demands of cooking different dishes and keeping the house clean are higher here. We know that in large families, newly married and younger women are given more housework. In some families, especially smaller ones, men may be more willing to participate in housework.

In general, however, housework is regarded as women's work. It is assumed that women are naturally suited for housework. Others may help them, but housework is seen primarily as women's responsibility. In our society, womanhood is defined by these activities. It is common to speak of women who are not good at these activities, or not interested in them, as 'un-womanly'. In fact, most people are shocked if household tasks are described as 'work' because doing housework is generally considered to be an expression of women's love for their families. Women are not expected to want appreciation, remuneration or anything else in return. The more selfless and service-oriented a woman is, the better she is considered. Even when women work outside of the home and earn money for the family, they are expected to take responsibility for the housework—to cook, take care of everyone and also work around the house. Even women who are incapable of doing housework, due to physical restrictions or professional commitments, are still expected to manage it.

Is Housework a Woman's Job?

We all know that there are no such similar expectations of men. Girls in a family are required to help with housework, but not the boys. Men are expected to earn and provide for the family, but not to share the work around the house or to look after the people in the house. Of course, some men and some boys do help around the house. They take care of repairs, drop and fetch children to and from school, and buy weekly and monthly provisions and often also shop every day for fresh food and vegetables. Some men also cook special dishes for the family on special occasions. Studies show that their numbers are growing. But even today, men doing housework as a matter of routine is not common.

The funny thing is that men do all these activities for money; and when they work for pay, they specialise in doing only one thing. We all know Sanjeev Kapoor, the famous chef, don't we? In hotels, housekeeping is a postgraduate specialisation. Male nurses, ward boys and doctors care for the elderly and sick. Washer people can be both men and women. Laundries are usually run by men. Tailors are often men. When young men rent a house together while pursuing an education or during their initial employment, they often cook and manage the house. Strangely, despite all this, the predominant message that men get from society is that they should not do housework. Men who help in the house may even be laughed at.

As we learnt in the unit on socialisation, women and men are socialised into this division of work from childhood. We grow up thinking that the work men and women do around the house is different but equal and complementary. This is not true. Women and men may do different things around the house, but women do the most time-consuming, tedious and routine tasks. When women are employed, they continue to do more work around the house than the men.

The time and energy women spend on housework is ***invisible labour*** because housework is considered to be their natural duty. This invisibility leads to non-recognition and undervaluation. This, in turn, deprives women of the free time necessary for physical rejuvenation and social life. We all know how important these are, don't we? Many makers of kitchen gadgets promise women freedom from drudgery. However, the responsibility of obtaining, using and maintaining the gadgets remains with women.

Many also argue that employing domestic workers has solved the problem of housework for middle-class women. However, women still have to manage and organise domestic workers. Furthermore, female domestic workers who do housework remain poorly paid (compared to drivers, gardeners and others) precisely because of its invisibility and undervaluation. We should also remember that they too have a house to manage after work.

Did you know?

According to a survey done by the United Nations, in every country across the world, men spend less time on household work than women. Men in some countries (such as Norway and Finland) spend more time sharing housework compared to men in other countries (for example, Mexico and Turkey). Men in India spend the least amount of time on housework. Indian women spend five-and-a-half hours each day on housework, whereas Indian men spend thirty to forty-five minutes!

According to unofficial estimates, there are nearly 40 lakh domestic workers in India. They do the chores in other people's houses: cleaning; caring for the children, the elderly and the sick; cooking; gardening; and driving. There are part-time, full-time and live-in workers. It is largely women and men from marginalised communities who are engaged in this form of labour. But they are not granted even minimal rights as workers. The National Domestic Workers Movement (NDWM) has been demanding that they be recognised as workers, and be given all the rights and benefits of workers such as minimum wages, weekly time off, overtime payments, and so on: 'The proposed Domestic Workers Regulation of Work and Social Security Bill, 2016, mandates minimum wages and social security benefits to be applied to these women and men.'

We rarely think about these issues in our personal lives because we believe that these divisions are normal. Men who cook at home or care for the children or the sick are rarely appreciated or encouraged. Similarly, we see few women openly protesting about housework. All of us would have heard our mothers, grandmothers or female cousins complain about housework at some point or the other. But such complaints are usually short-lived and are about specific instances or occasions. If we listen to women, we might learn to see housework from a different point of view.

Points to discuss:

1. Do you think the current method of completing housework is fair?
2. Do you think this division of household labour constrains the choices of women and men in, say, choosing careers? In what ways might it affect their choices?
3. What are the ways in which housework is made 'invisible' in, say, the media, popular culture and everyday conversations?

4. Do you think there will be more of a sense of sharing and joy in the house if everyone in the family works together to complete household chores?

5. Can you recall occasions when your father, grandfather or uncle cooked something special that you really liked? Did you or anyone else find it 'unusual' or surprising that they could cook so well? Describe the occasion and people's reactions.

Vantillu

Let us now read the following excerpt from the poem 'Vantillu' by the Telugu writer Vimala, translated by B. V. L. Narayana Row, and think about the above questions.

I remember the kitchen's
flavour upon flavour,
a mouth-watering treasury,
pungency of seasonings,
and the aroma of incense
from the prayer room
next door. Each morning
the kitchen awoke
to the swish of churning butter,
the scraping of scoured pots.
And in the centre, the stove,
fresh washed with mud, painted
and bedecked, all set to burn.

We saved secret money in the
seasoning box; hid sweets too,
and played at cooking with lentils and
jaggery.
We played Mother and Father,
in the magic world of kitchen
that wrapped childhood in its spell.

No longer playground for the grown-up girl
now trained into kitchenhood.
Like all the mothers and mothers' mothers
before her, in the kitchen,
she becomes woman right here.

Our kitchen is a mortuary.
Pans, tins, gunny bags
crowd it like cadavers
that hang amid clouds of damp wood smoke.
Mother floats, a ghost here,
a floating kitchen herself,
her eyes melted in tears,
her hands worn to spoons,
her arms, spatulas that turn
into long frying pans, and
other kitchen tools.
Sometimes mother glows
like a blazing furnace,
and burns through the kitchen,
pacing, restless, a caged tiger,
banging pots and pans.
How easy, they say,
the flick of the ladle and the cooking's done.
No one visits now.
No one comes to the kitchen
except to eat.

My mother was queen of the kitchen,
but the name engraved on the pots and pans
is Father's.

Luck, they say, landed me in my great kitchen,
gas stove, grinder, sink, and tiles.
I make cakes and puddings,
not old-fashioned snacks as my mother did.
But the name engraved on the pots and pans
is my husband's.
My kitchen wakes
to the whistle of the pressure cooker,
the whirr of the electric grinder.

I am a well-appointed kitchen myself,
turning round like a mechanical doll.

My kitchen is a workshop, a clattering,
busy, butcher stall, where I cook
and serve, and clean, and cook again.
In dreams, my kitchen haunts me,
my artistic kitchen dreams,
the smell of seasonings even in the jasmine.

Damn all kitchens! May they burn to cinders!
The kitchens that steal our dreams, drain
our lives, eat our days—like some enormous
vulture.
Let us destroy these kitchens
that turned us into serving spoons.
Let us remove the names engraved on the
pots and pans.
Come, let us tear out these private stoves,
before our daughters must step
solitary into these kitchens.
For our children's sakes,
let us destroy these lonely kitchens.

❖ ❖ ❖

In the poem, a woman tells the story of
women's lives. It is the story of the poet's
mother, and all 'mothers' mothers'. It is her
story as well. History brings no change to
women's lives. What was fun when children
played together turns into drudgery for the
grown woman who slaves away alone. We
never learn the mother's name, or even the
speaker's name. The mother is a ghost who
haunts the speaker's kitchen, her arms turned
into spoons and spatulas. The poet remembers
her as flaring up like a furnace sometimes. But
her anger did not start any revolution. In fact,
despite the lifetimes that women have given
to kitchens, even the names engraved on the
vessels are those of their husbands.

Modernity (which, political theory tells us,
promises freedom to all) brings the speaker a
fancy kitchen with modern gadgets, but belies
the promise of personal freedom since she
remains, like her mother, a slave to traditional
expectations and demands. Even though some
of the details in the poem may sound specific to
some families and communities, they highlight
the general nature of compulsion and drudgery
in everyday cooking.

Points to discuss:

1. How do you understand the line 'she
   becomes woman right here'? Can you
   relate it to what was discussed in Unit 2
   on socialisation?
2. Does the poem describe what happens
   in your own house? If not, can you
   describe for the class what happens in
   your house?
3. The poet's mother sometimes flares up
   'like a blazing furnace'. Does this happen
   with your mother? Why do you think
   this happens?
4. Is the kitchen in the poem always a place
   of drudgery? When is it not so?
5. The poet ends by saying, 'For our
   children's sakes, let us destroy these
   lonely kitchens.' What do you think she
   means by this? Can kitchens be places
   where men and women jointly work?

4.2 SHARE THE LOAD

We all know that working women and men
usually undergo a lot of job-related stress.
They worry about the stability of their job
and their future prospects. Men worry about
providing adequately for the family. Women,
in addition to these concerns, experience
conflict between what is expected of them as

wives and mothers and the demands of their workplace. Working for an income does not necessarily reduce their housework. They thus carry a ***double burden***. They are expected to prioritise the social roles of mother and wife at the expense of their work life. As a result, they experience stress and guilt. In this section, we will try to understand this double burden.

You Are a Wife, Daughter, Mother…

In a 2014 interview with *The Atlantic*,[1] Indra K. Nooyi spoke about the difficulties and contradictions of being a working woman as well as a wife, daughter and mother. On the day she was made president of the Board of Directors of Pepsico, one of the world's largest companies, she returned home full of excitement and was eager to share her pleasure and pride with her family. But before she could even enter her house and announce the news, her mother asked her to go and buy some milk. Nooyi protested. The milk could wait. But her mother brushed her complaints aside. Left with no choice, Nooyi went and bought the milk. She returned home and angrily shared her news. In response, her mother said: 'You might be President of Pepsico, … but when you enter this house, you're the wife, you're the daughter, you're the daughter-in-law, you're the mother.' The implication was clear. The world might celebrate her achievement, but at home the priorities were different. Her responsibilities as wife, mother and daughter, or daughter-in-law, came first. More hurtful was the fact that her mother did not seem to value her achievement. Because of such expectations (which are not there for men; who are appreciated if they simply 'help' at home) working women carry a huge burden of guilt. Many authors of this book have similar experiences. They teach, they write books, they give talks at seminars, they research, they supervise students' research, they help run organisations they work in, but they all carry a burden of guilt that they do not spend enough time at home or with their children (even if they spend much more time than their husbands do!).

If a mother misses a parent–teacher meeting, both the teacher and the child complain. Many still believe that mothers are supposed to be back at home to help children with their homework and ensure meals are ready on time and that they are always available for the children to talk to. If they don't manage all this, Nooyi says, they 'die with guilt'. She adds, 'You know, stay at home mothering was a full-time job. Being a CEO of a company is three full-time jobs rolled into one. How can you do justice to all?'

> ***Points to discuss:***
>
> 1. Does it seem strange to hear, 'when you enter this house, you're the wife, you're the daughter, you're the daughter-in-law, you're the mother'? Do you feel there is a problem with what Nooyi's mother says? If so, can you explain why?
> 2. Nooyi was expressing the disappointment and anger that a working woman feels when her public achievements are disregarded by her family, and instead her duties as a 'housewife' are emphasised. Do you think her feelings are justified? Why?
> 3. Try and describe the guilt that Nooyi is talking about.
> 4. Do you think this experience is peculiar to elite or upper-middle-class women? Or do you think women from other classes experience it too?

Wanted: A Wife

Let us now look at excerpts from a satirical essay titled 'I Want a Wife!' by Judy Brady, an American writer. It describes the fantasy of a working mother, who is a wife herself, who dreams about what she could do if she were to have a wife. The statement makes us smile, but it is also a shock tactic that forces us to acknowledge the many things wives do which go unnoticed because it is assumed 'that's what wives should do!' For example, in the USA, many wives work and use their earnings to support their families while their husbands extend or complete their education. This is regarded as a way of ensuring that he gets a better job (which will be good for the family), but in this trade-off, the wife has to give up her ambitions for further study or a better job. Intensely aware that a husband can leave the numerous daily nurturing tasks of childcare that require careful and minute attention to the wife, Brady says: 'I want a wife to take care of my children. I want a wife to keep track of the children's doctor and dentist appointments. And to keep track of mine, too. I want a wife to make sure my children eat properly and are kept clean. I want a wife who will wash the children's clothes and keep them mended.'

Brady points to what a husband takes for granted when she muses: 'I want a wife who takes care of the children when they are sick, a wife who arranges to be around when the children need special care, because, of course, I cannot miss classes at school. My wife must arrange to lose time at work and not lose the job. It may mean a small cut in my wife's income from time to time, but I guess I can tolerate that.'

It becomes more and more clear that it is this unequal share of work which frees the husband to study—or to take his 'work' seriously. She dreams on: 'I want a wife who will take care of my physical needs. I want a wife who will keep my house clean. A wife who will pick up after my children, a wife who will pick up after me. I want a wife who will keep my clothes clean, ironed, mended, replaced when need be, and who will see to it that my personal things are kept in their proper place so that I can find what I need the minute I need it. I want a wife who cooks the meals, a wife who is a good cook. I want a wife who will plan the menus, do the necessary grocery shopping, prepare the meals, serve them pleasantly, and then do the cleaning up while I do my studying. I want a wife who will care for me when I am sick and sympathise with my pain and loss of time from school.'

Brady's satire may seem excessive or strange at times, but it draws attention to the unsaid beliefs that operate in our daily familial lives. Those of you who are not married (girls as well as boys) may realise that you make such assumptions about mothers, even mothers who have full-time jobs. The roles 'wife' and 'husband' are supposed to be equal and complementary. If they are, why do the 'persons with wives' (in other words, 'husbands') get to enjoy privileges that wives cannot?

Points to discuss:

1. Can you list three important aspects of being a 'good wife' according to the quoted lines?
2. Can you list three important aspects of being a 'good husband' from the quoted lines?
3. Are your two lists different from each other or the same? Can you explain why they are the same or different?

4. This essay was written for the North American context. Discuss how you might adapt it for the Indian context.

Sharing Housework

As you have seen in this unit, there is an enormous amount of work that wives and mothers do which most people generally do not consider to be 'work'. Read the list of household tasks in the box that follows to get a sense of the sheer volume of work that needs to be done to keep a house running smoothly. We have listed those tasks that are typically done in the first half of the day; there are plenty of other things to be done in the second half of the day. You cannot miss the inequality present in assigning all housework to only one member of the family.

You may have seen some recent advertisements that try to raise this issue in a thoughtful manner. Take a look, for example, at the 'Respect for Women' series of advertisements for household products that Havells brought out in 2014.[2] You could also watch the advertisement for a washing powder that asks the question, 'Why is laundry only a mother's job?' and states, 'Dads #ShareTheLoad'.[3] These advertisements show that housework can be done easily and equally well by men, whether married or not. In fact, the Havells advertisements tell us that family or household life is not simply about living together, but about friendship, companionship, respect and jointly sharing everything, including housework. We need to move beyond earlier models of the family where only women served husbands, elders and children.

List of morning chores in a middle-class household

- Sweep the front yard and draw a *muggu*.
- Collect drinking water from the municipal tap and pour it into the water filter.
- Fill bottles with drinking water and store them in the refrigerator.
- Separately store water for washing and cleaning.
- Pick up milk packets and the newspaper.
- Clean the kitchen counters and mop the kitchen floor.
- Scrape the dry remains from last evening's dishes and put the dishes out for the maid to wash.
- Decide what to make for breakfast and lunch.
- Cut vegetables, boil milk and prepare tea or coffee.
- Make dosas for everybody and serve with chutney.
- Find and iron children's school uniforms and husband's office clothes.
- Look for misplaced socks and books.
- Cook lunch and pack boxes for both the children and the adults.
- Cook an extra meal or snack for the children to eat after they return from school.
- Drop the children off at the bus stop where they board the school bus.
- Make the beds—one's own and the children's—and put away dirty clothes.
- Clean the dining table, reading tables and beds of litter, pencils, papers, books and gadgets.
- Sort the clothes to be washed and soak them or put them in the machine for the maid.

- Hand over the trash to the trash-picker.
- Water the plants.
- Clean the bathrooms.

You have read the list of morning chores in a typical middle-class household. Can you prepare a similar list of chores for the maid who comes to work in that household?

NOTES

1. Read the full interview here: https://www.theatlantic.com/business/archive/2014/07/why-pepsico-ceo-indra-k-nooyi-cant-have-it-all/373750/

2. Watch the Havells' advertisement here: https://www.youtube.com/watch?v=TN_mGzEP6RM or here: https://www.youtube.com/watch?v=MaJf0mNMqos.

3. Watch Ariel's #ShareTheLoad advertisement here: https://www.youtube.com/watch?v=wJukf4ifuKs.

Missing Women: Sex Selection and its Consequences

5.1 DECLINING SEX RATIO

In 1990, the eminent economist Amartya Sen argued that ten crore women were 'missing' in the regions of South Asia, West Asia and North Africa. He remarked: 'These numbers tell us, quietly, a terrible story of inequality and neglect leading to the excess mortality of women.' This unit aims to understand the appalling story of these missing women by examining the role of *sex selection*. In the Indian context, sex selection is generally done by ascertaining the sex of the foetus through scanning—and then terminating the pregnancy if the foetus is female. This is called female foeticide or sex-selective abortion (SSA). Sometimes, the female child is killed soon after birth and this is called female infanticide. Both practices exist in our country.

There is a Tamil proverb which goes, 'Raising a daughter is like watering a flower in the neighbour's garden.' There are proverbs in many Indian languages that echo similar sentiments. Daughters are often referred to as *paraya dhan, parayi ghar ki* and so on to suggest that they don't really belong to their biological parents and, worse still, that they are a burden to them. The practice of patrilocality—when a woman marries and has to leave her parents and home to go live with her husband in his house or close to his parents—which occurs in most parts of our country, reinforces this idea. In the prose-poem, 'Girl', which you read in Unit 2 on socialisation, we see a daughter trained from a young age to be a skilled, obedient wife and daughter-in-law. Many parents still worry about having to pay a huge dowry to get their daughters married, and believe that only their sons will look after them in their old age. Many therefore dislike having daughters and prefer having sons. A sad example of such an attitude is the practice in rural Maharashtra of naming third or fourth daughters 'Nakusa' or 'Nakoshi', meaning 'unwanted'. This is done in the hope that the next child will be a boy. The girls who carry such names are scarred for life, growing up as they do with an acute sense of feeling unloved and unwanted. As a result of this preference for sons, many parents opt to commit female foeticide or female infanticide. This horrific reality is a grim reminder of gender discrimination in our society. It is also one of the reasons why there has been a lot of concern over our country's sex ratio.

Many of you must have seen advertisements like the one below or heard or seen slogans issued by the government like 'Save the Girl Child' or *Beti Bachao, Beti Padhao*. Have you ever wondered why the government issues such slogans and runs such campaigns? The answer lies in the discussion over sex ratio and sex selection.

What is Sex Ratio?

Sex ratio is the number of males to females in a population. In many countries, this is measured by counting the number of males per 100 females. In India however, it is measured by counting the number of females per 1000 males. Additionally, Child Sex Ratio (CSR) refers to the number of girls to boys, and Overall Sex Ratio (OSR) refers to the number of women to men.

In the decades since India gained its independence, the number of girls has been decreasing at an alarming rate. This has resulted in a ***gender imbalance***. The table below shows the CSR and the number of girls who survive

Stop Sex Selection, Save the Girl Child

Pre-conception, Sex Selection and Pre-natal Sex Determination is a Criminal Offence

PC&PNDT Act 1994: Salient Features

- **PROHIBITS** sex selection before and after conception
- **PROHIBITS** misuse of preconception and prenatal diagnostic techniques for determination of sex of the foetus
- **PROHIBITS** advertisements of such techniques for detection or determination of sex of the foetus, even through internet
- **REGISTRATION COMPULSORY** for facilities providing preconception and prenatal diagnostics capable of determining the sex of the foetus
- **MAINTENANCE** and **PRESERVATION OF RECORDS COMPULSORY** in the prescribed formats including Form F*

Penalties under the PC&PNDT Act 1994

For Doctors/Owners of Clinics
- Upto three years of imprisonment with fine upto Rs.10,000 for the first offence
- Upto five years of imprisonment with fine upto Rs.50,000 for subsequent offence
- Suspension of medical registration of doctors if charges are framed
- Cancellation of medical registration of doctor for five years by the State Medical Council in case of first offence and permanent cancellation in case of subsequent offence

For Husband/Family Members or Any other person abetting sex selection
- Upto three years of imprisonment with fine upto Rs.50,000 for the first offence
- Upto five years of imprisonment upto Rs.1,00,000 for subsequent offence

For Non registration of any organization using Ultra sound machine, scanner or any other equipment capable of determining sex of the foetus:
- Confiscation of equipment/machines/and further action as per the provision of Section 23

For any advertisement regarding sex selection:
- Upto three years of imprisonment and upto Rs.10,000 in fine

Appropriate authorities empowered with the powers for search and seizure for non-compliance of the Act

Every offence under the PC&PNDT Act is cognizable, non-bailable and non-compoundable.

Who all are liable?
- Unit in charge/owner of diagnostic facility
- Doctor/persons who perform the test
- Mediator abetting pregnant woman's access
- Husband/relatives of the pregnant woman
- Persons advertising sex selection in any form

The pregnant woman herself is considered innocent under the Act unless proved otherwise.

dropping from 983 per 1000 boys in 1951 to 918 per 1000 boys in 2011. This means that over the years the situation has grown worse for girls, with the country facing a gender imbalance of 37.3 million more men than women.

It was in the mid-1970s that demographers first took note of this gradual decline. The landmark *Towards Equality* report, which was prepared in 1974 by the Committee on the Status of Women in India, strongly emphasised the need for taking note of this 'shocking' and 'inexplicable' decline in the number of women.

OSR and CSR

Carefully go through the table below. It provides details of the steady decline in the number of women for every 1000 men (OSR) and the number of girls for every 1000 boys (CSR). The CSR in particular shows an alarming decline from 983 in 1951 to 918 in 2011.

The reason this was seen as shocking was because people believed that with modernisation and development there would be an improvement for everyone in all spheres of life. But, surprisingly, the situation for women was deteriorating.

You might think that the birth of a child is a natural process. After all, we have no control over the sex of a child. But you might be surprised to learn that, on average, more boys than girls are born. This means that the number of men and women in any population is never quite equal. This is why the sex ratio at birth is usually 950 girls per 1000 boys in many countries where sex selection is not widely practised. But a baby girl has a slight biological edge over a baby boy in terms of survival. Furthermore, women tend to outlive men at the other end of the life cycle. So, in most countries there generally tends to be more female children than male children and more women than men in the age group of 15–65.

Contrary to this, though, is the fact that India is among only a small handful of countries in the world, along with Nepal and China, where the number of girls who survive is lower than the number of boys. Our neighbouring country, Bangladesh, does not have this problem. Its sex ratio is similar to the world norm. This clearly indicates that, contrary to our perceptions, economic development does not necessarily have a positive impact on gender discrimination. Developed states like Punjab and Haryana have had very skewed sex ratios. Similarly, gender imbalance is more visible in urban rather than rural areas.

Table 1: Child Sex Ratios (CSRs) and Overall Sex Ratios (OSRs)

	1951	*1961*	*1971*	*1981*	*1991*	*2001*	*2011*
Overall sex ratio (OSR)	946	941	930	934	927	933	943
Child sex ratio (CSR)	983	976	964	962	945	927	918

	1951	*1961*	*1971*	*1981*	*1991*	*2001*	*2011*
Drop in overall sex ratio (OSR)	/	–5	–11	4	–7	6	10
Drop in child sex ratio (CRS)	/	–7	–12	–2	–17	–18	–9

Source: Mary E. John. *Sex ratios and gender biased sex selection.*

Why are Sons Preferred over Daughters?

The social and cultural attitudes that we mentioned in the beginning of this unit play a major role in determining the country's sex ratio.

Dowry is a significant reason why many families and communities do not want daughters. Female infanticide, a practice largely found in upper-caste communities earlier, is now spreading to all communities along with the practice of giving dowry.

The government's push to implement a two-child policy has convinced many to plan their families with at least one son and not more than one daughter. You may be interested to know that in China, the government's 'one child per family' policy led to many families trying to ensure that the one child they had would be a son, thereby contributing to a major gender imbalance in their country. Here, in India, the pattern of sons inheriting and managing property and businesses also makes daughters less desirable. Added to this, the cost of educating a girl and ensuring she marries into a good family discourages many families from having daughters.

Points to discuss:

1. Is the comment on dowry true? If the practice of dowry did not exist, do you think our society would be kinder to girls?
2. Are only sons entitled to inherit property? What does the law say? Find out.
3. Do you know of families or communities where the married couple stays with the girl's parents? Is this a common practice? How is such an arrangement viewed in our society?

5.2 DEMOGRAPHIC CONSEQUENCES

The Struggle against Sex-Selective Abortions

Social and cultural practices that privilege boys over girls have played a significant role in creating a gender imbalance in our country. Modern medical technologies, like the ultrasound, that are used to help detect physical abnormalities in the foetus, have also been used to determine the sex of an unborn child. Medical procedures like amniocentesis and chorionic villus sampling were used as sex-selection techniques in the 1980s. Together, these technologies and procedures have been used widely to discover the sex of the child before birth and have contributed to gender discrimination against girls because, once the sex of the child is known to be female, families might force the woman to undergo an abortion.

This process of selective abortion is called female foeticide. Female foeticide and female infanticide have contributed to a severe numerical imbalance between the sexes.

Many women's organisations have tried to address the issue of female foeticide. In 1982, a national coalition of women's organisations demanded a complete ban on medical tests that aided sex selection. Initially, there was very little public support, but this changed when reports of female infanticide from districts in Tamil Nadu became national news. The entire country was horrified, and this helped step up the campaign's pressure on the government. In 1985, the Forum Against Sex Determination and Sex Pre-Selection (FASDSP) was established in Bombay. FASDSP's systematic campaigning—using methods ranging from street theatre to Public

Interest Litigation (PIL)—and the support it received from women's organisations and health groups across the country turned the issue into one of national concern.

These campaigns led to the Government of India placing a ban on diagnostic tests that determined the sex of the foetus. Known as the Preconception and Pre-Natal Diagnostic Techniques (PC and PNDT) Act, it was introduced in 1994. The Act limits the use of pre-natal diagnosis to detect a list of selected congenital conditions and explicitly prohibits using these techniques for sex determination of the foetus (look at the poster on page 46).

The Supreme Court of India also issued detailed directives to national and state governments to raise awareness of the law on sex determination and called for increased surveillance of all clinics providing ultrasounds. You must have seen signs in the maternity wards of hospitals and in diagnostic centres urging people not to ask for the sex of their unborn child. The hospital staff are not allowed to disclose this information. Doing so is a punishable offence. This measure is aimed at preventing female foeticides. Despite this, there continue to be many cases reported in the media about the misuse of diagnostic tests resulting in the medical termination of female foetuses.

But is the Law Enough?

We know from other units in this book that the law alone cannot change everything. The law does lend support to those fighting against the discrimination of women and it does act as a deterrent to cases of sex-selective abortions. But local activists have reported that medical practitioners are ready to reveal the sex of an unborn child for as little as 600 rupees. Doing so is illegal, and discouraged by various campaigns, but it is almost impossible to fully enforce the law across the country. There is a strong demand for scans to reveal the sex of the child before birth, and enterprising technicians are able to evade the law by visiting villages with scanners on bicycles. Often slapping the father on the back and saying 'you're a lucky man' is hint enough that the foetus is male. It seems the introduction of a number of laws and acts has had limited success in improving India's sex ratio and mitigating the country's problems of female infanticide and foeticide.

In fact, some scholars argue that the law has not only failed in halting sex-selective abortions, but that it has been counterproductive as well; they claim that for fear of attracting criminal charges, many private clinics have stopped scanning altogether. This has led to a denial of essential diagnostic and medical services, thereby resulting in certain cases where there has been loss of life. All in all, it is quite clear that the real and long-term solution to the sex-ratio problem is a change in our attitude towards girls. The more we see them as human beings who have a right to life, to education, to employment, to choose their own life partners—in short, the more we see them as individuals who have a right to live as equal citizens—the less need for such laws.

> **Points to discuss:**
>
> 1. Have you heard people say they are lucky to have sons? Why do you think they believe this?
> 2. Do you really think it is bad luck to have a daughter?

What's Wrong with More Men?— The Social Consequences of a Skewed Sex Ratio

Researchers have noted that female mortality rates are higher in India than in other countries due to neglect of the health and nutritional needs of a girl. This means that even when a girl is born unharmed, she is more likely to die in her infancy than if she was a boy. In other words, in India, girls are more likely to die when young than boys. Some of you may still be grappling with the question: What is wrong with having more men? Many social science researchers have tried to address questions like 'What are the social consequences of a skewed sex ratio?' and 'Why should we be worried that there are close to more than four crore men than women in India?'

One of the adverse results of a skewed sex ratio is what sociologists and demographers have called the 'marriage squeeze'. In states like Rajasthan and Haryana, the gender imbalance has led to a shortage of brides and therefore a severe marriage crisis. Men who are poor, uneducated, unemployed, of a low status or disadvantaged in some other way are most likely to remain unmarried.

Some of us might wonder, 'If women are fewer in number, won't they be valued more?' This is unfortunately not the case. Another problem with a skewed gender balance involving more men than women is an increase in crime and violence. Due to the shortage of local women, there is often heightened competition to secure their hand in marriage by any means necessary. This shortage also means inter-caste or inter-religious marriages may not be tolerated, resulting in honour killings by bodies like caste *panchayats*.

Scholars argue that another social consequence of a shortage of women is that such an environment may actually reinforce traditional female roles like reproduction, domestic work and care work. This contradicts the ideal of providing women with the necessary opportunities to live their lives as equal citizens.

With increased violence against women, parents may withdraw their daughters from school and instead of prioritising education might concentrate their efforts on getting them married.

These are but a few consequences of the gender imbalance in India. We should therefore protect the fundamental right of every girl not only to be born, but also to lead a healthy, happy and fulfilling life. We should also recognise that a more balanced sex ratio is a primary requirement for the well-being of men, women and society in general.

Points to discuss:

1. Why do you think the number of girls for every 1000 boys is declining in India?
2. What are some of the negative effects of sex selection?
3. Do you think rethinking gender roles will diminish the number of cases of female foeticide?

Looking at Knowledge through the Lens of Gender

6.1 POINT OF VIEW

You may be surprised to learn that sensitivity to questions of gender has influenced academic disciplines ranging from anthropology to zoology. For example, in the 1970s and 1980s, women scholars pointed out that the authors generally prescribed for study in English literature syllabuses were all men, and that too men from elite backgrounds.

The word 'elite' here suggests a privileged, upper-class or upper-caste person. Elite men represent a tiny fraction of society. Their literature depicts the world as they see it, from their *point of view*. We should remember that 'point of view' here has two meanings: it refers to the position from which a person observes the world, and what can be seen (or cannot be seen) from that position; and it also refers to that person's interests. In other words, we often choose to see the world in a manner that suits us best.

Different points of view are welcome in a free society. They can make us think. They can even make us change our minds. Look at the drawing on the next page. A large number of people think that women who cover their faces and heads live according to the rules of a male-dominated society, no matter that other women are free to dress as they please. But as you can see in the drawing, there are other points of view. If we seriously consider what the woman on the right is thinking, we may change our minds about our perceptions of freedom.

Points to discuss:

1. Why does the woman in a bikini think the woman in a burqa lives in a male-dominated society?

2. And why does the woman in a burqa think the woman in a bikini lives in a male-dominated society?

3. Who is right?

Women Writers, Women's Worlds

Gender-sensitive scholars suggest that when an elite male point of view is taken to be the truth, other points of view appear less true or even false. This is one of the reasons why literary critics and syllabus-makers did not take women's writing seriously. In their opinion, women writers dealt with trivial, personal and domestic matters, while men wrote about important universal issues. They often dismissed women's writing as 'subjective' or 'emotional' or 'poorly written'. In fact, the power and dominance of this elite male point of view erases—in the sense that it makes invisible—the lives and experiences of all others.

New research shows that women writers and poets existed from the very earliest years of known history. An Egyptian inscription that dates back to the fifteenth century BCE records the edicts of a woman ruler. Among the earliest women poets in India were Buddhist *bhikkhunīs* (fifth to sixth century BCE) whose poetry is collected in the Therīgāthā. The following poem is by Bhikkhuni Mutta. She seeks freedom from the repetitive grind of kitchen work and from her 'twisted' husband's domination. And she finds what she is looking for in the liberation preached by the Buddha.

We should note here that Buddhist scholars and thinkers not only valued Bhikkhuni Mutta's poem enough to place it in such a collection, but also, in doing so, acknowledged and accepted her idea of freedom.

So free!

So free am I, so gloriously free,
Free from three petty things—
From mortar, from pestle and from my twisted
    lord.
Freed from rebirth and death I am,
And all that had held me down
Is hurled away.

❖ ❖ ❖

Mutta's poem, translated by Uma Chakravarti and Kumkum Roy, shows that an idea such as liberation—spiritual or political—can have very different meanings. For women, liberation may mean freedom from never-ending, unappreciated and unpaid kitchen work, from sexually demanding and tyrannical husbands or from exploitation by landlords or employers. Writings like Mutta's poem touch upon areas of human life that may not have received attention in modern scholarship. But when professors of literature chose material for syllabuses, they were not sensitive to this or had no interest in such writings. Why? We can understand why women writers, their experience, their worlds, their ideas were not considered important only when we ask: Who has the power to judge literature, to decide what is 'good', 'bad', 'important' and 'unimportant'? Whose values, interests and worldview is taken as universal, worthy of study, or even objective? How does the question of power affect the ways in which disciplines select and organise material for study?

It is possible to 'add women' to existing knowledge formations or disciplines, but this does not solve the overarching problem as the exclusion of women is connected with the powers that structure and control disciplines. This is very important to note here: making disciplines aware of women and accountable to women's interests requires fundamental changes—in ways of thinking, in education, in universities and workplaces, in the family and in public life. In fact, gender studies is not really a separate discipline. It is a critical perspective on all disciplines.

The account that follows is of an Urdu writer who, in the 1940s and 50s, wrote about gender issues in ways that even today we might find bold and progressive. Her work was labelled as 'controversial' and she was criticised by well-known male authors of her time as not attending enough to the art of writing. Decades later, readers interested in gender issues began speaking of her as a leading writer of her time. We hope you like Shankar Pamarthy's drawing of her.

Ismat Chughtai

When scholars began searching for writers sidelined by elite literary evaluation, they soon found rebellious ones like Ismat Chughtai (1915–91). Chughtai wrote about topics that were considered taboo. But more disturbing than her themes was her attitude. She cut through social pretensions and her stories flashed with irreverent humour. This outspoken, and therefore controversial, style of writing made her an inspiration to the younger generation of writers, readers and intellectuals. Her witty realism made for irresistible reading. Some of her stories and her novel *Terhi Lakir* (*The Crooked Line*, 1943) have now been translated from Urdu into English as well as other Indian languages.

Girls in Chughtai's time were raised to cook, sew and excel at a variety of domestic skills, but she preferred books—much to the irritation of her mother. Her father, however, encouraged her studies. She grew up in the company of her brothers and this, she says, is the source of her open and frank nature. She was the first Muslim woman in pre-Partition India to get a BA degree. Before she married the film director Shaheed Latif, she told him: 'I'm a very troublesome woman … I have been breaking chains all my life. I won't be bound in any chain now. It doesn't suit me to be an obedient, virtuous woman.'

Among her best-known stories are: 'The Wedding Suit', '*Choti Aapa*', 'The Quilt', 'Homemaker', 'Sacred Duty', and 'Scent of the Body'. Many of these are available on the internet—both in translation and in Urdu.

6.2 INEQUALITIES IN THE STRUCTURE OF KNOWLEDGE

As discussed, knowledge production, which can be thought of as the processes by which theories as well as the practical know-how in a discipline or area are systematised, invariably assumes different kinds of elitist viewpoints. However, social groups such as dalits, minorities and people with disabilities have, like women, begun to raise questions about the criteria and limits by which what is 'valid' or 'proper' or 'true' is decided.

In the field of Indian literature, an upper-caste point of view was dominant until very recently. Some of you may have heard of *Boosa Chaluvali*. Read about it below to understand how this movement raised some important questions about Kannada literature in education while also drawing attention to rich literary material produced by dalits.

Boosa Chaluvali

The *Boosa Chaluvali* movement began in 1974 when B. Basavalingappa, a well-educated and popular dalit minister in the Karnataka government, said: 'We should have Kannada pride, speak Kannada, strive to make it grow; but we get ideas, independent thinking and patriotic feeling[s] by reading English.' He went on to say that Kannada literature, which at that time was dominated by the upper castes, had a great deal of *boosa*, which meant chaff or cattle feed. He made this claim because he believed it did not contain democratic values and attitudes; it did not foster genuine nationalism based on the equality of citizens. Since literature is thought of as embodying the highest values of a culture, his statements enraged many professors, critics, established writers and students who took to the streets demanding his resignation. The uproar was so strong that it looked as though the government would fall. Basavalingappa was forced to resign. The elite represent a very small percentage of the population, but when they are supported by political, economic and cultural power, they can control a discipline or field of knowledge in subtle and deep-seated ways.[1]

Happily, there is another side to the *Boosa Chaluvali* story. The controversy led to the formation of the Dalita Sangharsha Samiti (DSS) and the flowering of dalit literature in Kannada in the 1980s. The poem 'The Dalits are Here' by Siddalingaiah, translated by M. Madhava Prasad, emerged from that movement and announced the 'arrival' of dalits in the modern world.

The Dalits are Here

The dalits are coming, step aside—
hand over charge, let them rule.

Minds burning with countless dreams,
slogans like thunder and lightning,
in the language of earthquakes,
here comes the dalit procession,
writing [history] with their feet.

…

For the thorn bushes of caste and religion,
they were as thorns in the side.
They became the sky that looked down at
the seven seas that swallowed them.

Since Rama's time and Krishna's time
unto the time of the Gandhis,
They had bowed low with folded hands.
Now they have risen in struggle

…

Under the flag of dalit India
stood the farmers and workers.

Flowers bloom in every forest,
thousands of birds take flight,
the eastern sky turned red,
morning broke for the poor.

The dalits are coming, step aside.
The dalits have come, give it up!

Dalit writers and intellectuals credit Basavalingappa for having lit the spark that led to the birth of a new literature. 'The Dalits are Here', by Siddalingaiah, who at the time of writing the poem was a student living in a social welfare hostel but is now a leading scholar and poet, can also be understood as a statement about dalits (and others) staking a claim in the field of knowledge. Their claim over knowledge leads to their claim over the nation, as equal citizens, that has hitherto been in the hands of the elite. The movement revealed new perspectives and rediscovered literature that had been dismissed and devalued as 'not good enough'. It also brought to attention important issues pertaining to cultural, social and political inequalities.

As many of you know, feminist and dalit writers have similarly challenged the dominant form of literature in other Indian languages as well.

6.3 ACROSS THE ACADEMY

Not just literature but even 'objective' and 'factual' scientific disciplines like economics, biology or medicine exclude many important issues related to women or other marginalised groups because their frameworks deny 'seeing' these issues as significant. In later units you will learn why the discipline of economics must take into account the importance of housework, child-rearing and home nursing of the sick and the aged—all work that women do for free—if the field is to understand the workings of the national economy. Since political theory and law treated the family as private, domestic violence was neither legally recognised as violence nor studied by political or legal theorists until the issue was first raised by women's movements in the 1980s. You will also learn how gender sensitivity has helped us think beyond the biological idea of two genders. Today we see that all forms of knowledge have been transformed by movements (race, class, caste, gender, sexuality, disability) that have asked pertinent questions about established and accepted ideas. If you ask your teachers, they will probably be able to give you more examples of how their disciplines have been influenced by gender studies.

In Search of a Dalit Journalist

It has often been observed that mainstream media is not alert or sensitive to dalit issues. We only read reports about dalits or tribals in the context of heinous atrocities, such as when dalit children are burnt alive or an entire family is hacked to pieces. We can understand this in terms of a dominant elite point of view—journalists write articles on issues which are in line with their own concerns.

How does this happen? Journalists and others in the media business are the people who decide, to a large extent, what is 'newsworthy' and what news should be prioritised or gain front-page coverage. Their own attitudes and assumptions shape how and what we read or receive as 'news'.

The excerpt that follows is from a 1996 investigation by B. N. Uniyal, a nationally renowned journalist. It explores how interests and prejudice, absent or present, are crucial to what is presented as 'news'. It also provides statistics from the Press Information Bureau booklet to show that, at the time, there were no accredited journalists that belonged to the

dalit caste. Ten years later, in 2006, when the Delhi-based Centre for the Study of Developing Societies created a list of the 315 most influential journalists in Hindi- and English-language media, there still wasn't a single dalit among them. Seventy-one per cent of the journalists were upper-caste Hindu men. This under-representation of dalits and other marginalised voices is part of the reason why there is a paucity of news and discussion about these communities in the mainstream media.

One morning last week, a correspondent of a foreign newspaper stationed in Delhi rang me up to find out whether I knew any dalit journalist from whom he could get a quote on Kanshi Ram and Mayawati's recent squabble with some media persons. 'Mr Uniyal, could you tell me if it would be offensive to ask an Indian journalist whether he is a dalit?' he began. . . .

'Well,' I hesitated for a while, struggling in my mind with my various selves to formulate a correct response on behalf of them all. . . .

Suddenly, I realised that in all the 30 years I had worked as a journalist I had never met a fellow journalist who was a dalit; no, not one. And, worse still was the thought that during all these years it had never occurred to me that there was something so seriously amiss in the profession, something which I should have noticed as a journalist. . . . I have journalist friends who are Christians or Muslims, and a few Jains and Sikhs too, but none who is a dalit. How strange! There must at least be a few in the profession here in Delhi, I told myself. I decided to find out.

I rang up an English-language columnist friend—a former editor of a weekly who knows and meets more journalists from among the younger lot these days than I do. 'No, I don't know any,' he said. I rang up another friend. He said the same, I rang up another friend. He said the same. . . .

I decided to call up another journalist friend—a trade-union activist of long standing. He must know someone, I told myself. But he felt upset about it all. He saw in my query a conspiracy to divide the journalist fraternity. . . .

That night I went to [the] Press Club and asked several friends and acquaintances whether they knew any journalist who was a dalit. Nobody did. . . .

Another friend of long years told me that journalists are journalists and should not be screened on caste basis. 'Do you mean to say the Press is really *manuwadi* as Kanshi Ram says? Do you think any of us writes or reports as a brahmin journalist, or as a kayastha or a Jain journalist?' asked another friend. I admitted that that was not true, though I was by now becoming unsure of such an assertion. Does it really mean anything not to have any journalist amidst us from among the dalits? I asked myself. . . .

I came home and began leafing through the Accreditation Index, 1996, of the Press Information Bureau of the Government of India, which lists the names of all the accredited correspondents who serve as the eyes and the ears of the nation in the capital city of Delhi. They are the ones who decide what is news and what is not; what is worth reporting . . . and what is not.

Though it is not they alone who decide what or whom to play up or play down in next morning's newspapers or in the next edition of their weeklies and fortnightlies, it is basically they who give the news the slant which shapes our attitudes towards men and women in the news. Everything depends on what questions they ask at a press conference and how they ask these questions. And, at the end of the day, it all depends on how they compose their reports.

The Accreditation Index was revealing. Of the 686 accredited correspondents listed in it, as many as 454 bore their caste surnames and, of them, as many as 240 turned out to be brahmins, 79 Punjabi khatris, 44 kayasthas, 26 Muslims with as many baniyas, 19 Christians, 12 Jains and 9 (Bengali) baidyas. I checked out the caste affiliation of the 47 of the remaining 232 correspondents at random, and none of them turned out to be a dalit either. . . .

What would journalism be like if there were as many journalists from among the dalits as there are from among the brahmins? I asked myself.

6.4 FURTHER READING

The profiles that follow are of women in and around the city of Hyderabad in modern-day Telangana. We hope these accounts will help you search for such people in your own areas. We write about a skilled and talented performance artist, the world's first qualified lady anaesthetist and a woman pilot, all of whom were extremely distinguished in their fields but remain largely unknown.

The sketch of Chindu Yellamma gives a sense of what is lost when the importance of artists like her are not appreciated enough. This dalit woman's artistry and skill at performing male as well as female roles should also draw our attention to the social and cultural (as opposed to the physical or biological) nature of gender identities. The photograph is of her as Narasimha Avatar.

Chindu Yellamma

Chindu bhagotam is an ancient rural performing art (*yakshagana*).[2] It celebrates rural life, economy and culture, all of which are crucial to the survival of the community. In fact, *bhagotam* performances bring the village to life in the minds of its inhabitants.

When people move out of the village and away from their community, they experience an intense and complex sense of loss. This is particularly so in our time when villages and their natural resources and surroundings are being transformed by industrialisation and urbanisation. As people move from villages to towns, the cultural bases of villages are eroded. The appearance of Hindu festivals like *Ganesh Chaturthi* and *Varalakshmi Puja* have overshadowed and marginalised local festivals and art forms. Dance forms such as *bharatanatyam*, which the upper castes took over from temple performers, are now regarded as national art forms and receive official support. But *chindu yakshagana*—a dalit art form which plays an important part in giving rural communities heroes, heroines and stories to celebrate and cherish—is neglected and ignored. Today, *chindu yakshagana* is a forgotten art. Only traces of it remain in modern culture. Let us see how this skilful and distinguished cultural practice has been gradually excluded from our cultural landscape.

We are often told that N. T. Rama Rao and Telugu films familiarised people with the physical appearance of Rama, Krishna and other Hindu gods. However, the eminent *chindu* performer, Gaddam Sammayya, argues that Rama Rao and the film industry were actually introduced to these figures by *chindu* troupes. In fact, these gods and goddesses were first made visible as human figures in *chindu* performance narratives. The *chindu*

community worked hard over generations to create these much-loved representations. They went into forests to collect plants, leaves, roots, stems and so on which they used to create the paints, ornaments, crowns, weapons and musical instruments for their performances. Their performances take place on a stage in the village square. Adorned with make-up and wearing costumes that glitter like gold, performers enter accompanied by drums and music and dance vigorously, leaving the audience entranced. The world of the gods is depicted in their performance, and the story of village life is woven into the story of the gods.

Every *chindu yakshagana* performance begins with a ritual where the artists pray to the leather worker's curing tank (madiga *landa*), the blacksmith's furnace (kammari *kolimi*), the potter's kiln (kummari *aamu*), and the carpenter's plane (vadla *badishe*). In her performance, Chindu Yellamma describes this ritual in verse:

'We should raise our hands in salute to the beloved kammari who gives us the knife, because we madigas have given the kammari his bellows. This is why, the kammaris and the vadlas have made the blade and handle of the crane-neck knife that rests in the goddess Yellamma's hand.'

Chindu artists are important because their performances celebrate the value of artisanal occupations and also keep alive in their descriptions each artisanal community's traditions and links with other communities. For example, their performances stress the value of implements and celebrate the importance of the working castes in providing food and agricultural produce to the world. Relationships between communities are orally narrated in the Jambava Puranam and the Yellamma Katha. Both these epic performances represent the history not only of the dalits but of all the other productive communities in the village. Their art is thus a repository of knowledge about rural economy as well as a village community's social and cultural relationships. When art forms such as these find no place in modern institutions and are left to die, then a community's sense of meaning and self-worth are also lost. In present times the Jambava Puranam is being interpreted as an anti-caste *purana*, and the Yellamma Katha is being framed as a dalit feminist story.

One actor who has played both male and female protagonists in major compositions and has dazzled the world and mesmerised audiences is Chindu Yellamma. A nationally acclaimed performer, Chindu Yellamma could reach deep into the hearts of her viewers and rouse them to dance. She stepped onto the stage in the role of the child Krishna at the tender age of four. By eleven she was performing the female roles of Rambha, Chenchulakshmi, Savitri and Sita, as well as male roles like Vali, Kushala, Narayanamurthy and Dharmangadha.

Yellamma took *chindu yakshagana* from the village square outside the bungalows of powerful landlords to auditoriums in Hyderabad and all the way to Delhi. The famous dancer Nataraja Ramakrishna, who revived the tenth-century art form *perini sivatandavam*, said this about her when she died: 'When I think of Yellamma, my grief knows no bounds. The spirit of her performance (*abhinaya*) appears before my eyes as I speak. When we first met at Armoor, she performed, along with her troupe, two stories—*Sarangadhara* and *Chenchulakshmi*. Her performance as Chitrangi in *Sarangadhara* was wonderful. Just as I thought to myself, "It is getting dark, I have to get home," she said, "Ramakrishna *garu*, two minutes," went backstage and returned in the form of Narasimhaswamy. Her performance as Narasimhaswamy, in the love scene after his marriage to Chenchulakshmi where he gives her betel leaves (*tamalapaku*), mesmerised me. I have never seen any other actor play both masculine and feminine roles in quick succession with such expertise.'

The sad thing is that even as Chindu Yellamma performed the roles of Rama and Krishna, she could not escape the poverty that shadows untouchability. In spite of her fame, she was ignored till the end. She spoke of her distress, saying: 'It has become difficult even for me to live. How can the *chindu* art survive? Give me two *bighas* of land. It doesn't matter even if you don't give me ten thousand rupees, awards, rewards. This will be a life support for me.'

She died of starvation on 9 November 2005 in her small, dilapidated hut. Yellamma's life and the shocking manner in which she died—impoverished, neglected, unrecognised—is an example of how some dance forms, such as *bharatanatyam*, have come to represent Indian dance, while ancient traditions such as *chindu* and their gifted artistes are disregarded, unsupported and left to perish.

Dr Rupa Bai Furdoonji

Dr Rupa Bai Furdoonji, a Parsee woman from Hyderabad, was the world's first qualified female anaesthetist. She pursued her medical education from 1885 to 1889. Women back then found it difficult to gain admission to medical schools, even in England and the US. Furdoonji, however, was able to study at the Hyderabad Medical School largely due to its principal at the time—Surgeon Major Edward Lawrie.

Furdoonji, along with Lawrie and Sir Thomas Lauder Brunton, participated in many experiments involving the administration of chloroform on animals and clinical studies on humans. She was a member of the second Hyderabad Chloroform Commission held in

1889 and received a special mention from Lawrie in his final report on the Hyderabad Chloroform Commission published in 1891.

In 1909, she was assigned a position in Edinburgh for further training. She travelled by ship from Bombay to Edinburgh with a letter of recommendation from Dr Annie Besant, who was at the time the president of the Theosophical Society in India. On her return journey, her ship was anchored for a few weeks at Eden, a port in what is now Saudi Arabia. Impressed by the high quality of her abilities, the British Resident—the highest-ranking British official in a small colony—wrote to his counterpart in Hyderabad to ask if they could spare Dr Rupa Bai. Qualified anaesthetists were rare, and Dr Rupa Bai's services were much needed in Eden.

Upon her return to India, she worked at various major hospitals in Hyderabad including Sultan Bazar Hospital, Afzalgunj Hospital and Zenana Hospital. She retired in 1920.

Aban P. Chenoy

It is remarkable that another Parsee woman, Aban P. Chenoy, was the first woman member of the Hyderabad State Aero Club to qualify for an aviator's licence, and that too as early as 1938. She was also the only woman back then among the 55 Indian members of this 70-member club. We were unfortunately unable to find out more about her life, except that she passed away in 2012.

However, even such fragments challenge us to rethink commonly held views about women in different fields. They also demonstrate that a new framework or perspective (such as the one provided by feminism) reveals new dimensions in an existing field and reintroduces us to forgotten or ignored knowledge.

NOTES

1. Read an account of the Boosa controversy here: https://dissensustestimonies.files.wordpress.com/2015/02/dissensus-catalogue.pdf. The material on the website was curated in 2015 by students at Jawaharlal Nehru University, New Delhi.

2. *Yakshagana* is a rural dance form that incorporates dialogue, spectacle and dramatic stage techniques. It is prevalent, in different variations, across the southern regions of India, and is thought to have originally been a dance form of 'lower'-caste artists, especially dalits.

Sexual Harassment: SAY NO!

7.1 SEXUAL HARASSMENT, NOT 'EVE-TEASING'

Generations of film songs have eulogised men chasing reluctant women as a legitimate form of courtship. Reluctant heroines almost always accept the hero's love after he sings. In many Indian films the hero pursues the heroine and declares his love by entering her classroom or workplace, following her home, making his friends speak to her or, in some cases, threatening to commit suicide. Watching these films, most of us have begun to believe that this is how romance works: men pursue reluctant women who only agree to marry them after a lot of persuasion.

But is this behaviour by men actually romantic? Be assured, in real life women do not think so! They do not like being followed to the bus stop. They do not want to hear comments from passers-by about their dresses, bodies or hair. They are extremely annoyed by catcalls and whistling. They hate being touched or groped by strangers.

Today, we hear or read about girls being pursued on Facebook and other social media platforms or receiving phone calls, messages or obscene pictures. It must be clear by now that we are not discussing the usual jokes and good-natured banter between groups of young women and men in colleges. Nor are we discussing friendly comments, warnings or declarations of interest. In friendships and romantic relationships, sometimes things work out and sometimes they do not; most men and women understand this. Rejections of love are pretty common in college settings. Those who are rejected—women and men—go on to find other, perhaps more suitable, partners or remain single and continue to live their lives. What we are discussing in this unit is harassment—behaviour that is not consensual, disturbs a woman, causes pain and anxiety and is wilfully continued despite knowledge of how it hurts and affects her. It is not just women who are exposed to harassment, but men as well, especially those who do not conform to societal expectations of 'being a boy' or 'a man'.

'Eve-teasing' is the term sometimes used in South Asia to describe such malicious behaviour, implying it is simply a case of boys having some light-hearted fun. But shouldn't any fun activity be enjoyed by everyone involved? When it is not enjoyed by everyone involved, talking about it as 'fun' is surely not right. Till a few years ago, ragging was depicted as a fun way to welcome freshers to college. But a number of people said it was hurtful, humiliating and psychologically damaging; it drove many to such despair that they committed suicide. It became clear that this type of 'fun' was not at all fun for everyone involved. Today we have laws that punish ragging in colleges. Similarly, the term eve-teasing misrepresents the experience of women. As the poem 'Stares' by the Telugu critic and poet Jayaprabha powerfully portrays, being stared at is not fun for women (this poem appears in the 'Further Reading' section at the end of this unit).

A more apt name for this kind of activity is *sexual harassment*. Sexual harassment is the term used by women's movements and the term used in our laws. Sexual harassment is the term used internationally for this sort of behaviour and the term we will be using in this unit.

A prevalent form of sexual harassment is stalking. This involves men following, pursuing and even persecuting women despite the women expressing clear disinterest and distress. Some men think that if they find a woman attractive, they can continue to chase after her no matter her feelings. Maybe like certain

kings of old, they believe that whatever they want must be theirs.

Unlike what many people assume, it is not just young men who harass women; many older men are guilty of committing sexual harassment. The offender can be a stranger on the bus, a neighbour, a relative, an auto or taxi driver, a hostel warden or colleague or senior person in an organisation. It could even be an online anonymous user on social media.

The list of possible harassers is a long one, and the scale of sexual harassment across the world was recently revealed by the *#MeToo* movement when millions of women took to social media to narrate incidents of harassment and abuse that they faced or continue to face. Some women shared their experiences publicly, some anonymously. Some of the incidents occurred a long time ago, some more recently. Some incidents were brutal and violent, some more insidious and subtle.

The #MeToo movement revealed that sexual harassment occurs frequently in relationships of authority such as those between teachers and students, doctors and nurses or patients, producers and film stars, employers and employees and so on. In many instances, the woman is a subordinate who is at risk of losing employment if she raises her voice or lodges a complaint. The #MeToo movement also brought fresh attention to the culture of male dominance, entitlement and privilege in workplaces and the public sphere.

At the heart of this problem is the idea that men have authority over women. When men believe in this idea, they no longer see a woman as a person; she is simply an object that they desire. What she thinks, feels or says is of no importance. If they want her, then she should be theirs. It is this authority that men exercise when they touch, grope or prod a woman (a woman they might or might not know) on a bus or train, in the middle of the street or at a traffic light, at a wedding function or at the office or, in fact, anywhere.

All these forms of harassment are now recognised by law as sexual harassment which, like ragging, results in legal action and imprisonment.

What Harassment Does to Women

Women's experiences have shown that such behaviour causes extreme discomfort and distress. It impacts their mobility, everyday lives and life choices. In order to avoid men who follow or harass them, women have to adopt several precautionary measures such as taking different routes to the bus stop, making sure they are accompanied by male family members when commuting or simply not travelling during the night. If sexual harassment occurs at the workplace, women may be forced to leave their jobs for their own safety. Such 'adjustments' often compromise their opportunities for education or employment, forcing them to settle for less. The scale and nature of sexual harassment is such that it puts women in doubt; they are not sure they will be believed or supported; they are anxious

they will be blamed and people will say things like, 'You must have encouraged it!' or 'What were you wearing?' or 'Why were you out so late?' They fear that harassers will abuse their positions of power to invalidate, contradict and negate their complaints, sometimes even by threatening to fire them or spread disreputable rumours. Women are left with the fear that their families may put an end to their education or career, or that they may be hurried into an early marriage where their actions come under extreme scrutiny and surveillance. Severely distressed, unable to cope with such behaviour, some women opt to take their own lives rather than continue to live with such persecution.

Many women have contributed to the #MeToo movement by sharing their experiences of being shunned at the workplace, of not being given work, of not being promoted, of being subjected to disciplinary action on frivolous grounds, of being targeted for unnecessary punishment and for losing their job after complaining of sexual harassment. While such experiences were spoken of in the past too, they are being shared much more widely through the recent online movement.

It has not been easy for our society to understand the emotional, psychological and physical costs of sexual harassment. In the past 15 years, new laws have been enacted to prohibit sexual harassment on the streets and at educational institutions or workplaces. The #MeToo movement has paved the way for unequivocal public condemnation of sexual harassment, and one can see that the movement is a response to previous legal mechanisms that were unable to prevent this type of behaviour. The movement is also a response to survivors and victims of sexual harassment who have been publicly humiliated or shamed.

In light of this changed outlook, women are now encouraged to not feel ashamed to talk about harassment and, if they wish, to share their experiences with trusted friends, family or even authorities. Men, rather than women, are now being made to feel shame for any disgraceful conduct and are being taught to change their behaviour and ways.

Points to discuss:

1. Can you think of an incident which happened to someone you know which involved their receiving anonymous phone calls or being followed? How did they deal with the situation? How did the people around them behave? Share this incident with the class.
2. Go online and read some of the #MeToo accounts that women in India shared. Present your views on sexual harassment to the class based on these accounts.
3. Do you think it is necessary to educate boys and men about more appropriate ways of social interaction? Why? Talk about this in class.

Popular Films: Harassment as Love

It is appalling to note that despite changing contexts, many popular films continue to perpetuate myths and untruths about male behaviour, promoting the idea of men pursuing reluctant women as a desirable form of romance. Through cheeky responses and popular songs, they suggest that women mean 'yes' when they say 'no'. These films exhort us to think that women do not know their own minds. In this section we will look at some South-Indian films and their recurring tropes and examine how they deal with questions of harassment and consent.

× When women say 'no', they really mean 'yes': This line features in a famous song from the Telugu film, *Missamma* (1955). It was also the title of a recent Telugu hit film. In the Telugu film *Gabbar Singh* (2012), the titular protagonist played by the star Pawan Kalyan declares, 'Listen, man! One girl might fall for you in a week's time, another might take a month and some girls might even need a year … But the fact is, finally every girl will fall in love. That's natural law!' In another recent Telugu hit, *Loukyam* (2014), the hero says, 'Every girl is waiting to fall in love, they are just waiting for the right man!' That may be true. What is not true, however, is his assumption that he is always the right man!

× Women actually enjoy obscene or sexually coloured remarks about them: In what was called a decent family film, *Seethamma Vakitlo Sirimalle Chettu* (2013), one of the male leads played by the popular Telugu star, Mahesh Babu, says to a young woman, 'Just think, when you turn sixty and look back on your life, don't you want some sweet memories of the comments made by fellows on the street? So, you should actually encourage men who pass comments about your appearance.'

× Women welcome abuse: In many Malayalam movies, the strong female character suddenly turns submissive and coy as soon as the hero forces himself upon her by kissing or hugging her. This change is presented as though she has been waiting all her life for such a violation. Manju Warrier's character in *Kanmadam* (1998) is a clear example of this trope.

× Women should be beaten because they are not trustworthy: In Kannada films that feature the actor Upendra, women are regularly beaten up, bruised or brutalised. They are forced to undergo life-threatening risks to prove their love and trustworthiness to the hero. In the film *A* (1998), the heroine Chandni has to stand in a circle drawn by the hero on the edge of a cliff and not move even as a jeep hurtles towards her. Time and again the women in Upendra films are told that if they don't love him or marry him, he will throw acid on them, destroy their homes or finish them off. In films such as *A, Upendra* (1999) and *Buddhivanta* (2008), the hero acts as a one-man army against women. It seems as if his battle is not against a villain like the father of the heroine, or a landlord, industrialist, politician or underworld don, but against women themselves!

× Women are just pretty dolls: Most heroines in hero-centric films are just glamour girls with no character, intelligence or individuality. As the heroine in *Seethamma Vakitlo Sirimalle Chettu* says, 'All I want is sound sleep and a good husband!' In the same film, the hero reprimands a short-haired girl who expresses her feelings for him by saying, 'It's a shame Indian woman have stopped plaiting their hair. If I give you a flower, how will you wear it?' Apart from a few exceptions, most popular films in the last decade have portrayed heroines as pretty and glamorous women with little intelligence and no goal or aim in life but to win the attention of the hero. These films don't seem to think that women have their own goals and desires and that they are real human

beings with different tastes, aptitudes and capabilities.

Points to discuss:

1. Do you agree with the above points? Can you think of similar examples in films you have seen?

2. Do you think more recent films depict women and romance differently? Can you think of any popular films in any language in which the leading male character treats women with respect and as equals?

7.2 CONSENT AND RELATIONSHIPS

The crucial issue that these relationships in films do not address is that of ***consent***. Now, what is consent and why is it important?

Consent is when a woman or man show an unambiguous willingness to engage in a physical and emotional relationship with someone else. It is permission which is freely given. It implies active interest to engage with the other person. It is built on the recognition that adult women and men have the right to engage in a relationship if they so desire and equally the right to reject a proposal for a romantic or sexual relationship. Women have the right to say 'no'. Unlike what popular culture suggests and is passed down as common sense, if a woman responds with silence to a relationship proposal, it does not indicate her acceptance. Her silence may be out of discomfort, shock or fear. Silence is not consent. It is therefore essential to ask for a clear and enthusiastic 'yes'.

Due to several cases of sexual harassment and assault, many universities across the world have made it mandatory for students to attend classes on consent as part of their orientation programme. These universities believe it is necessary to educate students on what does and does not constitute consent. Such classes aim to improve campus culture and enable women to feel safe and secure.

Chai pe ek aur charcha

The animated film *Chai pe ek aur charcha* (2015)[1] discusses the important issue of consent by making a metaphorical comparison between buying someone a cup of tea and showing interest in someone. It stresses the fact that consent, or unconditional willingness, is a key factor not only when it comes to drinking tea but also when it comes to romantic and sexual relationships. Watch the film and discuss the points it makes with your classmates.

7.3 COPING WITH EVERYDAY HARASSMENT

Women often receive so-called 'common sense' suggestions on how to avoid harassment. These suggestions are mostly about how women should conduct themselves. For instance, people say, 'Women should dress respectably. If they do so, nobody will make obscene remarks or bother them.' This advice is built on the assumption that what a woman wears can lead to sexual harassment. In response, the organisation Blank Noise, which is dedicated to eradicating sexual and gender violence and street harassment, conducted an interesting survey on the topic.[2] They asked women, 'What were you wearing when you were sexually harassed?' The answers are listed as follows: school uniform / capris / *churidar* / *salwar kurta* / trousers / shorts / jeans / burqa / *dupatta* / *sari* / long sleeves / short sleeves / sleeveless tee-shirt / a cute top / jacket / blazer / *ghaghra* / long skirt / short skirt / red lipstick / no lipstick / open hair / oiled hair / school socks / stockings / bare feet / kaftan / work uniform . . .

As you can see, there is no connection between sexual assault and what a woman wears. As a matter of fact, it turns out that contrary to what people generally think, 'respectably' dressed women are also harassed. Don't you think girls and women should have the freedom to wear the clothes they are most comfortable in and like?

Other advice and so-called 'common sense' suggestions women often receive to avoid sexual harassment and stay safe include the following:

- Avoid going out alone.
- Reach home before dark.
- Avoid late night work or outings with friends.

In many families, women face a strict night curfew. Because of this and the above suggestions, there are fewer women on the streets after nightfall. But such advice is simply impractical. Women need to work late or they have to shop in the evening or they may need or want to meet someone in the night.

Restrictions are also imposed on women who stay in hostels. Let us now look at the adapted account of an 18-year-old female student who studied in a college of Delhi University.[3] She, like many young women pursuing higher education, aspired to have greater mobility and more opportunities. She found such restrictions imposed on her unacceptable. In the name of safety, she could not visit the library for research after class hours, nor could she avail herself of basic medical facilities or simply visit her friends in the evenings.

❖ ❖ ❖

In the name of safety, women students in our university are controlled to a terrifying extent. We have no flexibility of movement. We are treated like children and our views are not respected or considered.

The girls' hostel is like a *zenana*. A brick screen shuts us off from all sides—hiding our verandas and open spaces from public view. We have two entrances, both guarded all day. We have a warden to whom we must apply for permission to stay out at night or for leave. This requires endless letters of permission from our parents or our local guardian. Male students do not require such permission.

We protested these rules and asked for an 'open campus' with the following conditions: that when we ask for permission, we should not be interrogated even after we have a permission letter from parents; that we should not be locked inside our blocks after ten p.m.; that women students deserve autonomy and certain freedoms.

I accept that there are rules that we need to follow while living in a hostel. . . . But what I am angry about is that male students face NONE of these rules! I am told that this is for my own good. I am not sure. On the contrary, I wonder if this is another way of controlling me.

Points to discuss:

The student's account raises some interesting questions:

1. Is it right to control the lives of women in the name of safety?
2. Do you think young women are not capable of thinking about their own safety? Aren't women, like men, capable of judging situations?

3. Is it not better to make all public spaces accessible and safe for women as well as men?

Culture of Silence

Another form of advice given to women is to keep silent about being harassed. It is true that some of the issues can be and are handled by women, while in other instances they may want the advice and support of others. But often they are told not to speak about it, not even to their close friends. Till recently, it was not possible for this issue to be raised or discussed in public forums, including classrooms, though this culture of silence has now come under severe challenge with the arrival of the #MeToo movement.

It is important to note that across generations women have devised varied methods to deal with harassment on the streets, in colleges or at workplaces. Even after new laws are enacted, not all women report incidents of harassment to the police. Some deal with it personally and some collectively. Some women write about it. Below is an example of the latter. Read a letter written by a student to her male teacher. (Note: This is a fictionalised letter based on our knowledge of experiences where we have heard from many young girls and women. It was inspired by the website blanknoise.org, which is devoted to ending gender-based and sexual violence).[4]

To the tutor who groped my breasts when I was 12 years old: I wish I had you thrown out of the house then and there. I will teach my sons and daughters to NOT keep quiet when men like you touch them, ever. I am not ashamed. I refuse to share your shame and make it mine.

You might think you are powerful, but you are weak and a coward. You were a teacher and a mentor. I looked up to you. I trusted you. But guess what? You just ruined everything. I can no longer trust anyone. I feel like every person out there is somehow trying to use me. And I constantly blame myself for what happened.

But … sir, wait a minute. I have thought about this again and again. I don't want to hate you, or pepper-spray you, or learn to defend myself with martial arts. I don't want to hang you or jail you. I refuse to harbour negative feelings.

I want to trust my teachers.

> ***Points to discuss:***
>
> 1. List some reasons why girls might find it difficult to speak about harassment they have faced to their friends or their family.
> 2. Do boys face sexual harassment? Discuss instances that you have come across in the newspapers or online.

Complaints Committee

It is now mandatory for colleges, universities and workplaces to set up a complaints committee. The mandate of such a committee is to address all complaints of sexual harassment—between teachers, between students and teachers, between students, between workers and so on. Female students, teachers and workers facing harassment can lodge a complaint with this committee. Known as the Gender Sensitisation Committee Against Sexual Harassment (GSCASH), this committee is not only responsible for hearing complaints, investigating issues and disciplining wrong-doers, but must also raise awareness about the issues of sexual and gender-based harassment, the impact it has on the community and those being harassed, and how people should refrain from such conduct.

The Ministry of Women and Child Development released an illustrated handbook on sexual harassment. This handbook provides a detailed account of how complaints should be heard by complaints committees.[5]

> **Sexual Harassment of Women at Workplace (Prevention, Prohibition and Redressal) Act, 2013**
>
> This special law was enacted to address the sexual harassment that women face in their workplaces. Working women often confront stressful situations where the terms of their employment are determined by harassment; many are forced to leave their jobs or apply for transfers to escape their harassers. Some of the salient provisions of the law are listed below.
>
> 1. Sexual harassment includes any one or more of the following acts either by the employer or by co-employees:
>   a. physical contact and unwanted advances
>   b. a demand or request for sexual favours
>   c. making sexually coloured remarks
>   d. showing pornography
>   e. any other unwelcome physical, verbal or non-verbal conduct of a sexual nature
> 2. The female employee who complains of sexual harassment need not be a permanent employee. She can be temporarily employed, a daily-wage earner, an ad hoc employee, a

trainee, apprentice, contract worker, probationer or even a volunteer. Domestic workers are also recognised as employees who can complain about sexual harassment.

3. The workplace is not limited to government offices and departments. It includes private-sector organisations, establishments, ventures, societies, trusts and NGOs, hospitals and nursing homes.

4. Every employer now has the responsibility to form an Internal Complaints Committee. The presiding officer of this committee must be a senior female employee and must be assisted by two employees and a member of an organisation committed to the cause of women or familiar with issues related to sexual harassment. Your college is legally required to have a committee of this kind to receive complaints and act on them. If this has not already been set up, you can ask for it to be set up.

5. An aggrieved woman can submit a written complaint of sexual harassment to the Internal Complaints Committee within a period of three months from the date of the incident. Upon receiving the report submitted by the Internal Complaints Committee, the employer must take action against the accused harasser as per the service rules applicable to the workplace. This can also include payment of compensation to the aggrieved woman.

'Take Back the Night' Campaigns

Women have challenged curfews and restrictions on their mobility in many countries by marching in the night. They point out it should be safe for them to do so, and furthermore, that they have a right to be out on the road, no matter the time. These campaigns are organised by the non-profit organisation 'Take Back the Night', which aims to end sexual violence. Such collective action has been quite empowering for women. After the December 2012 gang-rape incident in Delhi, many people across the country publicly protested by marching on the streets, chanting slogans and demanding safety, security and equality for women. In one such march held in Hyderabad, nearly 4000 individuals chanted the slogan, 'Free the night, it belongs to both men and women.' The march was a truly spectacular and inspiring event.

The demands made by the people who were in the march included cheap and accessible public transport, street lighting that reduced the possibility of harassment or violence against women, and functioning emergency helplines. Listed below are questions from a pamphlet distributed at the midnight march in Hyderabad.

- Why is it dangerous for women to walk at night?
- Why does a woman need to be protected by a man?
- Why can't men and women coexist on the streets at night as well?
- Why can't men be trusted not to abuse women?
- Why can't we make all spaces safe instead of keeping women indoors?

Points to discuss:

1. Think of an incident when a woman was harassed. It could be from a film, television show or time when you were

out with friends. Recall the clothes she was wearing. Do you think her appearance was connected to the harassment she faced? How so? Would it have been any different if she had been wearing something similar to what women in your family wear?

2. You, or someone close to you, may have had to go out late in the evening—to watch a film or visit a doctor. Describe the experience of that trip (whether you were alone, with family members or friends, etc.). Do you think it would be different (a) if it was a young boy travelling alone or (b) if it was a young girl travelling alone? If yes, discuss those differences.

Nirbhaya Act

In 2013, the Criminal Law (Amendment) Act, also known as the Nirbhaya Act, was passed by the Lok Sobha. The laws were related to sexual offences and dealt with those who followed women, pestered and sexually harassed or assaulted them. New offences have also been introduced to the Indian Penal Code recently: the act of stripping a woman and parading her in public is a common way of 'punishing' women for their transgressions, especially in rural areas, and is now a separate offence; likewise, acid attacks, which involve men taking revenge against women who have rejected their offers of love or marriage by hurling acid at them, is also now included in the Indian Penal Code. The Nirbhaya Act recognises and defines the following offences too:

1. Stalking: Any man who . . .
   a. follows a woman and contacts or attempts to contact her repeatedly for personal interaction despite receiving a clear indication of disinterest from her.
   b. monitors the internet, email and other forms of communication of a woman.
   c. watches or spies on a woman in any manner that results in fear of violence, serious alarm, distress or interferes with the mental peace of the woman.

2. Voyeurism: Any man who watches, photographs or disseminates images of women in various stages of undress or engaging in private acts.

3. Sexual harassment: Any man who . . .
   a. makes physical contact with a woman in an unwelcome or sexually explicit manner.
   b. demands or even requests sexual favours from a woman.
   c. shows pornography against the will of a woman.
   d. makes a sexually coloured remark or any other unwelcome physical, verbal or non-verbal conduct of a sexual nature.

4. Intent to disrobe a woman: Any man who tries to disrobe a woman or compel her to be naked in a public space.

The punishment for committing the above crimes is severe, with imprisonment ranging from one to ten years.

7.4 FURTHER READING

There is a clear line demarcating behaviour that is acceptable from that which is not. Take, for instance, staring at women and girls. Women do distinguish between looks that are appreciative, even admiring, and those that are not. Such looks may be considered harmless, but is that really the case? The following poem, written by the well-known Telugu poet Jayaprabha and translated by B. V. L. Narayana

Row, is about the stares women receive on a daily basis. The poem offers a clear sense of the anger a woman feels at unwelcome looks.

Chupulu [Stares]

Needle sharp stares
from two eyes
land on these lumps of flesh
and roam freely about.

Liar stares
that do not dare look into my eyes, but
crawl
like larvae on my body.

Eyes rich and poor,
young and old
stare
at women
alike.

Signalling
the hunger of a drooling dog,
the ugly grab of a wolf.
They haunt my dreams.

In the dense jungle
I cannot tell
light from darkness.
There is no escape
from these stares

On the road,
in the bus,
in the classroom,
they chase my step
snapping at me, here and there.
These poison fangs
knife me.

I feel scared.
I wish I could fly
or vanish into the void.

I've taught my eyes to stare back,
equally sharp.
Stares for stares.
That is how I wage my war now.

These cowardly stares
that cannot look me in the eye
flee to the underworld.

How I long for the day when
not only eyes, but
the whole body
of a woman
bristles.

NOTES

1. Watch *Chai pe ek aur charcha* here: https://www.youtube.com/watch?v=OTmu62peWw0.

2. Read about Blank Noise's survey here: http://blanknoise.org.

3. The student account has been adapted from an interview which you can read here: http://www.anveshi.org.in/a-conversation-between-a-daughter-and-a-mother/.

4. Read actual letters by young girls and women who have been harassed here: http://www.blanknoise.org/everything-i-want-to-say-to-the-harasser.

5. Access the complete handbook by The Ministry of Women and Child Development here: https://legislative.gov.in/sites/default/files/A2013-14.pdf. You can also print copies of the handbook and keep it in your office or library for reference.

Women's Work: Its Politics and Economics

8.1 FACT VS. FICTION

In today's world, financial security and social respect are closely related to jobs and income. Most of us enter college hoping to get a good job after we graduate. But women and men often receive very different messages about work. Society tells men they must work hard to earn enough money to support their families, which is a lot of pressure for young men to face, while society tells women they may consider taking up jobs as long as they ensure household work does not suffer. It seems as though society's message to women is that their work is not 'serious' work, and that their income is only 'supplementary' to the main income which is expected to be earned by the men of the family. In this chapter, we will discuss the above points and how we need to change the way we think about women's work.

Facts About Women's Work

If we look around, we see a large number of women engaged in many different jobs. These may include working as vegetable vendors, beauticians, corner-shop assistants, domestic help, television anchors, actors, lab technicians, doctors, accountants and clerks to name but a few. We also now find plenty of women in important positions of leadership: K. K. Shailaja, popularly known as Shailaja Teacher won national and international recognition for her work as Health Minister of Kerala state; Indra Nooyi served as the chairperson of the multinational company PepsiCo and was its CEO for more than a decade; Gita Gopinath is the Chief Economist in the International Monetary Fund; and Deepika Padukone and Priyanka Chopra are among India's highest-paid actors.

Let us take a quick look at some statistics on the number of women in India's workforce.

Table 2: Number of women in India's workforce

Sector	Number of Women
Agriculture	7.7 crore
Tobacco-related work (collecting and drying *tendu* leaves, rolling *beedis*, etc.)	1.2 crore
Textile work (traditional weavers, dyers and mill workers)	
Construction	57 lakh
Domestic work	19 lakh
Teachers	25 lakh
Sales	23 lakh
Personal services (beauticians, etc.)	17 lakh
Healthcare (nurses, hospital staff, etc.)	12 lakh
Government	11 lakh
Total	11.2 crore

Source: Lahiri, Tripti. 'By the Numbers: Where Indian Women Work.' *The Wall Street Journal.*

The census provides a figure of 35 crore women in the working-age group (15–65 years) in India. Among them, 11.2 crore women reported themselves as workers. The largest numbers are in the agriculture, textile, tobacco and construction sectors. 65% of Indian women are literate. In the last two decades, a lot more women have completed their school and college education. As is clear from the table, many of them have gone on to become teachers, nurses, saleswomen and government clerks. The sad part is that many women are unable to make use of expanding work opportunities. This is because, firstly, mechanisation and technological developments have rendered knowledge about and skills in certain fields of work redundant. While male workers have been able to secure remunerative work in other fields, female workers have suffered from a gender-segregated labour market, lack of training to enter such markets and the excessive burden of domestic responsibilities. This explains why the 19 lakh women displaced from agriculture (due to mechanisation) became domestic workers in urban areas (a job which does not require any special skills). Secondly, many professions are still considered 'unsuitable' for women.

Educated women therefore face a limited number of employment choices. And their numbers are not growing as fast as we would like them to. When these sectors stop generating new jobs, women are unable to find employment. According to one estimate, there are 22 million fewer women in the job market than there should be.

As of now, less than a third of India's 350 million women are out there earning an income. But there are a few problems with this figure as an assessment of women's work. One, it does not include homemakers (another term for housewives). As we learnt in Unit 4 on housework, homemakers are constantly on their feet, working. Two, it does not include family workers. In both rural and urban areas, household work includes many income-generating activities. But the work done by homemakers and family workers is not officially recognised as 'work' by the National Sample Survey Office (NSSO). The importance of these workers and their work for the economy is therefore invisible and undervalued. We will learn how and why this happens in the next section.

There are many professions and occupations in which women are extremely active, but their work is regarded as 'helping the family'. These include but are not limited to farming, repairing shoes, roadside vending, petty trading, etc. Let us take a look at the profiles of women who have joined traditionally 'male' professions.

- Gouher Sultana is a cricket player from Hyderabad. A left-arm orthodox spin bowler, she was part of the Indian women's cricket team and captained Hyderabad's senior women's squad. She has played for India in more than 40 international and T20 matches.

- Shanti Devi is a mechanic working on the outskirts of Delhi at one of the largest truck stopovers in Asia—Sanjay Gandhi Transport Nagar Depot. Along with her husband, she runs a workshop that fixes and changes tyres and undertakes other repairs. She is in her fifties and believes that women can be just as good mechanics as men if they put their heads to it. She is greatly respected by her colleagues.

- Devi Thangavelu runs a hair salon called Bhuvanadevi Hairlines in Palladam, a village near Coimbatore in Tamil Nadu. Having grown up watching her father working in the salon, she took over his responsibilities when he fell ill. Though her father's customers initially shunned her, they now queue up in front of her salon. She is highly sought after by young men keen for her to cut their hair in the same style as their film heroes.

- Vankadarath Saritha of Nalgonda started off as an autorickshaw driver, then became a taxi driver, and is now the first female public bus driver in the Delhi Transport Corporation. There is also a chance she may drive a public bus in Telangana with the Telangana State Road Transport Corporation.

- Sunita Patil was one of three women fire fighters who joined the Mumbai fire brigade in 2011. The three women were the first women to apply for such a position in 130 years! She was encouraged by her family to apply. Though the training is extremely difficult, she believes in the importance of her job and is pleased by the public show of support she has received.

- Ramya Krishna, better known as Racha Ramulamma, was a physiotherapy student who was persuaded by her friends to audition for the role of a television anchor. Channel V6 promptly picked her up, and she is now famous for her weekend shows and her *Teenmaar* news bulletins.

- Anuradha Naik is a trained conservation architect and architectural historian based in Hyderabad. She redesigned the City Museum in Purani Haveli, Hyderabad, and is currently involved in the conservation of heritage buildings and in various architectural history research projects.

Babai

Now watch the short film *Babai* (2014[1]), directed by Kavita Datir and Amit Sonawane. The documentary is about an 81-year-old woman in a Pune wholesale market who transports goods on a handcart.

Points to discuss:

1. List a few jobs or professions in which you do not find many women.
2. Why do you think you do not find many women in certain professions?
3. Can you list any assumptions about gender that the film *Babai* breaks? Would you consider *Babai* a feminist film?

8.2 UNRECOGNISED AND UNACCOUNTED FOR

Why is it that women's work remains undervalued, poorly appreciated and invisible, not recognised as 'work'? There are several reasons for this. When looking at women's work, the focus tends to be on work that is remunerative, that is, work which earns a salary. If a woman does not earn money, she is considered 'unproductive' or a 'non-worker'. Using this definition, the 2011 Census of India categorised most of the working-age women in India as non-workers. But, as we have seen in the unit on housework, women's work, unlike men's work, is not limited to activities that earn a salary. A large portion of women's work goes into income-generating activities to maintain household order. All this hard work does not earn them an income, but it may prevent them from taking on a salaried job. Let us see how this happens.

Unpaid Family Work

A worker is someone who is employed for wages or salary and typically works eight to ten hours a day. Many women currently categorised as non-workers actually work for family or household enterprises. Some of these household enterprises include farming, animal husbandry, weaving and dyeing, pottery, petty trading, hawking, catering, managing small hotels or *kirana* shops or family-run businesses. None of these enterprises can run unless the woman (or women) of the household shoulders a large part of the responsibility and work. However, this does not give the woman any control over the family's income, including the share she has earned. This kind of work is called ***unpaid family work***. It is seen as work which 'supports the family' and not as work that produces an income. A small proportion of men, too, are engaged in unpaid family work.

Some women work for wages, but from home. They engage in a number of activities that earn them money, from making *beedis*, *papads*, *agarbattis*, bangles, etc., to tailoring and embroidery. They may work as long as nine hours a day. This is called ***home-based work***. This type of work is specifically done by women as they must stay at home to manage the housework. Compared to unpaid family workers, these women have more control over their income. But much, if not all of it, goes into supporting the family. As they work from home, and think of themselves as only 'supplementing' the family income, many such women tend to not think of themselves as workers. The Census of India too does not count them as workers!

Most women in India are homemakers or housewives. Their labour is invisible and difficult to account for. Many of us know that housework is essential to a family's survival and well-being. But we should also know that it is equally essential to the functioning of the economy. Schools, factories, construction sites, farms, fields, colleges and offices would fail to run as efficiently as they do now if mothers, wives and daughters were to cease their housework and not wash clothes, cook and pack food, clean the house, take care of us when we are sick and so on.

According to 2012 statistics from the NSSO, 49.9% of rural and 61.1% of urban working-age women are engaged in housework, whereas only 0.5% of rural and 0.3% of urban working-age men are engaged in housework.

A Day in the Life of a 'Non-worker'

Kalpagam is a 45-year-old homemaker from a village near Pudukkottai. Born in a lower-middle-class family, she was educated up to class five. She got married at the age of 16. Her husband runs an auto-rickshaw in the nearby town. They have two sons.

Kalpagam's day is hectic. She wakes up at five in the morning. First, she sweeps and cleans the house and yard. Then she milks the family's cows and sends the milk to the cooperative. After that, she takes a bath. She then prepares breakfast, washes dishes, cleans the kitchen, washes clothes, prepares feed for the cattle and cleans the cattle-shed. She is fortunate that the family has a borewell, which makes it relatively easy for her to collect water. By this time, it is almost late morning. Kalpagam has to begin making lunch. She has to ensure her family gets lunch at the right time as her son needs to get back to his work in the field.

Kalpagam also works on the farm. In the afternoon, she takes the buffalos out, sometimes with the help of her two sons. If she has some time, she makes *beedis*. Before evening, she finishes her cooking. The family eats and goes to bed early as their day starts before sunrise. Kalpagam does the cooking and serves the family herself, though sometimes her second son helps her. She rarely has any free time for recreation and prefers to rest or sleep whenever she gets time off from her work.[2]

Points to discuss:

1. In Unit 4 on housework, we discussed how women's domestic work is often made invisible and is therefore undervalued. Do you think there are similarities in the way women's income-generating work is also made invisible and is therefore undervalued?
2. Can Kalpagam's housework be differentiated from the family's income-generating work? Why or why not?
3. Since Sunday is a holiday for everyone, should mothers also get the day off? Explain your answer.

8.3 WAGE DIFFERENTIALS BETWEEN WOMEN AND MEN

The most visible indicator of the undervaluation of women's work in the economy is wages or salaries. In many sectors, women are paid less than men. For example, statistics compiled by the NSSO reveal that in agriculture, women are paid at least 50% less than men. A similar situation exists in other sectors such as healthcare, entertainment, the arts, management and the software industry. A recent study found that female software professionals earn 29% less than their male colleagues. Why are women paid less than men? Some of the reasons we usually hear include:

- Men and women do different kinds of work.
- Men take on heavier tasks; women do lighter work.
- Men need to support a family.
- Men are more efficient.
- Men are more skilled.
- Women lack experience.

But if we think carefully about these points, we find much of the reasoning is untrue. Carrying bricks on top of your head is not any 'easier' or 'lighter' than laying them. Nor, for that matter, is laying bricks very skilled work. Most people can learn how to do it. As women gain more access to training, and as employment opportunities increase, women are moving into many jobs that were previously reserved for men. As you know and can see from the examples in this unit, women now drive tractors, buses, trains, aeroplanes and can run farms or work with heavy machinery. In an age of mechanisation, physical strength is irrelevant in many sectors. It is also not relevant in 'white collar' sectors such as medicine, software, accounting, management or teaching.

Differences in 'work experience' between men and women mostly arise due to women's social obligations of pregnancy and childcare. For many women, maternity and childcare become huge obstacles in their ability to continue work as they require time off before, during and after pregnancy. Across the employment spectrum, be it domestic work or software engineering, they drop out of paying work once they have children as there are no adequate social-support systems for childcare. This situation prevails even in the fast-growing software industry, in management or other corporate sectors which educated women are entering in greater numbers than ever before. Once women drop out of the workforce, it is difficult for them to re-enter it and acquire the same position. Women in the informal sector, after taking a break of this kind, largely turn to home-based or part-time work.

Wherever adequate childcare facilities and maternity benefits are provided in the world, women continue to stay and grow in employment. More importantly, men sharing the responsibility of childcare enables women to continue working. Take the example of Jacinda Ardern, the Prime Minister of New Zealand, who returned to work six weeks after she gave birth to a daughter while her partner became a stay-at-home parent. In fact, the option of paternity leave—a period of leave granted by a company to a male employee just before the birth of his child—is now being provided in many countries by many employers hoping to enable such a change. Around seventy-eight countries, including India, provide paternity leave, though only five countries provide it for more than two weeks.

Pay Inequality

In 2007, the organisation Catalyst, which works for inclusive workplaces in corporations and firms, began tracking 10,000 MBA graduates from top business schools in the US and found that women start out earning an average $4,300 less than men at their very first job. The gap keeps growing over time, and after only two to three years, Catalyst found it surpasses $40,000. Their study concluded that a gender gap exists from day one and women do not even start out on an equal footing.

Turning attention to India, female actors are paid on average only 10% of what male actors are paid. The inequality of earnings between men and women is the highest in healthcare, the arts, management, recreation and entertainment industries. The software industry has the lowest level of inequality of earnings between men and women. Usually, the higher the rank or scale, the greater the *gender pay gap*.

Points to discuss:

1. Conduct research and describe, on average in India, the different tasks women and men do in: construction or farming; in a brick kiln; a garment factory; a *beedi* factory; or a pharmaceutical company. How does the work differ? How does the pay differ?
2. Male film stars such as Shah Rukh Khan, Rajinikanth, Akkineni Nagarjuna or Mohanlal are paid much more than female stars such as Priyanka Chopra, Trisha or Samantha because the former work harder than the latter. Do you agree or disagree? Explain why.
3. Choose your college or a company or firm near your college. Check the leave policy—specifically, maternity and paternity leave—that the organisation has in place for new parents. Discuss whether or not you believe it is fair.
4. What are some of the factors that impact a woman's decision to work for an income?

Men as Breadwinners

Actually, men are paid more because of the idea of family wage. A wage is decided on the basis of what it takes to sustain a worker. The concept of family wage assumes that a man has to sustain a family and therefore pays him more. They are also paid more because of social (or, in other words, patriarchal) beliefs and practices that have very little to do with strength or efficiency. Wage differentials between men and women operate due to the persistent myth that men are and should be the primary breadwinners of the family. As we have already discussed, it is believed that what men earn is the main income while what women earn is extra to the family income. In India, this myth originated in the 1930s when the Wage Board proposed that a man should be recognised as head of the family and should therefore be paid a family wage—payment for his labour plus what is needed for the maintenance of his family. By contrast, what women earn was seen as only supplementary or supportive. So she should be paid only for her labour. This myth remains strong.

Even when women earn the same as or more than their husbands, society prefers to see it as extra to the husband's income. The man may, in fact, spend his income on himself while the family runs on her income, but the women will nonetheless continue to be paid as if what she earns is additional or supplementary income. Worse still, this is also true when she is the only income-earning member of the family (in a woman-headed household).

It is true that after 1947 the concept of family wage was revised. After a great deal of struggle, the principle of equal pay for equal work is now practised in government employment and a few other sectors. But equal pay is limited to an extremely small portion of the economy. The usual practice in large parts of the economy involves unequal pay for women and men. A ray of hope in recent times has been the Mahatma Gandhi National Rural Employment Guarantee Act (MGNREGA), a labour law which implements the principle of equal pay for equal work.

In nearly 40% of Indian households, women are the primary breadwinners. Even though a few of these households have land and other assets, a majority of them, known as woman-headed households, rank among the poorest of the poor.

> ***Points to discuss:***
>
> 1. Do you think paying women less than men helps the overall welfare of the family and the children?
> 2. In Unit 3 we saw how important the idea of being the primary breadwinner was to the idea of masculinity. How, in your opinion, does this relate to the gender pay gap that exists between men and women?

8.4 WOMEN IN THE WORKING ENVIRONMENT

A century ago it was considered inappropriate and disreputable for women from propertied classes to step out of the house to work for an income. They were only expected to work hard managing the house and kitchen. But modernity and education have made working for an income respectable in these classes. Now the majority of women who hold good jobs belong to these communities. And a good number of them have pursued higher education.

A century ago, for the women of landless families and communities, work was compulsory, and drudgery. In addition to working for an income they were forced to work without pay in the households of landlords. It was known as *vetti*, *begar* or bonded labour. After many protests over several decades, this was legally abolished under the Bonded Labour System (Abolition) Act of 1976. Now many women are free from *vetti* and may work for wages. A miniscule portion of such women have entered full-time salaried government employment due to the constitutional provision of reservation in education and employment institutions.

The majority of Indian women workers, however, work in irregular, insecure and low-paying jobs. They constantly fight for minimum wages, basic facilities such as functioning toilets, drinking water, childcare facilities, opportunities for breaks during monthly periods and for their dignity. In what follows we will read two accounts, both from Kerala, of such struggles. The first one is an excerpt from an article by Suresh P. Thomas.

They Sat Down for Their Rights

Kalyan Sarees is one of the most glamorous shopping chains in Kerala where scores of saleswomen work. In 2015, Padmini, a senior woman worker, along with 5 other colleagues, undertook a 106-day sit-in for basic facilities and minimum wages in their workplace. This is how she described the working conditions and the working women's problems:

My name is Padmini S. K. I started working as a salesgirl in 2005. It was a not-so-big shop at City Centre. My salary then was 500 rupees per month. I did not have many other options. On the first day itself, I was told about the rules of the job. First and foremost: a salesgirl should never think about sitting down. Not even when there are no customers. You don't have to ask why. That's just how it has been ever since there were salesgirls. So from 9.30 a.m. to 7.30 p.m., I should just stand there. No toilet breaks. In the showroom that I joined, there was not even a toilet. So I used to go out to a hotel or to the corporation office to relieve myself. That too only once a day, maximum twice. Sometimes, not even once.

After working in the showrooms of a few big brands, I joined Kalyan Sarees in 2012. By that stage I had worked my way up to be a sales supervisor. I was fortunate—the standard hierarchy among sales employees is that men will be the supervisors and floor managers while women will deal with the customers. This works well for the management because the women who work in this field are usually meek and are afraid to challenge the supervisors.

I was offered around Rs 8,000 in the interview. But when I joined, the management told me that even those with 10 or 12 years of experience would be given only Rs 6,500. They might have lied to me about my salary, but what they said about the salary of those people was true. Most were paid around Rs 4,000 to Rs 5,000, and the really experienced ones were paid around Rs 6,000. None of us knew that there was a Minimum Wages Act or that we were rightfully entitled to a minimum salary.

For a salesgirl, work starts at 9.30 in the morning. Imagine this: Rs 4,000 for a minimum of 11 hours of work. And from this, money is deducted for PF and welfare fund, and there wouldn't even be any legal acknowledgements. We were not given salary slips. We did not even know that, according to law, we should have got at least Rs 7,200. Or that, according to law, women were not allowed to work after seven in the evening. We have a lunch break of 20 minutes. It is on the fifth floor that we have to go and eat. We are not allowed to use the lift to go there. It is so bad that to even be asked to go and eat there is a punishment. If it rains, we get drenched. Many days, we don't even bother to have our lunch.

Even when there are no customers we are not allowed to sit. So what we do is this: we will put already folded clothes on the floor and then we will pretend that we are folding or arranging those clothes again, and in between we will steal a moment to sit. But now with cameras everywhere, these stolen moments have become rare.

And yet, despite all this, if we have to attend to a customer, we will be ready with our happiest, prettiest faces. It comes naturally to us, like an addiction that cannot be chucked. Even today, if I were to go to the showroom from this strike site, I will straight away start smiling.

Because we keep standing for hours, and because we hardly ever relieve ourselves at work, most of us have uterine problems, urinary infections, back problems and varicose-vein issues. Once, the varicose vein of a sales

woman burst and she didn't even know. The customer who saw the trail of blood on the floor fainted and only then did the woman realise what had happened to her.

Pembilai Orumai

The second account is about a recent strike by the women tea-leaf pickers in Munnar, Kerala. Pembilai Orumai (Women's Unity) plantation workers, who constitute the majority of the 13,000 leaf pickers in the Kanan Devan Hills Plantation (KDHP) in Munnar, went on the first-ever women-only strike in the history of plantations in September 2015. Why? Leaf pickers are paid the least compared to supervisors and managers, who are mostly men. But they have to work 12 hours a day. Unless they pick more than 20 kilograms of leaf, they do not get their daily wages. Protesting discriminatory working conditions—such as lack of fair wages, poor housing conditions and their children being denied admission to the company-run school—5000 women spontaneously went on strike on 7 September 2015. Calling themselves Pembilai Orumai, they said they would not allow men to be a part of the protest. 'Men don't do the work that we do,' they said. 'We are the ones who pluck the leaves, carry the burden all day and even load it onto trucks.' They insisted on negotiating directly with the company. They refused to agree to the compromise that the trade unions tried to negotiate with the company. They converged in Munnar from distant plantations to express their anger and demand better wages and working conditions. The strike was called off on 13 September only after trade-union leaders signed the deal the women had negotiated for higher bonuses, higher wages and better working conditions.

> **Points to discuss:**
>
> 1. Padmini says, 'The standard hierarchy among sales employees is that men will be the supervisors and floor managers while women will deal with the customers.' Why is this so?
> 2. 'None of us knew that there was a Minimum Wages Act or that we were rightfully entitled to a minimum salary.' What is Padmini referring to when she talks about the Minimum Wages Act?
> 3. 'But now with cameras everywhere, these stolen moments have become rare.' Why does Padmini think that cameras deprive her and the other sales women of brief moments of rest?
> 4. Explain the significance of the name Pembilai Orumai.

NOTE

1. Watch the film *Babai* here: https://www.youtube.com/watch?v=wILdFtwSnGs
2. This is adapted from an account in *Women's Economic Contribution through their Unpaid Work: The Case of India* by Natasha Choudhary, Ashutosh Tripathy and Beena George.

Domestic Violence: Speaking Out

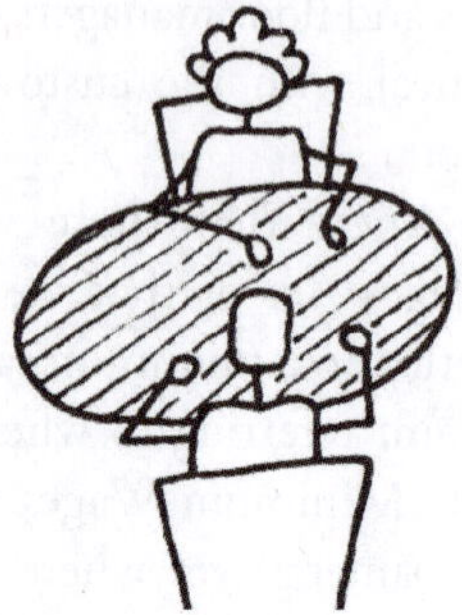

9.1 IS HOME A 'SAFE' PLACE?

In 2015, Rati Agnihotri, a famous actress who starred in the hit movie *Ek Duuje Ke Liye* (1981) with Kamal Haasan, announced that she was leaving her husband after 30 years of physical abuse. She said the violence started early on in her marriage and progressively got worse. She had hoped that the situation would improve. She did not want to deprive their children of a father's love. But she feared for her life and decided to report him to the police. Many people expressed surprise and disbelief at this announcement. People also wondered if she was speaking the truth. If this is true, some asked, then why did she stay in such a marriage for so long?

Some were suspicious of Rati's version of events because of her privileged status in society. People wondered how this could happen in a rich, educated family. But the fact is that almost every woman faces the doubts of others when she speaks out about harassment or abuse in her marriage. The general tendency is to assume that she might have done something which invited the abusive behaviour. In other words, the woman is blamed for the violence. And this is the case whether she is a worker in a factory or farm, a professor at a prestigious university or a middle-class housewife. Suspicion arises because of the strong belief in the goodness of family and marriage, the belief that families form the base of society and provide us with stability. It is also widely believed that a family should be headed by a man. A man's honour, prestige and worth are tied up with how he keeps the family and wife 'under control'.

What about women? People also believe that the responsibility of preserving a marriage and family lies with the woman as wife. In order to do this, a wife may have to bear her husband's irresponsibility, drunkenness, bad temper, physical and mental abuse and sexual torture. She may also have to manage with very little money. She may not be allowed to meet her family and friends. A good wife is supposed to suffer all this in silence.

It is also believed that a man subjected to humiliation, exploitation and oppression in the outside world often vents his frustrations at home. His wife and children may know this but suffer from the violence no less.

Society understands and even forgives such behaviour as a natural exercise of authority by the husband. The same society judges a woman's worth on the basis of how well she bears all this silently and privately. There are even common proverbs that refer to a husband hitting his wife as a sign of his love![1] When married women like Rati Agnihotri speak out, they are seen as women who failed to preserve their marriage. They are accused of being arrogant and selfish and violating the sacred institution of marriage.

A child who grows up in a house where they have to watch their father abuse their mother may end up traumatised. They may not understand what is happening at a young age, but as they grow older, they may feel guilty over their inability to stop such abuse. They may feel torn between the wish to protect their mother and the fear that doing so may further upset their father. They may fear losing his affection and love. But grown-up children often extend their support to their mother to stand up against such abuse. Such support is immensely enabling for mothers.

Points to discuss:

1. Men receive conflicting messages from society. They learn that a husband has to provide for his wife and family. But, as we learnt from Krishna Kumar's essay in Unit 2 and the excerpts in Unit 3, another message that frequently crops up is that real men keep their wives under control. Films and serials often show a man slapping his wife, and this is seen as justified chastisement. Do boys grow up into men, anxious and confused about their role in a marriage? Try to describe this confusion.

2. In our society, marriage is compulsory for almost all men and women. Women are prepared from childhood to bear pain and suffering. It is fairly common for a girl to be told, 'How will you manage in the in-laws' house if you can't bear pain?' Do you think it is this preparation (which we called 'socialisation' in Unit 2) that makes women like Rati Agnihotri endure years of violence? Or are there other reasons as well?

3. Try to imagine what it must be like for children growing up in a family of abuse. Discuss with your classmates the emotions such children must experience, and what can be done to help.

Are Family Matters Not Subject to the Law?

You may be surprised to learn that for a long time the societal rule of privacy and family honour was strengthened by the law. In a modern state, bonded labour, slavery, violence and exercise of arbitrary authority by one citizen over another is illegal and punishable. But even in early modern democracies, such as Britain, police often refused to intervene when women complained about domestic violence. 'This is a private matter,' they would say. Disturbed by this exception, J. S. Mill, the well-known British political scientist, asked the British Parliament in 1854 how a modern state like Britain, which claimed to be liberal, could leave its women to the arbitrary authority of their husbands. He was among the first to observe that family was the only sphere that remained outside the rule of law in the modern state.[2]

In India, this question was forcefully raised in the 1970s. Around this time, as a result of the efforts of the women's movement, domestic violence began to be openly discussed. The contradictions were obvious. On the one hand, the Indian Constitution gave equal rights to men and women. On the other hand, husbands and marital families could do what they wanted with their wives and daughters-in-law, including killing them or driving them to suicide, by claiming the act was a '*family matter*'.

Statistics from the National Family Health Survey (NFHS), 2009

- 31% of married women in India suffer from violence within their families. Such violence may involve being violently pushed or shaken, having something thrown at their face, having hair pulled or an arm twisted, being slapped, punched, kicked, dragged or beaten.
- 10% reported that their husbands tried to choke or burn them and threatened to attack them with a weapon.
- Almost 2 in 5 women suffered from cuts, bruises, sprains, dislocation of bones, deep wounds, broken bones, broken teeth, eye injuries and burns.
- Of the 31%, 1 in 10 women experienced sexual violence. They were forced to have sex or unwillingly perform other sexual acts with their husbands.
- Of the 31%, only 1 to 2% reported such violence to the police!
- Women's deaths in families are under-reported.

According to a study of emergency wards in public hospitals in India, published in 2009 by the well-respected medical journal *Lancet*, which collated material on accidental deaths by fire through detailed hospital records, more than one lakh women (1,00,016 was the figure given) died in kitchen fires. The largest number of them were married women between the ages of 18–35. This figure was six times the number recorded by the police that year.

During the late 1970s, newspapers in India began to increasingly report about newly married women found dead under suspicious circumstances in many middle-class homes. These women had invariably died due to severe burns. The police registered these cases as accidental deaths under the theory of 'stove burst'. Nobody asked whether other family members had died or been injured, or why those who died were all newly married women, or how stoves could burst in kitchens where families did not even use stoves to cook!

Women activists in India wanted these deaths to be investigated. The police were reluctant. It was a family matter, a private issue, they said. No outsiders, including the police, had a right to enter. But why were these deaths 'private'? Why did 'family' enjoy immunity from the law of the land?

Women's organisations across the country were shocked that the law did not recognise the harassment, mistreatment, torture and murder of married women by families as a crime. They pointed out that women in families were also citizens and therefore entitled to protection from the state. Lawyers argued that if the state did not recognise this violence and provide protection, it would amount to discrimination under the Constitution of India.

Just think—if anyone is burnt alive on a road, in an office or anywhere, it is considered a major crime. But if a woman is beaten up or killed within her family's home, then it is not.

Since the police were reluctant to investigate, women's organisations themselves gathered information about the cruelty and abuse that women experienced in families. In the late 1970s, and 80s, the evidence they gathered through their investigations and revealed to the public through press statements, reports and booklets shocked the country.[3] With this evidence they challenged the idea that the violence and suffering married women undergo is natural. They argued that violence in the family is a violation of the basic human rights of women. What was categorised as private suffering was made visible and public, and the law was forced to recognise women's suffering as violence.

Points to discuss:

1. Open last week's newspapers or search on the internet and see how many cases were recently reported of young women who died from burning. How many of them were married? Was anyone else in the family reported as injured? Share what you find with the class.
2. Did the newspapers or internet articles report the causes of their deaths? What are they? What are your thoughts on this?

Breaking the Silence 

For women, the most important step is to break the silence surrounding such violence.

As it is a taboo to speak about 'family matters' with neighbours, relatives or outsiders, women seeking help in these kinds of situations have to take two important decisions. The first is to mentally break free from the iron law of family privacy. The second is to overcome the shame associated with breaking the silence, as such abuse is often linked to one's so-called failure as a wife or a daughter-in-law or a mother. There is no reason to protect those who are supposed to love you and take care of you when they choose to abuse you.

In the 1980s, it was discovered that sharing experiences within support groups was hugely helpful for women. Groups such as Progressive Organisation of Women, Stree Shakti Sanghatana, Stree Sangharsh and Saheli in Hyderabad, and later, Stree Sangam (now known as LABIA) and Forum against Oppression of Women in Mumbai, Jagori in Delhi and Vimochana in Bangalore were all formed to provide physical, emotional and even legal support for women. The discussions in these forums enabled large numbers of women to understand that it was not their failure to be good wives, daughters-in-law and mothers that resulted in their beatings and abuse. It was not their fault. They were not to blame, and these support groups paved the way for measures which helped women.

There are now policies and social and legal measures in place that offer support to women facing such violence. Special courts and women's police stations have also been instituted by certain state governments. Importantly, society recognises that this violence—now known as ***domestic violence***—has devastating effects on the psychological and physical health of the women, men and children in these families. Government surveys such as the National Family Health Survey clearly prove this.[4] We also understand domestic violence more fully and richly through women and men who have written about it. Once the law recognised domestic violence as illegal, women started writing about how they themselves, or their mothers and families, suffered from it. A good example of this is Meena Kandasamy's autobiographical narrative *When I Hit You: Or, A Portrait of the Writer as Young Wife* (2017) in which she describes the marital abuse that she faced. Another example is Flavia Agnes's *My Story . . . Our Story of Re-building Broken Lives* (1984), from which an excerpt has been provided later in this unit. Though the violence itself has not stopped, our society is moving in small yet significant ways towards challenging the notions of privacy and honour that control women within families.

Documentaries and feature films are being made that explore domestic violence. Shabnam Virmani made a series of one-minute films titled *Bol* to help raise awareness about domestic violence. In each film, a woman makes a short, sharp statement about what she found absolutely unbearable.[5]

Nowadays, we also see many advertisements which condemn domestic violence. For instance, Bell Bajao,[6] a campaign against domestic violence, released a series of advertisements which featured someone on a street hearing an argument break out inside a house, with a man shouting and a woman crying in fear and pain. The person on the street gathers courage and rings the doorbell of the house. The shouting stops. A man answers the door, and the person asks him a question such as, 'May I use your phone?' The idea behind the advertisement is to promote awareness of domestic violence and to urge citizens to intervene and help put an end to it. Interestingly, the advertisements show a man ringing the doorbell and interrupting the fight. Why do you think a woman is not shown doing the same?

Domestic violence is gradually being recognised as an undesirable and unacceptable practice as a result of changes in the law and state policy combined with the struggles of women. Many wives and mothers are also learning to break the silence around their suffering in different ways. To stop domestic violence and to try and save the marriage, some approach caste *panchayats*. Some even go to court. Some fight vehemently while others are forced to give up due to a lack of support or external pressures. Parents may no longer be as quick as they were before to blame their daughters and send them back to their husbands. Some women eventually separate from their husbands and live with their children or with their parents. But each woman's struggles are excruciatingly slow, painful and halting, as society is still predominantly oriented towards upholding the idea of a male-headed family in law and in culture.

Most women therefore take a long time to decide to even complain. They take even longer to decide if they want to leave their husband. Leaving is the last option for many of them. For various reasons, if it is possible, they would like to save the marriage.

9.2 WHEN WOMEN UNITE

Not many people know that domestic violence was one of the key issues that gave rise to the famous anti-arrack movement in Andhra Pradesh. During 1991–92, the Andhra Pradesh government centralised the sale of arrack and began to supply it in small sachets to villages. What was till then available only in bottles and pots when the village distilled it (mainly during festivals or harvests) could now be had every day and even carried home. Landlords were persuaded by liquor contractors to pay a percentage of the wages to the agricultural workers using these sachets. This wreaked havoc upon the domestic economy of many families. The struggles that women within the district of Nellore endured to prevent the sale of arrack in their villages transformed their relations with men and slowly gave them a measure of control over their lives. And from there the movement spread.

Rural women attending adult literacy classes in Nellore read about a woman named Sitamma who committed suicide because she was unable to help her husband with his alcoholism and unable to prevent his abuse. This led to them examining their own lives and how their husbands, influenced by the easy availability of arrack, had become addicts. Their husbands were no longer able to economically support the family and had also become violent. One of the women recounted: 'We are wage earners. We produce gold from the earth. But what is the use? All our hard-earned money is spent on toddy and arrack. When our men-folk do not have money, they sell away our rice, butter, *ghee* or anything that fetches them arrack … They take away whatever they can lay their hands on … Apart from drinking, they abuse us, pick up fights with us, slap our children. They make our day-to-day existence miserable … Then we read the story of Sitamma's death. It started us thinking. Who is responsible for her death? We then told the *sarpanch* (head of the village council) to close the arrack shop.'

The rural women in several districts decided to boycott arrack shops, stop the supply of arrack to their villages, and protect themselves and their families from economic and physical destruction.

Now watch Shabnam Virmani's film, *When Women Unite* (1996). This is a docudrama about the anti-arrack movement and narrates the story of these protests through re-enactments, interviews and actual documentary footage.[7]

9.3 REBUILDING LIVES

As we have learnt, a married woman will often try her best to save her marriage, even in the face of severe violence. She might seek advice and try to reform her husband. Taking legal recourse is likely to be a last resort. The following two extracts relate to women's uphill struggles to keep themselves safe and alive in the face of domestic violence.

The Search for a Good Marriage Counsellor

This extract is from an autobiographical account by Flavia Agnes, who is today a leading lawyer in the country. When she was younger, she was a victim of domestic violence. Her autobiography, *My Story … Our Story of Re-building Broken Lives* (1984), speaks about her struggle to protect herself and her children from violence, and her attempts to rebuild her life. She went on to study and practise law in Mumbai, where she has been relentlessly fighting to secure women's rights in families. You can also read her articles and essays on such struggles for justice in newspapers and journals. In the following excerpt, she narrates how she sought advice from a variety of people to stop her husband from ill-treating her.

❖ ❖ ❖

I tried to be a better mother, better housewife, better wife. I must make this marriage work, somehow. I learnt all the housewifely skills. I learnt to stitch children's clothes. … Beautiful clothes with delicate embroidery. … I baked cakes, learnt to make pickles, jams, biscuits.

Later I started a garden in the balcony. Varieties of cactus, tomato, chilli, *kadi patta*, mint, *tulsi*. The garden grew but the marriage didn't improve. I had mastered all the skills. But they were totally ineffective weapons to check the violence. . . .

The search for freedom . . . has been slow and painful. I was trapped within the vicious circle of a violent home and a cruel world. I went round in circles. . . .

I appeared for the Bank of India test. I passed. [My husband] said, 'Working women are arrogant. They neglect the home. I will not allow my wife to work.' I didn't go back for the interview.

A doctor in the neighbourhood offered to give me homeopathic medicine, free of charge, and advised, 'Don't drink coffee.' . . . The doctor advised, 'Why don't you talk to the priests?' Once, when I was thrown out after a violent fight, I did. . . . I was told, 'Counselling cannot be done to one partner. Bring your husband along.' I thought, 'If my husband is the type to come along, then I don't need to come at all.' Father Dominic said, 'You can come and talk to me, but I cannot intervene. He might make false allegations against me. Then my reputation will be spoilt.' But he was sympathetic. At least I could talk to him and retain my sanity. After I suffered a fracture [due to domestic abuse], he advised, 'Why don't you make a police complaint?'

I went to the police station. The officer said, 'He is an educated man. If you press charges, it will be worse for you. He will not be scared of our warnings.' I said, 'I need a shelter.' They said, 'There is one. We can direct you. But they will not take the children.' I asked, 'What will happen to them?' 'They will be sent to the remand home or left with their father.' That settled the matter. I withdrew the complaint. . . .

I met another priest for guidance regarding divorce. He said, 'He is a sick man. Not a physical sickness, but a mental sickness. Supposing he has cancer, would you have deserted him? He needs your help to overcome this sickness.' . . . 'But his cancer of the mind is growing on my body, breaking it, deforming it, damaging my psyche. His cancer doesn't hurt him, just me.' I realised that I was being asked not only to stay on with him but also to be sympathetic and understanding towards him because he has a sickness . . . the sickness of beating me! The search for a 'good' marriage counsellor came to an end.

A Petition for Divorce

This second extract is from a petition for divorce filed in a Hyderabad family court in 2013. Rarely do we come across women who take the step of seeking divorce from an abusive husband or marital family. The petitioner, a qualified engineer with a well-paying job, arrived at this decision after a long battle.

I got married in the presence of the elders and well-wishers of both sides in Madurai. We lived in Chennai. Right from the first month of my marriage, my husband started harassing me. He abused me in filthy language saying that I was not up to his expectations and that my parents were poor. Many a time he beat me and manhandled me even without considering that I was pregnant. When I was in hospital for my delivery, no one from my husband's family came to take care of me. I did not have food to eat. My parents and my sister were not allowed to visit me.

Unable to live with my husband and his drunkenness, I decided to move with my child to live with my in-laws. To my misfortune, my in-laws too ill-treated me. They would not allow me to talk to anybody. Whenever relatives and friends came to our house, it was my duty to serve them coffee or tea, but I was not allowed to sit and talk to them. They would go off to functions without taking me. I was seen as an unfit daughter-in-law. They would lock up all the rooms in the house so I was forced to sit in the hall only. Even the telephone was kept inside so that I could not talk to my parents or any other friends. I was treated like a servant and never given any respect despite being the daughter-in-law of the house.

I was a qualified engineer. I soon took up a job. When I went for work, I left my child with my parents. Sometimes, when I returned from the office, there would be no food for me in the house. My in-laws did not take care of my son even for a little bit of time. When I went to the bathroom or the toilet, I would take my son along as they refused to take care of the child. My husband came to Hyderabad once every week or fortnight. I was terrified every time he came home, as he would forcibly have sexual intercourse with me. I was subjected to sexual torture, the shameful details of which I cannot even discuss. In case I did not cooperate with his demands, he would become suspicious and beat me up, saying that I was having an affair.

I complained to the police twice. Both times the inspector admonished him and sent him off with a warning not to repeat such behaviour. But my husband came back and repeated the same behaviour. I have lost all interest in marital life and I have become increasingly devoted to God. I have one son aged seven years. I undertake to look after him. He is my only source of joy apart from my God. Please do not separate me from my son.

I therefore pray to this Honourable Court to grant me divorce.

Points to discuss:

1. When a wife is beaten, it is common to hear that it happened because of some fault on her part, For instance, that she was not good at something. In the first extract, Flavia Agnes says, 'I had mastered all the [housewifely] skills. But they were totally ineffective weapons to check the violence.' Why are these lines significant? Why do you think she says them?

2. Flavia Agnes writes, 'The search for freedom … has been slow and painful. I was trapped within the vicious circle of a violent home and a cruel world.' Discuss what she means by this.

3. Do you think the advice Flavia Agnes received from the priests, doctors and policemen was useful or correct? Give your reasons.

4. The general attitude in our society is that a relationship between a husband and wife is a personal or 'private' matter, even if the husband is physically abusing his wife. Do you agree with this statement? Do you think it is fair?

5. After reading the second extract, think about what inhibited the woman from seeking legal remedies. Was loneliness one of the reasons—loneliness caused by shame and an inability to change the situation? List your reasons and discuss each one in class.

9.4 FURTHER READING

New Forums for Justice

In the past twenty years, there have been scattered but interesting experiments in dealing with domestic violence in certain areas of Gujarat and Tamil Nadu by collectives of women.

In the state of Gujarat, these women's collectives are known as ***nari adalats*** (women's courts). We all know that community *panchayats* are traditionally all-male with women granted only a meagre presence and voice. *Nari adalats* came into existence to counter such traditional setups. Its members are elected from each village and the *adalat* meets and sits on a particular day near the district collector's office. Families may meet with the *adalat* to lodge a complaint. Sometimes the aggrieved woman may appear as well. The outcome of these hearings depends on the willingness of the concerned parties to change. In cases where there is no hope for the marriage, dowry and *stree-dhan* (women's wealth) are returned. Treating women as equal partners in a marriage, *nari adalats* have arbitrated more than 700 cases. This initiative came up under the Mahila Samakhya Programme supported by the government.

In the state of Tamil Nadu, we have another extremely interesting example of a women's collective tackling issues of domestic violence. This is a ***women's jamaat***. Traditionally, a *jamaat* is an institution that settles disputes among Muslims. Like any other traditional community *panchayat, jamaats* too do not have female members. But in the Tamil Nadu district of Pudukkottai, a group of Muslim women led by Sharifa Khanam decided to form *jamaats* made up of poor, rural, Muslim women. Dissatisfied with the way the all-male community *jamaats* were dealing with the concerns of women's education, dowry and domestic violence, they decided to step in. Religion, they discovered, did not form an obstacle, but male dominance did. In the process, they also learnt about the rights Muslim women held according to their faith and how to use such knowledge to question injustices and violence. Over time, male community leaders changed their viewpoint on the collective and began to accept the verdicts and resolutions offered by the women's *jamaat*. The sense of bringing justice to suffering women through a collective effort is captured by the song they composed, which has been recorded and translated by C. S. Lakshmi below.

The life we have lived begging,
Is not a life worth living
These are times when we have to demand
Let us come together
And dare to question—
No more succumbing with bent heads!
Every day feels like death
Due to this double-faced justice
When we make the law for men
Then will they learn!
Let us talk of a common justice
And attain our victory . . .

Protection of Women from Domestic Violence Act, 2005

In India, physical and mental cruelty has been recognised as grounds for divorce since the Dissolution of Muslim Marriages Act, 1939. But it was also made into a criminal offence in 1984. After India signed the Convention on the Elimination of all Forms of Discrimination Against Women (CEDAW), an international treaty put forward by the United Nations in 1981, women's organisations pushed for comprehensive laws against domestic violence. India and 59 other countries passed a law against domestic violence between 2005 and 2011. Now 144 countries have such laws. Passed in 2005, the Protection of Women from Domestic Violence Act defines a wide range of actions by husbands and their side of the family as domestic violence. These include: beatings, insults, physical or mental or sexual abuse, threats, excessive suspicion, demands for dowry, perverse sexual behaviour, financial deprivation and sale of household assets. A wife experiencing such violence can approach the nearest magistrates' court and seek the following:

- Protection order: If the wife lives separately from her husband, then her husband can be ordered not to enter her home, or disturb her at her workplace or attempt to communicate with her. This includes communication by email or phone calls.

- Maintenance order: The husband can be directed to provide financial support to the wife and children.

- Residence order: If the wife is living in her husband's home, the court can decree that she should not be evicted or thrown out of her husband's home. This order can be passed even if the wife does not own the house.

- Joint property: The husband can be directed not to sell joint property, such as the house, nor operate bank accounts and bank lockers used by both the husband and wife.

- Custody of children: If the wife is anxious that she will be separated from her children, the court can grant her a protection order. If the children are not with the wife, the court can direct that the children be returned to the wife or enable her to visit them.

- Compensation: The magistrate, in the final stage, can direct the husband to pay compensation to the wife for any physical and mental harm that she suffered on account of his conduct.

A violation of any of the orders passed by the magistrate is an offence. The husband can be punished with a sentence of up to one year in jail along with a fine. In addition to the above, the wife can also complain about domestic violence to the local police station. The provision of law is Section 498A in the Indian Penal Code.

NOTES

1. For instance, a popular Telugu saying, '*Kottina cheyye koru, korina cheyye kottu*' means, 'A hand that beats you desires you, and only a hand that seeks you beats you.'

2. Read J. S. Mill's essay, *The Subjection of Women* (1869) here: http://www.earlymoderntexts.com/assets/pdfs/mill1869.pdf.

3. An example of such work can be seen in Subhadra Butalia's *The Gift of a Daughter* (2002). In the book, she describes how she and her friends investigated the suspicious deaths of young brides from 'stove bursts' in the 1970s. Radha Kumar's *History of Doing* (1993) vividly describes the efforts by women's activists to convince the police to investigate such suspicious deaths.

4. Learn more about the government surveys on domestic violence in India here: https://www.livemint.com/Opinion/eIFZC21AWB1D0YXD4sDy8H/Are-Indian-women-safe-in-their-homes.html.

5. Watch the *Bol* series of one-minute films here: https://www.youtube.com/channel/UC8Qa7DzvcQslFxzRWJOb5Nw/videos.

6. Made by Breakthrough in 2008 in collaboration with the Ministry of Women and Child Development, UNIFEM and the UN Trust Fund, the 'Bell Bajao' films are available for viewing on YouTube. Here is the link to one such advertisement: https://www.youtube.com/watch?v=eh7WXBrEcSQ.

7. Watch *When Women Unite* here: https://www.youtube.com/channel/UC8Qa7DzvcQslFxzRWJOb5Nw/videos. For those interested, the full film is longer and available for purchase.

Whose History? Questions for Historians and Others

10.1 RECLAIMING A PAST

We asked a student from Class 10 to name some of the key people she remembered from her history lessons on the Indian nationalist movement. She struggled for a while and then the names, 'Mahatma Gandhi, Jawaharlal Nehru, Sardar Patel,' tumbled out of her mouth as if they all belonged to one person!

You can see there are no women on her list. Nor did she list anyone from the south of India, nor any dalits (not even Babasaheb Ambedkar), Muslims, Sikhs or Christians, even though all these different groups of people were importantly involved in India's freedom struggle. History as she learnt it, which is also history as popularly remembered, appears to be only about certain leaders and rulers.

In the poem 'A Worker Reads History',[1] the German writer Bertolt Brecht points to the many dimensions that are hidden and overlooked in popular history. Brecht's worker asks a number of questions, such as: 'Who built the seven gates of Thebes?' Did kings ever help haul stone to build monuments? What happened to the masons after the Great Wall of China was built?

This worker has many questions—questions which historians have either not thought of or deemed unimportant to ask. Initially, it seems as though the questions are about small, insignificant things such as who carried stones, built walls, cooked, found places to sleep in, etc. We soon realise these questions point to the fact that the life and work of the vast majority of people are missing from what can be described as 'mainstream' history. It is clear that such an omission is serious.

These questions, asked 'from below', also offer a working person an idea of his or her own true importance. Without workers, none of the great men would have achieved what they did. In the end, the poem almost implies that the contribution of workers may have been more significant than the contributions of great men. The sense of self-worth and pride that it instils is one of many reasons why history is considered so important.

We will discuss another reason later in this unit, but for now, let us consider the question: Could Brecht's worker be a woman? It is possible. Brecht does not identify the narrator as a man. But as you might surmise after studying the previous units in this course, the questions do not appear to cover many issues that would have specifically concerned a woman worker. It does seem as though Brecht imagines the 'worker' as a man—though he never actually says so. It is true and must be remembered that women also break stones and carry them, fight in armies, work in construction sites and cook. In addition to which they look after men, bear children and raise new workers, care for the sick and the aged. Yet somehow these vital contributions have remained invisible and forgotten. When history breaks this 'thought-barrier' and begins to think of women as well as men, it becomes more gender sensitive. The world expands. New areas open up.

Women's History

Brecht's poem speaks of history as seen from a working-class point of view, and it is important to remember that developments in the study of history have generally been inspired by people's movements. Take, for example, the women's movement which motivated historians to ask questions about women's achievements, their experiences, changing ideas of masculinity and femininity, the suppression or oppression of women, violence against women, the 'double

burden' of work inside and outside the household and other related topics. Meanwhile the dalit movement has pointed out the critical importance of dalit labour and the fact that nearly all folk art and craft in this country is originally the work of dalits. Their movement also raised questions regarding caste violence, discussed dalit thinkers and writers who had been forgotten or sidelined and documented important events in the development of dalit consciousness.

> **Points to discuss:**
>
> 1. Can you think of some questions Brecht's worker would have asked if the worker was a woman?
> 2. Try writing these questions as a poem. Don't feel nervous. You can work in groups if you prefer. Consider the following when you compose your poem: the 'double burden' women face of doing the housework and cooking and taking care of the child while also working at the construction site; wages for time she has to take off after giving birth; missed days at work and missed wages because she is caring for a sick husband, child or aged person; the constant threat of harassment or rape principally by her employers or overseers; the unreasonable tasks she has to undertake; her desire to become the planner or the architect of the city.

On a Larger Scale

Moving from an individual woman's experience to the broader sweep of history, we find women's contributions to many fields are inadequately appreciated. For instance, women were key agents in the development of medical knowledge in India. Midwives or *dais* were like present-day doctors who looked after the health of the village. These people knew about locally available medicines, helped pregnant women deliver their babies and generally cared for the sick. Yet their scientific contributions to medicine and pharmacology have been devalued and forgotten. What about technology? Women were central to many family professions in rural areas. For example, they tanned hides and made shoes, wove cloth, crafted pots, worked on metal, built houses. They were also involved in developing India's world-famous technologies in pottery, metal and textiles. In addition, they kept alive a vast 'folk' literature and an impressive musical repertoire through songs, dances and stories. It is only in the last few decades that these contributions are being recognised and documented, mostly by feminist historians.

That is not all. Village women were also witness to major events: floods, droughts, wars, famines. These often led to migration. When that happened, they cleared new lands, planted new crops, helped to build water tanks, roads, forts, palaces. They battled over land and produce. We know that even when they were not allowed to touch books, they secretly studied. They left home to join religious and political movements. Why are their experiences and perspectives on important events not part of India's history?

In modern times (late nineteenth century onwards), middle-class women moved into almost every field of employment. Indian women were among the very first qualified doctors and lawyers in the world. There were also well-known writers, scientists, theatre artists, painters, intellectuals and political leaders. We also know that women were active in many movements. In the Telangana rebellion between 1946 and 1951, women participated in large numbers. Many of them

were leaders. There are photographs of them training with weapons and evidence of letters that they wrote. But official histories of modern India say little about these women or many others who fought in such movements in other parts of the country.

10.2 HISTORICAL AND CHANGEABLE?

Remember when we said there was another reason why history is important? Here is the other reason—history helps us appreciate that many things which people often regard as natural and therefore unchangeable were different at other times in history. This is important because if they are shaped historically, they can also be reshaped. Importantly for us here, when a woman's role is understood to be socially constructed within a specific historical context, rather than natural and universal, it is open to change.

In fact, a surprising number of things we consider natural or traditional may actually have taken that shape only fairly recently. For instance, the six-yard *sari* that Indian women now commonly wear is considered 'traditional'. But we know that even today this unstitched piece of cloth is draped in different ways in different regions and by different castes. Temple sculptures show the cloth is draped in elegant and often revealing ways. Women who work in the fields wear it at calf length. The style of draping the five-and-a-half meter-long cloth that we think of as the 'Indian' *sari* today is only just over a century old and is a modern creation, developed because the clothing earlier used by women in elite families was considered immodest.

Read what Soudamini Khastagiri had to say about this in her article 'Striloker Paricchad' from the Bengali magazine *Bamabhodini*

Patrika in 1872: 'Any civilised nation is against the kind of clothing in use in the present time among women of our country. Indeed it is a sign of shamelessness. Educated men have been greatly agitated about it, almost everyone wishes for another kind of civilised clothing … there is a custom here of women wearing fine and transparent clothing which reveals the whole body. Such shameless attire in no way allows one to frequent civilised company … such clothes can stand in the way of our moral improvement.'

The idea that a *sari* was to be worn along with a 'blouse' and a 'petticoat' (notice that we use English words for these) was developed in the late nineteenth century by a Bengali woman from the Tagore family who drew inspiration from the Parsee way of draping it and from European costumes. This new and more modest style was welcomed as a corrective to earlier ways of dressing that were regarded as 'indecent'. This is the style that we think of today as 'traditional'.

In *The Feminine Mystique* (1963), a book which is often cited as having started the feminist movement in America, Betty Friedan analyses the prevailing assumption that women naturally find fulfilment in housework, marriage, sexual passivity and child rearing. 'Truly feminine' women did not desire higher education or careers and were not interested in politics or public life; they found complete fulfilment in the domestic sphere. Friedan suggests that this idea of womanhood arises in a specific moment in the history of the US.

During World War Two, when the men were called away to serve in the army, women took on the jobs they left behind. Initially it was the working-class women who took over the jobs, but soon middle-class women joined them. Women did every kind of work. They even worked in factories that produced munitions.

The iconic image of a muscular 'Rosie the Riveter' celebrates this experience. Friedan argues that after the war, when the men returned, women moved out of the factories and public life. Middle-class women retreated into the family and the household. Their task was to provide emotional support to men traumatised by war and to produce more children. The image of the slim and attractive suburban American housewife, immersed in cleaning, cooking and childcare, was celebrated in the films, popular literature and comic strips of the time. The suburban housewife was presented as the epitome of womanhood and the envy of the world. Friedan argues that this image was also part of the Cold War propaganda used against Communist Russia. In contrast to the 'feminine' suburban housewife who epitomises American women, Russian women were represented as muscular, manly and unfulfilled because they worked outside the home alongside men.

Betty Friedan displaces the idea that it is natural for women to be housewives, spending their lives in the service of the family, with a convincing historical interpretation of the figure of the suburban housewife. Her analysis shows that the confinement of women to domesticity is recent. She thus makes it possible for people to express their dissatisfaction with this ideal and to dream about, maybe even fight for, change.

Moustache Styles

In many cultures, a moustache is considered an expression of masculine authority and power. This is why in villages like Puliyangudi in Tamil Nadu, dalit men were not allowed to grow moustaches until recently. In other places policemen were encouraged to grow moustaches. The illustrations on the next page are an attempt to gather evidence for and depict a social history of the moustache.

As discussed in the unit on masculinity, the idea of what is appropriately masculine is different in different societies and also changes historically. Perhaps in your grandfather's time being masculine meant being aloof, stern, strong or even violent, expecting to be served by women. But today, men who are violent are generally not respected or liked by most people. The term *toxic masculinity* was developed to describe such disrespectful behaviour. In fact, nowadays many men share and enjoy the responsibility of taking care of their child or children. Some also cook and know how to run a household. They do not think this affects their masculinity.

10.3 SOURCES HISTORIANS USE TODAY

Historians need records and evidence. In the past, they often only used official archives. But such archives tend to preserve documents connected with governments and rulers. Are there other such 'archives' that can be used or created when there are no official texts or written materials? The answer to this question is fascinating. Feminists and others, working on history 'from below' or from the perspective of ordinary people and not the elite (an approach also known as *Subaltern Studies*), have made many pioneering contributions to historical methodology. Sometimes they read official history very carefully, 'against the grain', looking for what it does not say or tries to hide. They ask questions about whose point of view is being presented, whose interests are being served, what is left out and so on. They use letters, unpublished autobiographies, recipe books. They look through household account books, old bills, court notices and hospital records. They study paintings and photographs. They look at objects, artefacts and buildings.

Songs

When there are no written records available, women's songs and stories can also prove to be a source of valuable information. For example, when a well-known mythological epic like the Mahabharata is orally recounted in a village performance, local references are generally inserted. So, the mighty Bhima from that narrative will fight thugs who are likely to be recognised by the audience as people in their area. Facts about their daily life and work, events that disrupted their routines, experiences that made them happy or sad are all preserved in folk performances and songs. These songs can also tell us about their culture—agricultural practices, ways by which crops were sown and reaped, how they smelt metal, how they wove designs in cloth, fairs where things were bought and sold. They may also reveal more common everyday interactions by poking fun at landlords or husbands. In addition, they may report on larger-scale issues like famines, earthquakes and wars.

Hymns preserved and still sung by dalit groups in religious meetings in Kerala have been used to document the harsh lives of their ancestors who were slaves. An example of one such song is about a baby eaten by termites.[2] The baby was placed in a cloth tied to the branch of a tree while the mother worked in the field. The master refused to let her off even to feed her child. When people sing this song and retell this story, women who are listening often remember their own many sorrows and cry. This is also another reason why history is so important; it allows us to honour the past while preparing for the future.

Assignment

Sit down with your grandmother, grandfather or any other elderly person. Ask them about their childhood. With their permission, take notes on the conversation. Can you identify two ways in which the understanding of gender has evolved since their youth?

Family Histories

Many madiga families follow the tradition of sitting down in the evening and sharing stories about their ancestors. These stories help them remember their family history. But family histories can also be about a great many other things.

In his memoir, *My Father Baliah* (2011), the well-known academic and co-founder of the Centre for Dalit Studies, Y. B. Satyanarayana, remembers his childhood. His story focuses on his father, who starts off with a minor job in the railways and eventually secures a regular post. The family moves from the dalit section of their village to the railway housing, and then from their village in Nizamabad to Secunderabad. The children are sent to school and then college. Satyanarayana's memoir is a rich and moving history, not only of his family but of dalits in India and the opportunities that opened up for them during colonial times. It is also a social history of the railways in India.

Oral History

Oral historians extract history from the memories and recollections of others. For example, they might speak with people who have been in social and political movements, or experienced a tsunami, or worked under difficult circumstances such as perhaps in a coal mine. Historians sometimes crosscheck oral accounts for accuracy. But even when that is difficult to do, such accounts prove important as memories. *Manaku Teliyani Mana Charitra* (1986; the English translation, *We Were Making History*, was published in 1989), a pioneering book on women's history, relied on oral sources to recover information about women who had participated in the Telangana rebellion of the 1940s.

That movement fought against the forced labour (*vetti*) system, cruel landlords and the Razakars (a volunteer force that operated between 1947 and 1948 and defended the Hyderabad State against internal and external threats). The movement fought for rights over land and won. When historians spoke with women about the movement, they shared their stories and also dwelt on the difficulties they

faced. Short excerpts from the afore-mentioned narratives are included in the 'Further Reading' section of this unit. It is important to remember that such movements could never fully reach or help women without discussing issues such as sexuality, relationships, children, women's labour as well as women's participation in political discussions and decision-making.

10.4 FURTHER READING

Missing Pages from Modern History

In this section, we share the profiles of people from various walks of life whose lives and work are significant for a more egalitarian and nuanced understanding of social reform and political effort in modern India. Today, some of them are remembered by a few small circles, while others sadly remain largely unknown.

Small organisations started by ordinary people in villages or towns often have a significance that is only fully appreciated much later. For example, the Prathyaksha Raksha Daiva Sabha (PRDS), which translates to 'God's Church of Visible Salvation', was started in 1909 by the philosopher-activist Poikayil Appachan, but is only now beginning to be appreciated, that too largely as a result of questions raised by the dalit movement. This religious group provided spiritual and communal support to slaves in central Kerala. It also grew into a movement that advocated the emancipation of slaves and the annihilation of caste. PRDS drew on the memory of the suffering experienced by slaves to build a community and articulate a response to slavery.

Another example of a movement that had a wide-ranging impact, particularly on Tamil Nadu's growth and culture, was the early twentieth-century, non-brahmin, Self-Respect Movement. This movement against brahminism was founded in 1910 and headed by E. V. Ramasamy, more commonly known as Periyar. Until recently, we knew very little about the women in that movement and the issues they raised and wrote about. One of the profiles in this section discusses these women.

The remaining profiles focus on Chityala Ailamma and C. K. Janu. Chityala Ailamma's angry reaction to the landlords destroying her crops was the starting point for a very significant peasant struggle for land in the Telangana region in the 1940s. The oral history reproduced here vividly recreates the tension and drama of that time. C. K. Janu, the adivasi woman who led a successful struggle for land in Kerala, caught the attention of the world during the *Kudil Kettu Samaram* [build huts] agitation in 2001. But her work and her analysis of adivasi issues and the questions raised by adivasi struggles for land in many parts of India is not part of our understanding of Indian political life.

These profiles give us a feel for the forgotten or overlooked past of our country and create a history that resonates with contemporary concerns such as gender or caste or class. We hope they also give you an idea of local histories which you yourself can investigate and write about.

Poikayil Yohannan

Poikayil Yohannan (1879–1939), now reverentially referred to as Poikayil Kumara Gurudevan or Poikayil Appachan, founded the PRDS in 1909 in Eraviperoor, a small village in Kerala. Today, the PRDS is a significant dalit social and religious movement.

Born to dalit parents named Poikayil Kandan and Lechi, who were both slaves of a Syrian-Christian landlord family, he grew up like other slave-caste boys working in the landlord's fields and household. At a very early age he learnt to read and write. He is remembered for reading the Bible and explaining it to his friends as they grazed their master's cattle. He was charming and stood out among the other slave-caste children.

He initially worked as an itinerant preacher with various missionary organisations, leaving one after the other because of caste prejudices shown by upper-caste Syrian Christians who dominated these organisations and churches. During 1909–10 he mobilised parayas, pulayas and other dalit castes to establish an independent religion of their own. This new religion spoke of liberation and laid equal emphasis on the spiritual and material dimensions of life. Spiritual progress was to be achieved through new rituals and ideas that included *rakshanirnayam* (a vow of salvation). This involved lengthy discourses, mainly on biblical themes. It also involved, for the first time, a recounting of the history of these slave castes.

Since their extreme deprivation and suffering were the result of a caste society in which dalits were not allowed to own property and had no right even to their own person (as slaves they were bought and sold), Yohannan felt the need to transform their lives by helping them acquire land and become land-owning peasants. Efforts were made to purchase land and teach and learn skills such as weaving that were new to dalits in that region. He also set up a weaving centre at Eraviperoor, bringing in trainers from Balaramapuram, a village known for handloom manufacturing in southern Kerala. As mentioned before, the PRDS tried to engage creatively with both the spiritual and material realms, especially in the context of dalit communities emerging from centuries of caste slavery.

PRDS sermons and discourses combined Christian themes and ritual practices with elements drawn from dalit life to create a new religion. In particular, they made imaginative use of the dalit oral tradition to provide a historical interpretation of the dalit past. The remembrance and lament of the life of slavery became part of a project of salvation. In addition to being a sociopolitical project, it also became a mission of personal liberation and salvation.

European missionaries in nineteenth-century Kerala wrote extensively about slavery as a social evil. But in the early decades of the twentieth century, PRDS was able to transform slavery into a subjective, emotional category that fuelled a desire for liberation. 'Rememorialisation' refers to the process by which the present generation, who may not have experienced slavery, undergoes the suffering and pain of slavery through discourses and reconstructions of the slave experience. After Yohannan's death, the community kept alive this concern with history. This is exemplified by the oral and written narratives that are now in circulation. The movement was also an important dalit effort to negotiate modernity by making equality (as against the more conventional nineteenth-century focus on reform and uplift) their major concern.

In summation, the PRDS movement tried to engage with problems of caste hierarchy and exploitation, and strove to achieve social equality along with material and spiritual progress. The movement began against the backdrop of missionary Christianity, but it critiqued the missionary project and moved beyond its limits. With a sizeable section of his followers turning to Hinduism under the leadership of his second wife and leader of the movement, Yohannan came to be referred to as Sree Kumara Gurudevan.

Yohannan was nominated to the Sree Moolam Popular Assembly of Travancore in 1921 and 1931. He used the legislative floor to articulate the demands of all oppressed castes, including asking for access to modern education, cultivable land, employment and other facilities for a dignified life.

Self-Respect Movement

The Self-Respect Movement (1926–40) was a social movement that challenged the caste system and the supremacy of the brahmins in Tamil Nadu. It was a deeply rationalist movement popularly associated with E. V. Ramasamy Naicker, better known as Periyar. His influential writings and the movement's journals, *Kudi Arasu* and *Puratchi*, played an important role in creating a non-brahmin, Tamil public sphere. The movement also strongly advocated women's rights to property, work, divorce, remarriage and contraception. In the last couple of decades, historians have begun to unearth and understand the significant role played by the many non-brahmin lower-caste women in this movement. These women participated in meetings, gave public speeches, wrote insightful articles and emerged as powerful voices in their own right.

Trichi Neelavathi, a prominent Self-Respect woman, argued in her 1930 article, 'Is Widowhood a Question of Faith?' that 'India is notorious for its double standards. It is one justice for men and another for women. Our people are obsessed with "fate" as they are with gods and temples. They claim that everything happens in accordance with the dictates of one's *talaividhi* [fate] ... This thing called fate has forced us into slavery.' Describing the unhappy and miserable lives that widows were forced to lead in the society of her times, Neelavathi vehemently dismisses the differential treatment accorded to them. While widowed men are married off again with alacrity, the women have to suffer for the rest of their lives. 'They do not get to eat tasty food. They are not allowed to wear good clothes. They are not even permitted to enjoy the cool breeze that blows outside! Their lives are completely circumscribed. There is little space for happiness or pleasure in their lives!' Around the same time, a Tamil Muslim woman named Alhaj Subako wrote with equal passion of the suffering of Muslim widows and argued that their plight was no better than Hindu widows.

Many women imagined and hoped for a different world from the one they lived in. Writing in 1934, Jayasekari, another Self-Respect woman, argued eloquently for the recognition of women as workers. She envisioned a socialist society in which all work is shared and there is no artificial division between 'men's work' and 'women's work'. She wrote: 'You cannot chain the women of the future to the home! A healthy capable woman would never rest content with this . . . Both education as well as work, therefore, are gradually becoming part of a common public sphere. Inevitably, women's work will also move outside the confines of the home. Shops, factories, schools and cultural centres—these will constitute the new sites of women's work. In place of the separate category we now label "women's work", we will see a new category emerge—the work of the human race. In the socialist world of the future, everyone will share in the housework.'

The Self-Respect women were as eloquent in pointing to other dimensions of inequality and subordination. In 1930, Mu Maragathavalliyar wrote an essay titled, 'The Sufferings of the Adi-Dravidas' in which she said, 'The disease of untouchability has spread far and wide among our people. The adi-dravidas are the worst hit . . . People have decreed that adi-dravidas should not draw water from the common wells in the village. They cannot use the village pond either. Adi-dravidas, people insist, should live outside the boundaries of the village in small

huts built from palm leaves. Occasionally, an adi-dravida makes enough money to build a house with a tiled roof. He does this by working twice as hard as others. You can be sure that villagers will gang up against him. If he dares build this house despite threats from them, the villagers will not hesitate even to set fire to his house! "A parayan building a house with a tiled roof! Does he think he is equal to us?" they will exclaim. If we watch the situation closely, we will realise the difficulties that the rich and the powerful place in front of the adi-dravidas. The latter are forbidden from wearing the *veshti* and shirt; they cannot wear the *talapa*, use an umbrella or wear slippers. As for the adi-dravida women, they are forbidden from wearing a blouse. They cannot use brass utensils or pots. They are not permitted to wear gold jewels. Such are the cruel prohibitions they are forced to endure!'

Such writings are an important reminder of the many women in the past who have shaped our public culture by questioning and challenging existing social inequalities and hierarchies. Remembering them is one way of thinking about and examining our own society today to see how far ahead we have travelled on the paths they dreamed for us all.[3]

Chityala Ailamma

Between 1946 and 1951, the Telangana region of the Hyderabad State, which was then under the Nizam, saw a peasant uprising. Ailamma was the first to defy the landlord's attempt to take over the land she had cultivated for many years. When the landlord sent *goondas* to destroy the crops she had painstakingly cultivated, she threw stones at them and chased them away. Following this brave response, a movement took shape and spread. She is remembered as the person who started what is known as the Telangana Armed Struggle or the Telangana rebellion. This is an excerpt from the book *We Were Making History*.

❖ ❖ ❖

My name is Chityala Ailamma ... The whole of Isnur came to know ... Listen, let me tell you, the musclemen with their stout sticks had all arrived. Isaka Naligadu, the clerk, Abba Salim and that Guttalam Ramreddy—they wrought havoc. Believe me, they wrought such havoc, turned everything upside down ... We had put up cattle sheds. They tore them down. We ploughed and we worked the land but they ran roughshod over our labour. That bearded fellow—they took away the seven acres he had ploughed. The buffaloes went one way, the cows went another. Nearly sixty or seventy sheep, they were all taken away. So I thought—my land—take it all away, drive the cattle all away, after all, we owe you 500 rupees from when we built the house. Now take it all away. So the cows went and then the buffaloes ...

We suffered so much even God knows about it. We never touched one bit of folk's property ... [crying]. We never interfered with anyone ... The fight for the fields had started. We had taken the field from the Mallampalli *karnam* on lease ... We worked in that field after leasing it. All this land you see here ... all this around here is mine. Do you see, it's all mine....

The land was there before the Sangham came. It was there already. We had already leased it somehow. We had had it for nearly twenty years. When we kept it, they couldn't bear it and took it away from us. To those who had a title, no one said anything. They snatched away what we took. Where did we have the papers? After all, we had only leased it. So when it all came to a head we said we won't give it up, but they wouldn't give it up either. 'You should leave the Sangham,' the landlord's men said. We said we wouldn't....

They didn't give me the land in my name. They distributed it all. They didn't give it, may their bellies burn! They didn't give it, what does it yield? They gave four bags of paddy. How will I live on four bags of paddy? ...

We wandered house to house begging ... There was a blanket the landlord had given us, we took that blanket around to the fields where the harvest lay, collecting handfuls of grain. We lived eating that ... I was so proud of the Sangham. They said that the Sangham meant that the poor would be equal and their kingdom would come. Now it is the ones who have eaten who keep eating. Do they feed the poor? May his belly burn, he keeps eating. Do the poor get anything? We fought in the struggle. So what? Are the people who struggled here? They're gone! They are all dead, the ones who struggled.

C. K. Janu

Across many Indian states, adivasis have been displaced from forests that provided them with shelter, food and the basis of their culture and forms of worship. Over the last few decades, adivasis have protested this displacement and the takeover of their lands for mining, plantations, tourism and settlement by non-adivasis. One of the most important movements in Kerala is led by C. K. Janu of the Adivasi Gothra Maha Sabha (AGMS). The AGMS demands land, stressing that land is integral to adivasi survival as well as to their identity, culture and forms of worship. In 2001, Janu led a 'build huts' movement in which adivasis built shelters in front of the secretariat in Thiruvananthapuram and lived there for 48 days. The movement attracted world attention and the government finally agreed to give them some land. The promise, however, was not fulfilled. Those of you who are interested can read on the internet about the subsequent 2003 Muthunga struggle and other initiatives. In this excerpt from a 2010 interview, Janu tells us about adivasi life and their efforts to acquire land.

❖ ❖ ❖

Rekharaj: Can you tell us something about your childhood, special memories and adivasi life at that time?

C. K. Janu: When I was a child, slavery was a reality, our slavery under landlords. If one slogged from dawn to dusk, the payment would be some paddy. It used to be measured out in a hollow bamboo measure called *maanam*. For working from dawn till night, women used to get three *maanam* of paddy. Men used to get five.... We used to go to the forest and look for some special roots and tubers and that would really be our staple food ... But with the new laws, adivasis could not enter the forest whenever they wanted. Nowadays it is enough for an adivasi to pass near the forest boundary and a false case will be slapped against him or her for stealing wood.... What was traditionally available to them in the forest has become unavailable to them now.... Earlier, one could cultivate anywhere, change houses as and when required; celebrations would last for three to four days ... all these together constituted adivasi life. [Also,] these days, all adivasis [have moved into resettlement colonies and] have to do daily wage labour. Starvation deaths are on the rise. When such deaths occur, political parties claim that they are not due to starvation but due to the lack of a nutritious diet, use of polluted water and so on ...

[*Reporting on how the adivasi movement for land began and went on to succeed*] In the evening, after we had eaten, we would sit for three to four hours and discuss various things. We never used to discuss things that were taking place in far-off places. We focused on our own day-to-day problems. Water, connecting roads, and other such things. It was through these discussions that we began to see that the main problem was land....

We noticed when we visited the colonies that in many cases people in one house would not speak to people in other houses. If we called for a gathering in one house, some others would not participate. Very often the reason behind these quarrels would be trivial. All these houses are situated in two to four cents of colony land. Their roofs touch each other. Someone from one house would wash dishes and pour that water into the yard of the adjacent house. Kids from one house would urinate into the veranda of another. All these would lead to squabbles. When we enquired further into these quarrels, we hit again upon the fact of land hunger. It is an important point that these people do not have the material circumstances to survive. Space to just walk around, a good house, latrines or privacy—none of these is there. This is precisely the basis for most of the fights—not thefts or individual resentments. . . .

Most of the adivasis in the colonies are forced to do very hard daily labour to survive . . . we realised that if people have some land, they can at least survive by cultivating some tapioca, yam or other tubers even when there is no wage labour available. Because they do not have land, they are forced to go searching for wage labour every day. . . . In the early stages, under the auspices of the AVPS [Adivasi Vikasana Pravarthaka Samiti], we submitted numerous applications and complaints to the government. After that, whenever we met any minister or people's representatives, we would give them memorandums. Everyone who received the complaints would say, 'Of course, we will find a solution immediately.' But those would be just words and no action would follow. Fed up with this, we took the decision that there is no need any more to run after anyone for land. From now onwards, just locate where there is land, go and build a hut there and just start living. No need to check what land it is. . . . Let the authorities do whatever they want. . . . To do this, there was a lot of preparation necessary. The first step was to locate land where there were no people living. Following this, for the first time, under the banner of the AVPS, we built huts in Kolikkampali in Vellamunda *panchayat*. . . . The night before we took over the land, I went to the adivasi colony. . . . It was the season of the heavy monsoons. I said: 'Don't bother about the rains. Tomorrow itself you have to go to that place and erect huts.' Ten families

went to that place and built huts. There was only a little less than an acre of land there. This land acquisition became a problem. The village officer, police, everyone came. We said the problem was that we didn't have land. Finally, the adivasis got that land. Ten families got ten cents of land each. They also got the title deeds. . . .

When the adivasis first fought for land, the government said that there was no land available. Their argument was that Kerala's area had been reduced. . . . When we began the build-huts struggle, we discovered that private groups like the Tatas, Birlas and Harrisons, which had been given the land, had retained it even after the stipulated time period was over. Like that, we could convince the public as well as the government that a lot of land was available, and that this was being illegally kept by private groups. This was at the heart of the success of our struggle. . . .

Rekharaj: In various parts of Kerala, land transfer and 'build-huts' movements are happening. What is your view of these developments?

C. K. Janu: I feel really proud about that. The protest that we conducted has now become a wave. Even for the political parties which come to power alternately in Kerala, we could open up a fresh method of struggle. . . . Women's movements, rights, they are all good. But they don't come under a single banner of unity. I feel other women's issues get highlighted and dalit-adivasi women's issues get ignored. . . .

Rekharaj: How do you see dalit-adivasi women's issues? Do they have special problems?

C. K. Janu: I feel mainstream women ignore these issues. Among adivasis, there is no big woman–man distinction. The main problem is the atrocities committed by outsiders. Among adivasi families, the woman and the man both go for work together and take decisions together. In tribal groups, women are allowed to speak first. But the responsibility of the home and family rests fully with the woman.[4]

NOTES

1. The full version of Bertolt Brecht's 'A Worker Reads History' can be found here: https://allpoetry.com/A-Worker-Reads-History.

2. You can watch an interview and listen to the song about termites here: http://forums.ssrc.org/ndsp/2014/04/15/dalit-christian-prayer-songs.

3. This account has been adapted from *The Other Half of the Coconut: Women Writing Self-Respect History, An Anthology of Self-Respect Literature (1928–1936)*, edited by K. Srilata and published in 2003.

4. Excerpted from *No Alphabet in Sight: New Dalit Writing from South India, Dossier 1: Tamil and Malayalam* (2011), edited by Susie Tharu and K. Satyanarayana.

Gender Spectrum: Beyond the Binary

11.1 TWO OR MANY?

We are all familiar with the boxes 'M' or 'F' in application forms. Most of us tick one without thinking about it for a second. We assume that human beings are divided into two sexes—isn't that the most natural thing in the world? But there are people for whom this isn't such a simple matter. They cannot simply tick one box or the other. They may be identified as male or female at birth and brought up as such, but their own sense of self is different from their assigned gender. Recognising this, in 2009, India's election authorities allowed transgender people to select 'other' as their gender on ballot forms. In May 2014, the Supreme Court of India declared the transgender community as a third gender and ordered the government to provide transgender people with reservations in jobs and education in line with other minorities. 'It is the right of every human being to choose their gender,' the Supreme Court in the Union of India vs. the National Legal Services Authority (NALSA) said, in granting rights to those who do not identify themselves with the gender assigned to them at birth, that is, as either male or female.[1]

This recognition by the government and the law enables us to undertake a long-overdue process of discussing and understanding the complexity of gender. In Unit 2 on socialisation we discussed the processes by which society moulds us into men and women. Early feminists thought that sex was natural while gender was social and cultural. However, that is only one part of the story. In this unit we learn that maleness and femaleness are not even biologically stable features. Surprising but true! Gender is extremely complex. But, generally, we have not scientifically and rationally investigated this complexity. We simply take it for granted that gender is a binary. It is high time we moved beyond such an understanding.

What we learn from most science textbooks is that biological factors such as chromosomes, genes, gonads (tissue that could become testicles or ovaries) and hormones decide whether a person is male or female. Less emphasis is given to factors such as social roles, behaviours and identities most of us adopt to conform to the masculine–feminine norms in a society at any given time. This unit provides some information about the variation that exists at both biological and societal levels. It highlights the fact that the strict male–female dichotomy is grossly inadequate to characterise all human beings. Instead, we need to engage with the idea of a *gender spectrum*.

Most of us have learnt that if the fertilising sperm contains an X-chromosome, the egg will develop into a female. If the fertilising sperm contains a Y-chromosome, the egg will develop into a male. But it is not that simple. Six weeks after conception, the gonads of both sexes appear identical. The process of sex differentiation is not complete even at birth.[2] Anne Fausto-Sterling, a well-known professor of Biology and Gender Studies, points out that 'chromosomes, hormones, the internal sex structures, the gonads, and the external genitalia all vary much more than most people realise'. In this unit we will learn there are many reasons why we need to rethink the gender binary of male–female and move towards the more inclusive idea of a gender spectrum.

Most of the time a person's biological sex and gender complement each other. (The term *cisgender* is used to denote people designated at birth as females or males, who are also generally comfortable with these identities.) However, every society has a percentage of *intersex* people born with ambiguous biological characteristics. There are others who feel uncomfortable with the biological sex they were assigned at birth (male or female) and the gender associated with it. They identify as *transgender* and some of them choose to change their sex through medical intervention. Many others choose to present themselves as the gender they desire to be. For instance, this could be done through attire, a change of name, specifying the pronoun they prefer to be used to identify themselves (he/him, she/her, they/them), etc.

The Process of Gendering

Young children often dress up in clothes belonging to the opposite sex or try to perform the part of the opposite sex by walking, talking and behaving differently. They do this for fun. Many families tolerate such behaviour until the age of puberty. Around puberty, considerable physical and physiological changes take place. Let us take the example of voice pitch. You may have noticed that the voice pitch of four- to five-year-old boys and girls is similar: it is very high with the fundamental frequency measuring around 400 Hz. Fundamental frequency (Fo) refers to the rate at which vocal cords move in and out as we speak. The length and thickness of the vocal folds are not very different in young children. By puberty, however, the influence of hormones results in boys tending to have thicker vocal folds than girls. This leads to a reduction in the movement of the vocal folds, which in turn leads to their pitch falling to 100–120 Hz (whereas with girls, their pitch falls to 200–250 Hz). There are variations: some boys do not see their pitch fall so drastically, while some girls do see their pitch fall drastically. Former Prime Minister Manmohan Singh and the cricketer Sachin Tendulkar are examples of men with high voices. And the much-loved singer Gangubai Hangal is a good example of a woman with a low voice. The point here is that there are tremendous physical, physiological and cultural variations among even cisgenders in relation to the pitch of their voice.

In addition to changes to voice pitch, other examples of physical changes that take place during puberty may include the growth of pubic hair, the onset of acne, boys developing facial hair and girls growing breasts. All this is exciting. But it can also be worrying because with such change comes great social and commercial stress on the differences between girls and boys. Beauticians might lose a lot of business if women stopped worrying about body hair, and gyms might close down if men did not worry about their physique! In fact, almost everyone has some worry or the other about whether they properly fit into society's definitions of 'male' or 'female'. We worry about our physical appearance because it has considerable influence on how we perceive ourselves, and how we are perceived by others. Such anxiety is central to one's development of gender identity, which is about wanting to be masculine or feminine in conventional, socially defined ways, and need not be related to one's sex assigned at birth.

However, despite such anxieties, most people are comfortable with one or the other of the conventional male–female gender identities (these are cisgender people). Many are not as comfortable with their assigned sex or gender or both.

As a result of movements for sexuality rights and transgender rights, we know today that there is a spectrum of gender identities and sexual orientations.[3] It is important to seek out this information because, all around us, society puts a great deal of effort into emphasising and enforcing a strict male–female

dichotomy. This enforcement may be physical, but more often it is ideological—in other words, it works through the mind and emotions. Both kinds of pressure come from numerous sources including families, schools, advertisements in print and electronic media, social media, films, stories and even textbook lessons. We are bombarded by messages about gender in our everyday world. For instance, such messages about gender can be found in the language used to refer to males and females, the toys girls and boys are encouraged to play with, the clothes they are expected to wear, the domestic chores they are asked to complete, the professions they are expected to pursue, the games they are permitted to play, and so on.

All of these constantly reproduce dichotomous views about masculinity or femininity. In doing so, they erase the shades of difference that exist between the gender identities of individuals in a society. Gender is a dynamic concept. In fact, one could say gender is an interrelationship between (1) an individual's biology, (2) the internal sense of self as male, female, both or neither—the gender identity, (3) outward appearance and behaviour—that is, gender expression, and (4) the gender roles assigned to males and females in a given society.

In the early 1970s, psychologists and sociologists tried to come up with lists of 'essential' masculine attributes (for example, being athletic, forceful, aggressive, etc.) and feminine attributes (for example, being shy, sensitive, maternal, etc.). However, they soon realised that such efforts were pointless as many people possess both sets of qualities.

We can see that what we in fact deal with, on an everyday basis, is not a dichotomy but rather a spectrum of genders. Study the information provided on the next page.[4]

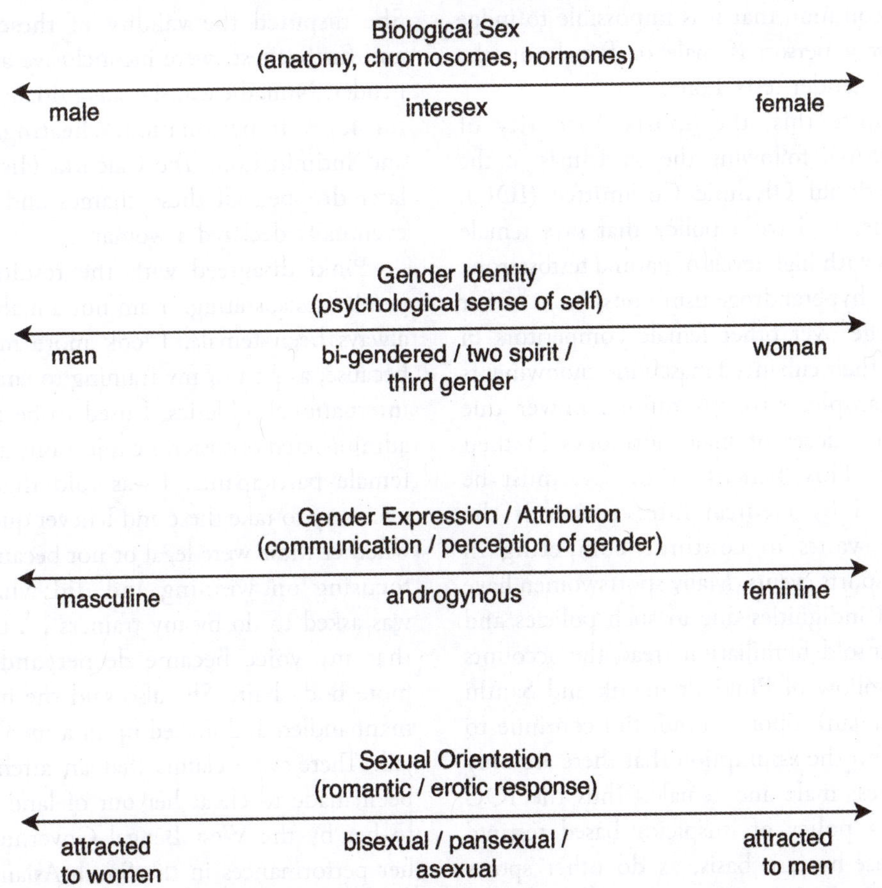

11.2 GENDER DISCRIMINATION

When a person's identity and/or sexual orientation is not in line with those associated with their biological sex (male vs. female), such a person is often subjected to discrimination. Let us read a little more about the gender spectrum in order to understand the experiences of people who do not belong to a strictly defined male–female dichotomy. This will help us relate to their struggles against discrimination and empathise with them. Also, when we do meet a person whose gender appears ambiguous, we should keep in mind that gender is a sensitive topic and the person should be treated with respect.

As discussed earlier, maleness and femaleness are not only culturally different and therefore different in different societies, but even biologically there are many variations in sexual characteristics and gender identities. But this fact was poorly understood until recently, and as a result, athletes regularly faced discrimination and various other injustices. However, gender verification tests were suspended in the Olympic Games in 2000. This was done after enough evidence had emerged to prove that 'atypical chromosomal variations' are not atypical at all. This is true of certain hormone levels as well. Such variations are so common that it is impossible to judge whether a person is male or female on the basis of gender tests alone.

Despite this, the Sports Authority of India (SAI), following the guidelines of the International Olympic Committee (IOC), continues to have a policy that says female athletes with high levels of natural testosterone ('female hyperandrogenism') possess an unfair advantage over other female competitors in view of their enhanced masculine endowments (for example, stronger muscle power due to higher doses of male hormones in their bodies). This 'benefit', they say, must be regulated by medical intervention if the athlete wants to continue competing in female sports events. Many sportswomen have suffered indignities due to such policies and faced untold humiliation (read the accounts which follow of Pinki Pramanik and Santhi Soundarajan). Sports authorities continue to work with the assumption that there are only two sexes: male and female. Thus the IOC retains a policy of 'suspicion-based testing' on a case-by-case basis, as do other sports governing bodies. This policy has resulted in different female athletes from different competitive events being disqualified after winning medals—the South African middle-distance runner Caster Semenya and Santhi Soundarajan are two examples of athletes who have failed 'gender tests'.

Pinki Pramanik

Pinki Pramanik (born 10 April 1986) is an Indian track athlete who, from the age of 17, has won several medals for her performances both at home and abroad.

In 2012, there was a complaint of sexual assault filed by her female friend. It led to medical tests being conducted to determine her gender. Initial tests declared she was male. She disputed the validity of these results, and further tests were inconclusive about her gender. Nonetheless, she was initially charged for rape, impersonation, cheating, assault and intimidation. The Calcutta High Court later dropped all these charges and she was eventually declared a woman.

Pinki disagreed with the results of the gender tests, stating: 'I am not a male. I have always been female. I look more male now because, as part of my training to compete in international athletics, I used to be regularly administered testosterone injections like other female participants. I was told that it was necessary to take these and I never questioned whether these were legal or not because I was focusing on winning and did whatever I was asked to do by my trainers … but after that my voice became deeper and I grew more body hair.' She also said she had been manhandled and locked up in a men's cell in jail. There were claims that an attempt had been made to cheat her out of land granted to her by the West Bengal Government for her performances in the South-Asian Games and Asian Games.

Santhi Soundarajan

Born into a dalit family in Kathakkurichi of Pudukkottai district of Tamil Nadu in April 1981, Santhi Soundarajan is a track-and-field athlete. She has won 11 international awards and over 50 national awards, and is the first Tamil woman to have won at the Asian Games. Soon after winning a silver medal in the women's 800 metre race in the 2006 Asian Games held at Doha, she had to undergo a gender test. The results revealed that she did not possess certain sexual characteristics of a woman. For this reason, she was stripped of her silver medal. Of this, she said: 'I am treated as an outcast and am unable to even go out of my house. . . . I was shunned by my own local community after being stripped of [the] silver medal and I was banned from competing by the Indian Olympic Association . . . I feel it is unfair to [determine] the quality of [a person] based on chromosomes. . . . It is unethical and biased. It was a very bitter and humiliating experience for me and my family.'

The media reported that she was born with Androgen Insensitivity Syndrome (AIS), a condition in which affected people are genetically male while possessing external female genitalia. This means that Santhi was identified by her family as a girl at birth and was brought up as such. Santhi too always considered herself a female. Neither she nor her family was aware of the genetic variation.

In September 2007, Soundarajan was reported to have attempted suicide by consuming poison. Fortunately she survived. Two months later she started her own coaching academy with 68 students, and also worked as a daily-wage earner at a brick kiln, receiving Rs 200 per day.

Her experience, as well as the experiences of other athletes in similar situations, raises a host of questions for us today. If a body has female genitals, this does not necessarily mean it will have predominantly female chromosomes or hormones. Most bodies (including yours and ours) marked 'male' and 'female' in this world would not pass gender tests if a congruence of these three factors were examined. The point is that in everyday life, gender tests are not routine because once a sex has been assigned at birth, most of us live our lives accordingly. It is mainly in sex-segregated activities like competitive sports that the question arises, and even then, only for women, because it is assumed that possessing male characteristics is an advantage in physical activities.

Of course, women athletes who are disqualified for some chromosomal, hormonal or physical variation that casts doubt on their 'femaleness' are not categorised as 'men'. They are still excluded from men's sporting events or professions exclusively reserved for men. We know all men do not run faster than all women; all men are not stronger than all women. This is why Nivedita Menon points out in *Seeing like a Feminist* (2012) that it has often been suggested by feminists that athletes should be categorised on the basis of physical characteristics relevant to the sport (like height or weight), rather than on the basis of sex. Our discussion of gender and sports is largely derived from her book.

Dutee Chand

Previously established societal norms are now being challenged. Dutee Chand, a young Indian sprinter, became the first to refuse to abide by the verdict of the Sports Authority of India. The SAI had conducted hyperandrogenism tests on her in July 2014. When the results came in, she was told that if she wanted to compete again, she would need to reduce her testosterone levels either through surgery or drug therapy. Chand rejected both options. Instead, she decided to challenge the guidelines at the Court of Arbitration for Sport (CAS), an international body with its headquarters located in Lausanne, Switzerland. In July 2015, the court suspended the regulations by the governing International Association of Athletics Federation (IAAF) regarding hyperandrogenism, stating there was not enough scientific evidence to warrant such tests. Noting that 'sex in humans is not neatly binary', the court asked the IAAF to submit more persuasive scientific evidence within a two-year period or else risk having the regulations declared void. More importantly, the IAAF was asked to create a procedure whereby athletes could compete in either the female or male sporting events and not be excluded as a 'consequence of the natural and unaltered state of their body'. Even though Chand had to miss the Commonwealth Games and the Asian Games, she was eligible for the Olympics in 2016 and won a silver medal in the women's 100-metre race at the Jakarta Asian Games!

11.3 TRANSGENDERISM

Transgender people have a strong physical and mental discomfort with the sex assigned to them at birth by doctors and their family, and with the gender identity they are supposed to conform to based on this assigned sex. Transgender (sometimes shortened to 'trans') is an umbrella term used to describe a wide range of identities whose appearance and characteristics are perceived as gender atypical—including transsexual people, cross-dressers (sometimes referred to as 'transvestites'), and people who identify as third gender. Transwomen identify as women but were classified as males when they were born, transmen identify as men but were classified as females when they were born, while other trans people don't identify with the gender binary at all. For transgender people, life can be painful and difficult. For those who have understanding friends and family who support them, things may be slightly easier. Some transgender people opt for medical intervention via surgery or hormone therapy to change their sex to align with their identified gender. This change or transition could be either male to female (MTF), or female to male (FTM). They often undergo this transition due to what is known as ***gender dysphoria***, where they feel extremely distressed about their assigned sex and gender, though the costs and risks involved make this difficult. Gender dysphoria is not universal, due to which many transgender people do not pursue medical intervention to transition.

The reality is that transgender people are often subjected to discrimination and harassment. For example, they may be denied access to housing, or it might prove difficult for them to find employment even if they have impressive qualifications. We should be aware of the need for legal protection for people whose cultural and emotional experiences do not match the physical and biological sex they are assigned at birth.

According to one estimate, India has about 20 lakh transgender people. *Hijras* are the most commonly visible among the transgender community in India, though the term is also used to describe transgender people, transsexuals, cross-dressers and transvestites. Most of them face discrimination and live in dire poverty on the fringes of society. Many earn a living as singers and dancers. Many are forced into sex work. According to the Telangana Hijra Intersex Transgender Samiti

(THITS): 'There have been physical attacks and brutalities on over 60 transgender people in Hyderabad alone in 2014. *Hijra* and transgender people are fighting for their lives on the streets because of discrimination and exclusion from jobs, education, housing and all welfare measures.'[4] The Telangana Hijra Intersex Transgender Samiti, in an attempt to advocate and protect *hijra* rights, issued the following demands:

- Implementing a reservation quota in jobs and education for the *hijra* community.
- Implementing laws that prevent any form of discrimination towards sexual and gender minorities.
- Establishing a statutory National Transgender Commission and state welfare board to help the *hijra* community access existing government welfare schemes, especially medical care, housing, jobs and education.
- Sensitising government organisations, educational institutions, etc., to help in the acceptance and inclusion of all sexual and gender minorities.

Manabi Bandyopadhyay

In June 2015, Manabi Bandyopadhyay became the first transgender college principal in India. Coming from a lower-middle-class family—her mother was a homemaker while her father was a factory worker—she studied in a school on the outskirts of Kolkata before attending college to pursue a degree in Bengali.

In 2003, Manabi decided to undergo hormone therapy to change her sex from male to female. She also wrote her thesis on transgender people in West Bengal. However, in 2006, after she changed her gender and name, she encountered many difficulties. Authorities refused to recognise her new gender and name. She was denied a pay raise at the college where she taught. 'They could not come to terms with my altered gender,' she said. 'There were taunts at work about my sex change. At home, my parents and siblings were worried sick whether my body would be able to cope with the changes. It took five years for the government and society to recognise my status and give me my identity. . . . I have always been popular with my students, but my colleagues and peers were not so favourably disposed towards me after I changed my gender.'

In 2015, she was appointed as the vice-chairperson of the West Bengal State Transgender Development Board, which is a government body. 'Now I will have some authority to help members of my community when they reach me in distress. Even today parents think that this is a mental-health issue. A few days ago, a boy from Burdwan committed suicide when he couldn't stand the pressure from his parents, who wanted him to take psychiatric help because he was a transgender,' she said. As a child, Bandyopadhyay was a victim of repeated rape. She said: 'I know of so many transgender people who have faced similar abuse. They have nowhere to go. I hope this board will give them a space where they can report their mental and physical abuse.'

filmmaker travels with his partner to Kolkata to shoot a documentary on a yesteryear actor and female impersonator.

- *Tamanna* (1997) is a drama set in Bombay in 1975 which tells the story of Tikku, a eunuch and *hijra*, and Tamanna, the girl he finds abandoned on the streets.
- *The Adventures of Priscilla, Queen of the Desert* (1994) is an English comedy-drama about two cross-dressers and a transgender woman who travel across Australia in a tour bus and perform their entertainment show at various venues.

Write a review on one of these films, or on any film that you know of that touches upon issues related to the gender spectrum.

11.4 HOMOSEXUALITY

Similar to gender identity, sexual orientation or desire is also best understood as a spectrum. Sexual attraction and sexual relations between men and women (seen as opposite sexes) is considered 'normal' by many people. It is also often believed that sex between men and women is natural as it is procreative and therefore serves as the basis for family. Family is understood as heterosexual by definition. Viewed through such a lens, homosexuality or sexual desire between people of the same sex is viewed as both abnormal and unnatural. Many countries criminalised homosexual relations and subjected homosexuals to inhumane and cruel treatment. Increasingly, this perception and treatment is being challenged by many across the world. There are movements which fought and continue to fight for homosexual

rights and an end to the discrimination they face. Over the past forty years, these movements have changed social attitudes towards sexuality, gender and sexual orientation. As a result, many countries have decriminalised homosexuality and changed their laws to legally uphold marriages between people of the same sex.

In India, the legal battle for the decriminalisation of homosexual relationships and equal rights began in 2001 and has resulted in an extremely important and historic judgement which we will discuss later in this unit. But first, let us read a brief discussion by Shad Naved, a scholar of comparative literature, cultural studies and gender studies, of a film that tells the story of a homosexual man.

My Brother ... Nikhil

My Brother ... Nikhil (2005) is one of the first films in India that shows the life of a man who loves another man. But it doesn't use the words 'gay' or 'homosexual' for its main character, Nikhil, who has two secrets in his life: he is a champion swimmer but swims only to please his father; and he loves a man, Nigel, a fact which he hides from his family. His two secrets are tragically revealed when he is diagnosed HIV-positive. His father disowns him and he is thrown out of the swimming team where he was a state champion. Not only that, the government forcibly places him under quarantine because there is panic about the spread of AIDS. His only ally is his sister, Anamika, who engages a sensitive woman lawyer to battle with the courts and government to grant Nikhil his freedom.

Nikhil asks the lawyer to fight his case not just in his name but on behalf of all HIV-positive people. He accepts the collective identity of people suffering from HIV and sees his suffering as that which is shared by others too. In the film, we have Anamika, Nikhil's other family members, friends, team members and his lover speaking to the camera, that is, directly to the viewers, about Nikhil. This establishes Nikhil's identity as a brother, son, friend, lover and team member and as somebody who may even be known to us. The film similarly puts Nikhil's sexual orientation on a spectrum of social identities. He dresses like a man. He sings. He is a popular person, including with women. He loves Nigel but doesn't talk about it. There is no one way in which his sexual orientation is expressed.

In a memorable scene from the film, when news of his diagnosis spreads, people rush out of the swimming pool he is in. We are then shown Nikhil swimming in the sea, in whose vastness he is just another vulnerable body. The film thus questions the notion that only normal, healthy bodies are touchable and lovable. It also questions family as the only source of care and love in our lives. Except for his sister, Nikhil's family rejects him precisely when he needs them most. Nigel takes care of him at home during the final months of his painful illness. He never tries to find out how Nikhil contracted HIV, and the film as well does not reveal that information. The disease is a disease and not a moral judgement against the person suffering from it. At the end, Nigel remembers he and Nikhil used to wait on the beach for sunrise, and it is during that hour, when there is both darkness and light, that Nikhil dies in his arms. The film suggests that sexual identity is hidden yet visible, scary yet pleasurable in our lives, and there is no single identity we can attach to a man who loves another man.

Valuing Difference: The Legal Story

In India, queer activists or the LGBTIQ[5] movement have been actively challenging the prejudice, discrimination and violence that queer people face in our society. Their first demand is that homosexuality be accepted as that which is as natural and as normal as heterosexuality. In many countries this is already the case. Scholars Ruth Vanita and Saleem Kidwai, who co-authored the book *Same-Sex Love in India* (2000), argue that before British colonial rule, homosexuality was not seen as unnatural or illegal in India. They cite many examples from ancient and medieval Indian literature to demonstrate this. Many modern Indian writers too have written about homosexuality. Their writings reveal to us the complexity of gay lives as well as the injustice of a law and culture that treats their sexual orientation as abnormal and criminal.

Section 377 of the Indian Penal Code is a law that was introduced by the British colonial government. It considers sex between men as unnatural and a punishable offence. Since the 1990s, queer activists have been actively challenging this law. In response to a petition filed by the Naz Foundation (India) Trust, the Delhi High court ruled in 2009 that sex between two consenting adults is not a crime and therefore not illegal. This was a landmark judgement in Indian history. The court stated: 'The criminalisation of homosexuality condemns in perpetuity a sizeable section of society and forces them to live their lives in the shadow of harassment, exploitation, humiliation, cruel and degrading treatment at the hands of the law enforcement machinery.'

However, following a counter-petition, the Supreme Court overturned this ruling in 2013 and reinstated Section 377. A slew of petitions by LGBTIQ activists and organisations challenged this judgement and once again appealed to the court to review this law. The petitioners included prominent artists, activists and other public figures including Navtej Johar, Ritu Dalmia, Akkai Padmashali, Sunil Mehra and Ratna Kapur. They pleaded that they were 'lesbian, gay, bisexual citizens of India whose rights to sexuality, sexual autonomy, choice of sexual partner, life, privacy, dignity and equality, along with the other fundamental rights guaranteed under Part 3 of the Constitution [were] infringed by Section 377 of the Indian Penal Code'. The Supreme Court appointed a five-judge constitutional bench that, in September 2018, ruled that Section 377 was unconstitutional and a threat to the dignity and equality of queer people. Gautam Bhan, a well-known activist lawyer, pointed out that constitutional morality in contrast to dominant social norms of morality enabled equality on the basis of sexual orientation and gender identity. Writing about the judges' verdict, he said, 'As a gay man, what I heard them [the judges] say that muggy day in July was that I was not just my sexual orientation. That my worth and my rights were not meant to be my responsibility alone. That I could expect, demand, get respect. That I could dream not just of a life free of violence but one of personhood, of joy. That our lives as queer people could hold rights and dignity without needing either extraordinary courage or immense privilege. That I would not have to hold my breath so often, whether in fear or regret. That the cost of freedom would not be loneliness.'

As further reading, you might want to check out the book, *Because I Have a Voice: Queer Politics in India* (2006). Edited by Arvind Narrain and Gautam Bhan, it is a collection of thoughtful essays, autobiographical accounts and fictional narratives which offers an insight into the queer community.

NOTES

1. Details of the Supreme Court's judgement on the transgender community are available here: https://www.lawyerscollective.org/wp-content/uploads/2014/04/Transgender-judgment.pdf.
2. For a pictorial demonstration of how biological sex is determined, visit the following website: https://www.pbs.org/wgbh/nova/body/how-sex-determined.html.
3. Learn more about the gender spectrum here: http://www.genderspectrum.org.
4. For more information on global transgender issues, visit the following weblinks: http://www.tgforum.com or http://www.qrd.org/qrd/culture/.
5. Lesbian, Gay, Bisexual, Transgender, Intersex and Queer

Thinking about Sexual Violence

12.1 BLAMING THE VICTIM

The word *rape* usually conjures up images of strange masked men swooping in on unsuspecting women in some lonely place, late at night. In this scenario, the women are young and unmarried. The men are sexually depraved, morally corrupt, or simply criminal. Only two questions are raised about such incidents:

1. Why were the men so sexually depraved?
2. Why were the women out in the night, alone and unprotected?

But the above-mentioned scenario suggests that we need to ask some other questions as well to gain a better understanding of why rapes take place:

1. Do rapes only occur in isolated places or at night? (No. They can happen in workplaces, homes, schools, etc.)
2. Are the victims of rape always young women? (No.)
3. Are rapists usually strangers? (No. Many victims know their rapists.)
4. Are older women and children raped? (Yes.)
5. Do women lose their honour as a result of being raped? (Certainly not! The personal accounts that follow are inspiring examples of this.)

It is difficult to talk about rape because it is a sensitive topic and is often surrounded by secrecy, shame, anger and disgust. In recent years, however, this has slowly changed with public debates and discussions about women's safety, rape laws and medical procedures. Norms have evolved for dealing with such issues in the media and in court.

Earlier, people were reluctant to speak about rape because the very word was shrouded in darkness and shame. Only the danger or threat of rape was referred to, and that too vaguely. But it has always been clear that girls and women have had to take great care to avoid this danger. The threat of attack has also been a way of controlling women's lives. Additionally, the dominant culture in our society quickly blames women. This dominant culture harbours the strong belief that a raped woman is somehow responsible for what happened to her and that she is now 'impure'. Additionally, there is the fear that if a young woman is raped, she can never marry. And if an older woman is raped, there is the fear that she will not be allowed back into her family. It is a strange culture that blames the victim. Should we also hold onto such baseless fears and beliefs?

> ***Points to discuss:***
>
> 1. We have discussed a few misconceptions about rape in this unit. Try to add to the list with notions about rape or sexual violence that you may have heard as you were growing up or seen in films or news programmes.
> 2. We have discussed how girls are brought up to feel fear and shame about sexual violence and rape. Girls, what are the fears that you grew up with? Have you ever discussed them with anyone else? Boys, have you heard girls talking about their fears before? How do you feel after hearing them now?

Facts about Sexual Violence

Most of you may have heard of the Nirbhaya gang rape that took place in Delhi in December 2012. The woman was so badly injured that she died despite receiving the best possible medical treatment. The incident gave rise to a lot of anger among both men and women and there were protests across the country. These protests challenged the culture of secrecy and shame associated with rape: lack of safety for women in public spaces including on public transportation and in the streets; insensitive responses by local police to complaints of rape; widespread use of outlawed medical tests to collect evidence; and low rape conviction rates. A question that was repeatedly asked was: Why should the victim and not the rapist carry the stigma of rape? In newspaper articles and discussions on television talk shows, a number of shocking points came up for consideration:

- Rape is not a rare phenomenon. It is prevalent across all sections of society.
- The majority of rape incidents are not reported to the police.
- In most cases, the rapists are not strangers. They are family members, friends, neighbours or people who have authority over the rape victim. Regarding the latter, this might include the rape victim's boss, teacher, warden in a hostel, contractor, etc.
- The victims belong to all classes and all age groups—infants, children, teenage girls, older women and even women above 60 years of age.
- There is increasing evidence that boys and men are also subjected to sexual violence, especially by men.
- In incidents involving mob violence, for example during communal or caste riots, women are raped in order to teach their community a lesson. Such incidents are rarely recorded as crimes, despite the victims' willingness to complain to the police.
- Several instances of sexual violence against women have been reported and investigated when the armed forces

have been called in to quell civilian disturbances. The victims often cannot approach the courts for justice due to the immunity enjoyed by the armed forces.

- Sexual violence is prevalent within marriages. Forcing a wife to have sex, even when she is unwilling, is common. In other words, non-consensual sexual intercourse in marriage (another term for this is *marital rape*) is common. The fact that it is common, however, does not make it any less violent or acceptable.

What do we learn from this?

- Rape does not happen by accident. Nor does it happen due to men's so-called uncontrollable sexual desire.
- Rape is the result of an imbalance of power—between men who feel they have power and are stronger, and women who are made vulnerable by their circumstances and unable to resist the physical advances upon their bodies.
- Rape is a violation of a woman's body. It is a form of violence.

Society fails to recognise this inequality and imbalance of power. Instead, we are often told that it is the woman's responsibility to protect her chastity at any cost. This is due to the strange notion that a woman's character lies in her body and its sexual 'purity'. In the case of rape, many believe a woman's body is defiled and loses its worth. According to this strange logic, the cost is borne by the victim, not the aggressor. We can see how this is unjust. It is like blaming a murder victim for not preventing their own murder. Additionally, if rape 'defiles' a woman, then this implies that a woman is not really a person (a human

being capable of feelings—a mother, a friend, a sister), and that she is only a sexual being.

This misguided societal understanding of rape has prevented us from seeing it as systematic violence against women. It has prevented us from adequately addressing the issue. As a society, we are only beginning to recognise the physical and psychological damage done to rape victims and the need to provide them with necessary support and services. But we are yet to come up with ways to educate men that such conduct is inhumane and damaging to all.

Points to discuss:

1. We have learnt that sexual violence against women occurs in a variety of situations involving different intentions. Still, society continues to blame women. Do you think this helps us understand the problem? Why or why not? Can you think of ways by which we can challenge the dominant perception that rape is the woman's fault?
2. We have learnt about the notion of consent in Unit 7 on sexual harassment. See if consent is present in the different scenarios of sexual violence described above.
3. Have you come across any reports where the victims of rape were not blamed? Or accounts where the victim was supported by their friends or family?

12.2 MASCULINITY AND SEXUAL VIOLENCE

As we learnt in the units on socialisation and growing up as a boy, a traditional upbringing in India often involves boys and men being encouraged to be aggressive and even violent. This is seen as an expression of their masculinity. Such pressures may result in any of the following disastrous consequences in social relations and personal life:

- The fear that they may not be considered 'manly enough' can push men into a vortex of fear, isolation, self-punishment, anger, self-hatred or aggression. Often boys and young men try to 'prove' their masculinity to each other by indulging in risky behaviour in gangs or by harassing women and girls. In some instances, this may lead to sexual violence committed by individuals or groups against women, girls or other men.

- The pressure to be masculine might leave a man obsessed with proving his sexual prowess. As a result, he might disregard the wishes of his partner or wife in their sexual life. This obsession also corrodes his ability to relate to his partner or wife as a friend, or to interact with them with tenderness. It can lead to unhappiness in a marriage and cause serious mental-health problems.

- Traditional socialisation inculcates in a man a sense of entitlement and an expectation of obedience or even subservience from the women in his family. He hangs onto this entitlement as a symbol of his manhood. He feels threatened when his partner or wife wants equality in their relationship. Modernisation and migration often undermine traditional entitlements. As a result, some men resort to sexual aggression and violence to reassert their masculinity.

White Ribbon Campaign

The White Ribbon Campaign (WRC) was formed in Canada in 1991 by men who believed that men and boys can and should play a vital role in reducing violence against women. It happened after a gunman shot dead 14 female engineering students in Montreal. The campaign has now spread across many countries and continents. It works with schools, churches, corporations, trade unions and prominent activists and individuals to pledge to end violence against women. The founder of the campaign, Michael Kaufman, is quoted as saying: 'From the start, the primary goal of the White Ribbon Campaign has been to encourage men to look at our own attitudes and behaviour, and to learn to challenge other men to stop all forms of violence against women. We believe that as more men and boys take responsibility for challenging ourselves and others, then the epidemic levels of violence against women will finally end. . . . We purposely used something that employed a simple symbolic language: wearing a white ribbon didn't require reading ten books or attending an eight-week men's support group.

On the other hand, this did not make wearing a white ribbon a simple act. How many times did we hear stories like this: "The first year, I thought you guys were a bunch of male bashers and the whole thing made me angry. The next year I started listening to what you said and it seemed to make sense, but there was no way I was going to wear a ribbon because what would the other guys think? Finally, in the third year I got up the nerve to wear a white ribbon.'"

An important area of focus that this campaign chose was the education system—schools and colleges. Male teachers who enrol in this campaign are able to inform students of the fear and anxiety that women live under through exercises such as the one which follows. Before you read them, consider this: Do you know of any men's campaigns in India which aim to fight violence against women? Search online for them and discuss them in class.

An Exercise in Changing Perceptions

One day, a workshop was being held for men and women. The workshop was about protecting oneself from violence. The coordinator of the workshop asked, 'Men, what do you do to protect yourself from being raped or sexually assaulted?'

None of the men answered. There was silence in the room. Finally, one man said, 'Nothing.'

The coordinator then asked, 'Women, what do you do to protect yourself from being raped or sexually assaulted?'

Nearly all of the women raised their hands. One by one each woman spoke. Some of their answers included:

- I don't make eye contact with men when I walk down the street.
- I always go out with a friend or two.
- I cross the street when I see a group of guys walking in my direction.
- I speak loudly into my phone.

The women went on for several minutes. The coordinator wrote down their responses on one side of the blackboard until it was completely full. The other side of the blackboard, which was the men's side, was blank.

Points to discuss:

1. Boys, imagine you were in these women's shoes and constantly needed to think about your every movement and interaction in a public place. How does it make you feel? What do you think it would do to you?
2. Girls, discuss the precautions you take on an everyday basis in a public place.
3. In Unit 2 on socialisation we learnt about the importance of public places, especially streets, for boys and men. Do you think women's fear of streets and public places has something to do with the way men and boys occupy them?

12.3 FURTHER READING

We have learnt about the need for everyone to understand what women undergo during incidents of sexual violence and the costs that they bear. Let us now read an account of a woman who survived rape and fought for a life of dignity. Perhaps in the future men who have experienced a similar kind of violence will also speak out.

Sohaila Abdulali

I was gang raped three years ago, when I was seventeen years old. My name … appears with this article.

I grew up in Bombay, and am at present studying in the USA. I am writing a thesis on rape and came home to do research a couple of weeks ago. Ever since that day, three years ago, I have been intensely aware of the misconceptions people have about rape, about those who rape and those who survive rape. I have also been aware of the stigma that attaches to survivors. Time and again, people have hinted that perhaps death would have been better than the loss of that precious 'virginity'. I refuse to accept this. My life is worth too much to me.

I feel that many women keep silent to avoid this stigma but suffer tremendous agony because of their silence. Men blame the victim for many reasons, and, shockingly, women too blame the victim, perhaps because of internalised patriarchal values, perhaps as a way of making themselves invulnerable to a horrifying possibility.

It happened on a warm July evening. That was the year women's groups were beginning to demand improved legislation on rape. I was with my friend Rashid. We had gone for a walk and were sitting on a mountainside about a mile-and-a-half from my home in Chembur, which is a suburb of Bombay. We were attacked by four men who were armed with a sickle. They beat us, forced us to go up the mountain and kept us there for two hours. We were physically and psychologically abused, and, as darkness fell, we were separated, screaming, and they raped me, keeping Rashid hostage. If either of us resisted, the other would get hurt. This was an effective tactic.

They could not decide whether or not to kill us. We did everything in our power to stay alive. My goal was to live and that was more important than anything else. I fought the attackers physically at first, and with words after I was pinned down. Anger and shouting had no effect, so I began to babble rather crazily about love and compassion. I spoke of humanity and the fact that I was a human being, and so were they, deep inside. They were gentler after this, at least those who were not raping me at the moment. I told one of them that if he ensured neither Rashid nor I was killed, I would come back to meet him, the rapist, the next day. Those words cost me more than I can say, but two lives were in the balance. The only way I would ever have gone back there was with a very, very sharp instrument that would ensure he never raped again.

After what seemed like years of torture (I think I was raped ten times, but I was in so much pain that I lost track of what was going on after a while), we were let go, with a final long lecture on what an immoral whore I was to be alone with a boy. That infuriated them more than anything. They acted the whole time as if they were doing me a favour, teaching me a lesson. Theirs was the most fanatical kind of self-righteousness.

They took us down the mountain and we stumbled onto the dark road, clinging to each other and walking unsteadily. They followed us for a while, brandishing the sickle, and that was perhaps the worst part of all—escape was so near yet death hung over us. Finally we got home, broken, bruised, shattered. It was an incredible feeling to let go, to stop bargaining for our lives and weighing every word because we knew the price of angering them was a sickle in the stomach. Relief flooded into our bones and out of our eyes and we literally collapsed into hysterical howling.

I had earnestly promised the rapists that I would never tell anyone, but the minute I got home I told my father to call the police. He was as anxious as I was to apprehend them. I was willing to do anything to prevent someone else having to go through what I had been through. The police were insensitive, contemptuous and somehow managed to make me the guilty party. When they asked me what had happened I told them quite directly, and they were scandalised that I was not a shy, blushing victim. When they said there would be publicity, I said that was alright. It had honestly never occurred to me that Rashid or I could be blamed. When they said I would have to go into a home for juvenile delinquents for my 'protection', I was willing to live with pimps and rapists in order to be able to bring my attackers to justice.

Soon I realised that justice for women simply does not exist in the legal system. When they asked us what we had been doing on the mountain, I began to get indignant. When they asked Rashid why he had been 'passive', I screamed. Didn't they understand that his resistance meant further torture for me? When they asked questions about what kind of clothes I had been wearing, and why there were no visible marks on Rashid's body (he had internal bleeding from being repeatedly hit in the stomach with the handle of the sickle), I broke down in complete misery and terror, and my father threw them out of the house after telling them exactly what he thought of them. That was the extent of the support the police gave me. No charges were brought. The police recorded a statement that we had gone for a walk and had been 'delayed' on our return.

It has been almost three years now, but there has not been even one day when I have not been haunted by what happened. Insecurity, vulnerability, fear, anger, helplessness—I fight these constantly. Sometimes when I am walking on the road and hear footsteps behind me I start to sweat and have to bite my lip to keep from screaming. I flinch at friendly touches, I can't bear tight scarves that feel like hands round my throat, I flinch at a certain look that comes into men's eyes—that look is there so often.

Yet in many ways I feel that I am a stronger person now. I appreciate my life more than ever. Every day is a gift. I fought for my life, and won. No negative reaction can make me stop feeling that this is positive.

I do not hate men. It is too easy a thing to do, and many men are victims of different kinds of oppression. It is patriarchy I hate, and that incredible tissue of lies that say men are superior to women, men have rights which women should not have, men are our rightful conquerors. . . .

We must stop mystifying rape. We must acknowledge its existence all round us, and the various forms it takes. We must stop shrouding it in secrecy, and must see it for what it is—a crime of violence in which the rapist is the criminal.

I am exultant at being alive. Being raped was terrible beyond words, but I think being alive is more important. When a woman is denied the right to feel this, there is something very wrong in our value system. When someone is mugged and allows herself to be beaten in order to survive, no one thinks she is guilty of willing consent to be beaten. In the case of rape, a woman is asked why she let them do it, why she did not resist, whether she enjoyed it. . . .

I am a survivor. I did not ask to be raped and I did not enjoy it. It was the worst torture I have ever known. Rape is not the woman's fault, ever. This article is one contribution towards exploding the silence and the comfortable myths which we build up to convince ourselves we are not potential victims, thus consigning actual victims to the most agonising isolation a human being can know.

Mathura

In 1972, a tribal girl named Mathura was allegedly raped by two policemen in a police station in Maharashtra. After a series of court battles, the Supreme Court acquitted the accused policemen in 1979. The Supreme Court did not believe Mathura had been raped and held that Mathura's body bore no marks of injury and that she was silent during the rape. According to them, this proved that she agreed to the rape.

Four professors of law in Delhi read this judgement and were anguished by the stand taken by the Supreme Court. They wrote an open letter to the judges of the Supreme Court and pointed out the fallacy of the judgement. They asked: How could a woman fight back or raise the alarm when she was held down in a police station? Why was it so hard to believe that a woman might consent to rape in an extreme state of fear? Why should every rape be accompanied by injuries?

The Mathura rape case became a rallying point for the women's movement in India. Several cases came to light where courts had disbelieved women's complaints of rape. These cases revealed there existed a systemic and severe bias against women in the judicial system. Police were insensitive and doubted women's accounts of rape. It was also discovered that women not only lost cases but were also subjected to humiliation in the courts. Protests by women's groups led to several changes in the rape law in 1983. These changes also paved the way for discussions on a hitherto taboo topic. The next set of changes in the rape laws came in the year 2013, following the Delhi gang rape case.

Nirbhaya

On 13 December 2012, a young woman in Delhi was brutally gang raped. The assault was so severe that she died within a week. The gruesome incident led to massive protests across the country with people taking to the streets to condemn the number of sexual assaults against women. The intensity of the countrywide protests forced the government to pass a new set of laws, and the following is a brief introduction to the scope of these laws which are popularly known as the Nirbhaya Laws:

1. It is rape if any part of the woman's body is penetrated, against her will, by a penis, body part or foreign object. The minimum punishment for rape is seven years and the maximum is life imprisonment.

2. It is custodial rape if a public servant or government official rapes a woman in a police station, jail, hospital, children's institution, etc. (The same is true of relatives, guardians, teachers or any person who is in a position of authority and capable of controlling or dominating a woman.) Custodial rape is a punishable offence with a minimum imprisonment of ten years and the maximum of life imprisonment.

3. Special cases of rape have been defined as such:

   a. rape of a woman suffering from a mental or physical disability

   b. rape of a woman incapable of giving consent

   c. rape of a woman during situations of communal or sectarian strife

4. If the rape results in death or the woman entering a vegetative state, like a coma, then the minimum punishment is twenty years and the maximum is life imprisonment.

Bhanwari Devi

In the past few years there have been several reported instances of sexual violence and rape committed against dalit girls and women in Haryana and Uttar Pradesh. In nearly all of the cases, the girls and women were targeted and kidnapped to teach a lesson to the dalit communities contesting upper-caste dominance over their lives and resources. Patriarchal logic dictates that if men from an upper caste shame and violate a woman from a lower caste, then the men of the lower caste will submit to the will of the upper-caste community. But many women and their communities refuse to obey this logic and fight for justice. The following text is about Bhanwari Devi, an inspiring woman who struggled for justice against sexual violence in Rajasthan. Her fight brought sexual harassment at the workplace to the fore for the first time in India.

Bhanwari Devi is a woman from the kumhar caste. She is from the village of Bhateri, Rajasthan, and worked as a *saathin*—an employee of the Women's Development Project run by the Government of Rajasthan. One of the main tasks of her job was to prevent child marriages in her village. The practice of child marriage was rampant in Rajasthan and in an effort to put an end to it the government had started a public campaign. However, this campaign was actively resisted by local communities and was seen as interfering with private matters. In 1992, one of the upper-caste gurjar families attempted to get their nine-month-old daughter married. Bhanwari Devi tried to prevent this child marriage.

News of the marriage attempt reached the local police station. The police travelled to Bhateri and stopped the child marriage. As a result of this, the gurjar community in the village was left feeling insulted and bore a grudge against Bhanwari Devi. She and her family were shunned by the village and not allowed to draw water from the well, sell their pots or their milk. On 22 September 1992, this social boycott went a step further. When Bhanwari Devi and her husband were working in their field, five gurjar men attacked her husband, beat him and then raped Bhanwari Devi.

Despite the fear of backlash, Bhanwari Devi decided to report the incident at the local police station. She lodged a criminal complaint of gang rape against the five gurjar men. It was not easy for a woman of her caste to file such a complaint against upper-caste men. The police were hostile and doubted her account. Her medical examination was so delayed that valuable evidence of the rape was lost.

In the meantime, in her village, gurjar men spread malicious rumours that Bhanwari Devi fabricated the rape account. She was subjected to humiliation and was once again socially ostracised. She received threats and was told to withdraw her case. Even some of her family members insisted she compromise and settle the case. In such a hostile atmosphere, Bhanwari Devi stood her ground and countered that she would withdraw her case if the gurjar men publicly acknowledged their crime and offered her an apology. By then the women's groups in Rajasthan came to know about the case and supported her in her struggle for justice.

The trial was held in a district court. In November 1995, the judge delivered his verdict: he disbelieved Bhanwari Devi's story and called her a liar. In his judgement he wrote that (i) upper-caste men could not have raped a dalit woman, (ii) an uncle cannot possibly rape in the presence of his nephew and (iii) her husband could not have passively watched while his wife was raped. On these grounds, the district judge acquitted all five gurjar men of the charges of rape.

The unfairness of the judgement led to a nationwide campaign for justice for Bhanwari Devi. Though she was subjected to rape, the discussion and the significant legal changes that happened as a result of her case were about sexual harassment. Vishakha, a network of women's organisations in Rajasthan and Delhi, filed an appeal against the judgement. They also filed a case in the Supreme Court against the Government of Rajasthan for not supporting Bhanwari Devi, who was their employee. They argued that this was a clear case of sexual violence at the workplace; that Bhanwari Devi was raped in the course of her employment while her employer, the Rajasthan government, did nothing to protect her from violence nor support her in dealing with it; and that she, as an employee, should not be left to deal with the consequences all by herself.

Bhanwari Devi's struggle, thankfully, was not in vain. In 1997 the Supreme Court held that sexual harassment was a form of discrimination against women and that it was a violation of the constitutional right to equality. The court held that the employer has the responsibility of defending its employee and punishing those who sexually harassed the employee. The court put together a set of guidelines to be followed by every employer with respect to its women employees in cases of sexual harassment. This is how the Vishakha Guidelines came to be enacted. This was followed in 2013 by a special law on Sexual Harassment at the Workplace, making it mandatory for all institutions (offices, universities, factories, etc.) to have an internal complaints committee to address all issues of sexual harassment at the workplace.

Becoming Man

13.1 INTRODUCTION

In Unit 3 we discussed how boys are taught to become boys. In this unit, we discuss the idea of *masculinity*. What is masculinity? Is it a quality that all men naturally possess? Having read the units on socialisation and boyhood, we know by now that masculinity, like femininity, is produced by society. This means that masculinity is shaped by our ideas and beliefs and therefore when new ideas gather force the idea of masculinity can change. As the sociologist Sanjay Srivastava remarks: 'The notions of "making" and "producing" are crucial to the study of masculine identities, for they point to their historical and social nature. The various discourses of "proper" masculine behaviour—in novels, films, advertisements, for example—would be unnecessary if it was a naturally endowed characteristic.' He further points out that masculinity is not something

you achieve once you become an adult; rather, it is a constant process and needs to be constantly reinforced through various means. The *chethu* style discussed in Unit 3 offers a glimpse of this process.

Advertisements tell us that certain shampoos, deodorants, cars or motorbikes will make men more masculine and attractive. Indeed, as we all know, hairstyle is a very important part of our personal appearance and gender identity, and although nowadays women wear their hair long or short (of course, long hair is still much desired!), most men keep their hair short to emphasise their male identity. This is true not only of boys and young men but also of many older men who pay close attention to the type of haircut, moustache and beard they sport. Look at the poster on page 134 of men's hairstyles, and read the interesting discussion in section 13.2 to understand the significant link between masculinity and hairstyle. If you remember, this link was touched upon in the story 'Rinku's Hair' from Unit 1.

Cinema, too, is another popular source of images of 'ideal' masculinity. Consider, for example, a film poster you might have recently seen. More often than not these posters feature a young, rugged, muscular hero wielding a weapon and wearing an expression of rage or aggression, ready to battle villains. Sometimes this young man is wearing sunglasses which cover his eyes and turn his face into a mask. There may also be a scantily dressed woman, or two women, standing behind or beside the hero and looking admiringly at him. The young man is clearly the centre of attention. In a film, a hero like this can singlehandedly beat up the villain and his henchmen.

In our hearts, we know that very few people are like the hero in the poster. But we also know that the young man represents an ideal of masculinity which a lot of men attempt to emulate, even though it is far removed from their everyday lives. There is a desire to be the hero—to walk like him, talk like him, dress like him, even behave with girls the same way he does. Such efforts often reveal the many insecurities men feel. In section 13.3, Singaraju Ramadevi's analysis describes how and why the model of masculinity that most South-Indian films depict today is quite dangerous. This is, however, not the only model of masculinity we have. For example, Devdas, the failed lover, is an enduring figure in Indian cinema, as are men in certain romantic films where the hero is shown as caring and gentle. Melodramas often feature troubled men dealing with the crises facing their families. The account in this unit discusses the transition from the 'angry young man' figure of the 1970s, as represented by Amitabh Bachchan, to the type of man represented by Shah Rukh Khan in the 90s and 2000s. It is an interesting story of the shifting images of masculinity in Bollywood.

Indeed, as women's movements have pointed out, masculinity and femininity are related terms. As Srivastava argues: 'Now, more than ever, we require an understanding of masculine cultures that is informed by feminist methods and perspectives. Gender is always a relationship between women, men and other genders, and unless we have a sense of how boys are socialised as men, our understanding of the ways in which gender oppression unfolds will always be incomplete.'

Many other social scientists too have felt that the growing violence against women has something to do with our society's understanding of masculinity. The feminist legal scholar Ratna Kapur believes that because many families value sons over daughters and often treat daughters as unwanted or burdensome, boys grow up with a sense of entitlement and privilege and assume they need to be respected and obeyed. But in today's world, more women are capable of pursuing an education and securing well-paid and highly respected jobs. This growing number of confident and independent young women is demanding equal respect and recognition for their contributions. However, many men are unable to cope with this new situation and feel threatened, even emasculated! The best way to handle this situation, Kapur argues, is neither through stricter laws (such as the death sentence for rapists), nor by providing more protection to women. Instead, she says, 'We need to think about how we can handle women's equality in ways that are not perceived as threatening [to men]. That demands greater responsibility on the part of parents as well as society not to raise sons in a way in which they are indoctrinated with a sense of superiority and privilege. There is also a need on the part of young men to be actively involved in their schools and communities in advocating women's equality rights.'

This is why we need to seriously consider alternative models of masculinity which recognise women as equal human beings and respect their freedoms and rights. We need to realise that there are many different ways of being a man. This is not an easy process. For a boy or a man, failure to follow the dominant codes of masculinity can sometimes result in physical, verbal or emotional abuse and alienation. One of our contributors, R. S., recalls how he changed from being a weepy boy to a ruthless bully in order to find acceptance among his friends. It was only when he was an adult and lucky enough to discover another kind of relationship, one that was based on mutual respect, that he reflected on his actions and the violence built into the routine rituals of manhood—in schools, college campuses, hostels and within male groups at large. His account gives us much food for thought. Unit 14 offers many examples of relationships between men and women that are based on a foundation of mutual affection and respect.

13.2 WHAT DO HAIRSTYLES TELL US?

Should men and women have long hair or short? Is facial or body hair desirable or undesirable? These are questions that have different answers depending on the culture and period of time. That being said, hairstyle has undoubtedly been a key factor in the creation and maintenance of gender differences. You may be surprised to learn that during the French Revolution—which gave the world the famous motto, 'Liberty, Equality, Fraternity'—the male Jacobin revolutionaries thought that long hair was a sign of virtue.

They considered haircuts a form of vice and also a sign that one was paying too much attention to their appearance. However, they did make it a point to shave because beards were associated with the 'ancient regime'—the rule of monarchs that the Jacobins had just overthrown!

The Step Cut

In the account below, cultural theorist M. Madhava Prasad recalls how in the 1980s certain barbers in Bangalore were reputed as 'step-cutting experts'.

I remember accompanying my friend to a place at least three kilometres away from where we both lived, where many boys were queuing up to submit to the special skills of the guy inside who was, unlike the barbers we were used to, quite fashionably dressed. What I can't recall clearly now is whether it was before or after the hippie era, which was like the Great Depression as far as barbers were concerned because boys defied parents and grew their hair long. Even hearing the Kannada superstar, Rajkumar, make fun of long-haired boys on screen didn't dampen our enthusiasm. But I think the triumphant return of the barber was after this low period and it was the step cut that aided the recovery.

In an earlier age, mothers, no doubt inspired by screen idols, would finish combing their sons' hair by creating a little puff in the front. Some boys would continue to give themselves this puff long after their mothers stopped combing their hair, but the rest of us went for step cuts and the downturned moustache which signalled to the world that there was nothing cheery about life. Tejaswi, the Kannada writer, lived through a time when boys began to get modern, short haircuts instead of growing their hair long like girls. Initially this haircut must have seemed no different from a full shave because people used to call such boys 'talkie baldie', implying that the style was copied from the movies. Being from 'the generation that never [or hardly ever] oiled its hair', I still find it quite disconcerting to see grown men sitting in salons and giving detailed instructions to the barber about how they want their hair cut. And after the haircut, they want the dye, the scented powders and whatnot. And what is worse, I have a suspicion such men are in the majority!

Indeed, many young men today do spend a lot of time styling their hair to get just the right look that will make them cool, desirable and masculine. Take a look at the following poster.

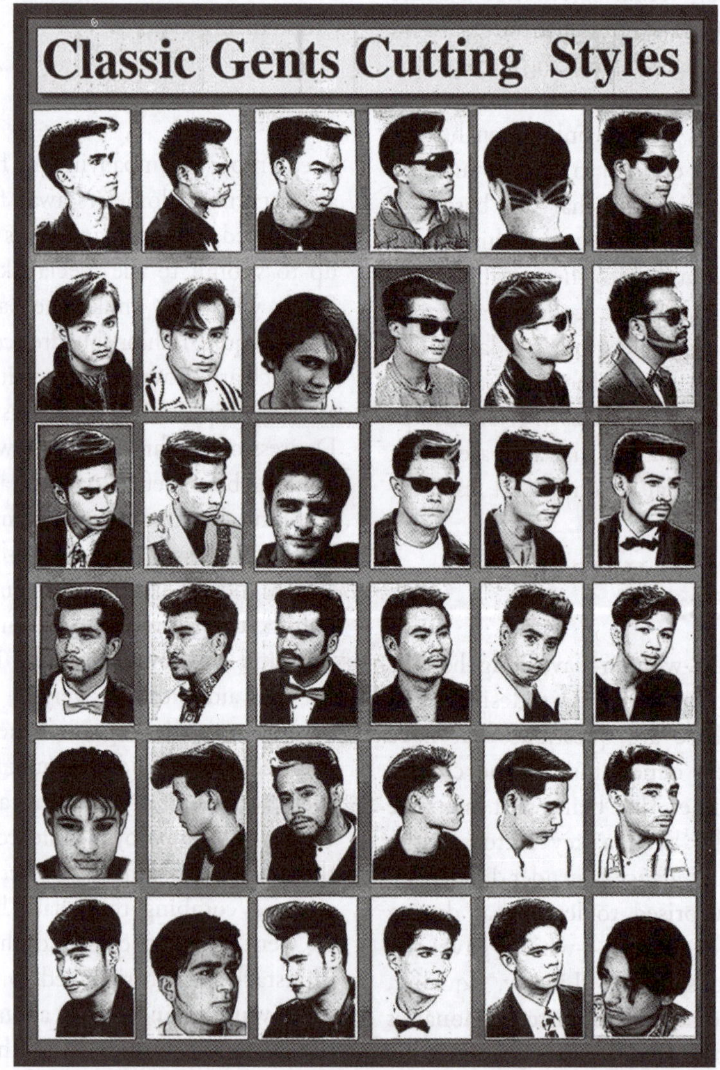

At first glance, many of the styles seem the same; not one style extends below the nape of the neck. But look closely and you will notice there are many small and subtle differences in the way the hair is cut and shaped on the sides and the front.

> **Points to discuss:**
>
> 1. Take a picture with your mobile phone of the latest hairstyle posters for men at your local hair salon or beauty parlour, and the latest hairstyle posters for women. What are the differences between them?
> 2. What does a man with long hair represent to you? Why? (For example, a man with long hair could be a priest, a traditional village landlord, a Sufi pilgrim, a rock star, a holy man, etc.)
> 3. Do men and women experiment with hairstyles now?
> 4. How important is hairstyle today in maintaining gender differences?

13.3 A DANGEROUS MODEL OF MASCULINITY

In many South-Indian films made in the last decade, the hero is depicted as a violent and aggressive man. Indeed, the model of masculinity these films project is a problematic one for young men. Read below Singaraju Ramadevi's humorous yet revealing account of contemporary Telugu cinema.

'I know you are wondering whether I'm a good guy or a bad guy! One thing is for sure, I'm definitely not a good guy,' says the hero of a recent box-office hit in Telugu.

Most of the recent successful films in Telugu revolve around the themes of love, enmity, revenge, violence and comedy. The same themes are endlessly rehashed in film after film and there is hardly any scope for new kinds of themes and narratives to emerge. In fact, the story as such has disappeared from most films and the importance given to the male protagonist has grown to such an extent that it subsumes the story and the other characters. The other characters in the narrative either exist to sing his praises or to provide a few laughs through their antics. The role of the antagonist is to ignite the flames of vengeance in the hero's heart, and the heroine exists as lover or wife to proclaim and reaffirm his sexuality and masculinity.

If the hero of yesteryear Telugu cinema was criticised for being a paragon of virtue with hardly any flaws, today's heroes have successfully laid to rest such criticisms. However, we would be mistaken if we were to conclude that they are now more realistic or down-to-earth. Far from it, they are now *Pokiri* (film released in 2006; the title means 'vulgar vagabond') or *Julayi* (2012; 'good-for-nothing') and *Idiot* (2002). Listed below are the typical traits of a Telugu film hero:

- He gets drunk, abuses and beats people, and generally creates a nuisance in public (*Venky*, 2004).
- His life's mission is not to become a lawyer or collector—like Telugu film heroes used to before—but to become a mafia don. (*Don Seenu*, 2010, and *Businessman*, 2012).
- He has no respect for the law, even when he himself is a policeman. Very often, he takes the law into his own hands and beats or even kills people. (*Gabbar Singh*, 2012, and *Temper*, 2015).
- If the girl he desires is the sister of a gang leader, he joins the gang, participates in their illegal and antisocial activities

and succeeds in winning the girl's heart. (*Dhee*, 2007, and *Loukyam*, 2014).

- As for smoking or excessive drinking, our current heroes are great proponents of these unhealthy habits. (*Don Seenu*, 2014, and *Gunde Jaari Gallanthayyinde*, 2013, and *Resu Gurram*, 2014)

- And, of course, every hero is a strong, muscular man (with a six-pack) who wields all kinds of weapons (from axe to gun), operates every mode of transportation (from horse to aeroplane) and is capable of singlehandedly beating up twenty men, all while showing off his superhuman masculine prowess.

> **Points to discuss:**
>
> 1. Can you think of examples from other language films of heroes who are similar to the ones described above?
> 2. Can you think of heroes in recent films who are unlike those described above? How are they different?

13.4 CHANGING MASCULINITIES IN HINDI CINEMA

We now turn to a more in-depth analysis of the portrayal of male heroes in Hindi cinema and how this has been changing over the years.

Who does not know the superstar Amitabh Bachchan? Popularly known as the Big B, he is perhaps the most famous and influential star in the history of Indian cinema. Even today, when he is more than 70 years old, crowds gather outside his palatial bungalow, Pratiksha, in the hope that they might catch a glimpse of their idol.

Did you know that Bachchan introduced a particular brand of machismo to Hindi cinema? In the late 60s and early 70s, the film industry in Bombay was ruled by Rajesh Khanna, known as the Prince of Romance, who had an irresistible smile and twinkling eyes. He had women swooning over him, some even marrying his photograph! And then in 1973 *Zanjeer* happened, marking the arrival of the 'Angry Young Man'—Amitabh Bachchan. As the brooding Inspector Vijay, Amitabh acts as a vigilante cop driven by a desperate hunger to avenge his parents by finding the man who murdered them. He does have a romantic interest in Mala, played by Jaya Bhaduri, but romance is only a small part of his life. The arrival of Inspector Vijay marks the end of the romantic excesses of the Rajesh Khanna era.

What really changed?

Let us try to understand the 'Angry Young Man' phenomenon in its historical context. By the late 60s, the promise of independent India—of equality and progress for all citizens irrespective of class, caste, gender or community—had not materialised. Wealth and prosperity remained limited to a miniscule group. The gap between the rich and the poor continued to widen day by the day. By the 70s, prices plummeted and food riots broke out in several parts of the country. There were massive strikes with workers in railways, factories and mills demanding better wages and living conditions. The countryside witnessed revolts by poverty-stricken peasants and agricultural labourers seeking freedom from feudal modes of oppression.

Sooner or later, the simmering discontent of the people was bound to find its way into cinema. Bachchan's film persona was that of a young, working-class man whose life mirrored the hardships the country faced in the 60s and 70s. The angry young man's rugged body represented the physical labour that a majority of men in India had to do to earn a living. During this period, Bachchan acted as a dock worker, miner, police officer, rebellious lawbreaker, etc., taking on roles that were primarily of lower-class young men. As film theorist M. Madhava Prasad points out, in Hindi cinema before Bachchan, the roles of aristocratic and upper-caste heroes were played by actors carefully chosen for their looks, which had to match a standard ideal of the heroic. Bachchan, on the other hand, was too tall and lanky and looked almost ordinary. His films did not really bank on his looks. However, his anger and pain brought an intensity to the screen that had never been seen before. In *Deewaar* (1975) he plays the role of Vijay. Vijay's father, Anand, is an upright union leader who is forced to sign an agreement going against the interest of the workers when the mine owners threaten his family. Unable to bear the humiliation that follows, Anand leaves his family. The workers, angry at Anand's betrayal, tattoo the words '*Mera baap chor hai* [My father is a thief]' on Vijay's left arm. This line serves as a permanent reminder to Vijay of the injustices he and his family suffered. It is also a marker of the particular brand of masculinity that Bachchan symbolised for almost two decades—a lean, angry, rebellious social outcaste who fought the system. Bachchan would influence a generation of everyman heroes in Indian films, including Hindi actors such as Anil Kapoor, Jackie Shroff and Ajay Devgn; Malayali actors Mammootty and Mohanlal; Telugu actor Chiranjeevi; and Tamil actors Kamal Haasan and Rajinikanth. These male actors embodied an underdog masculinity often in the form of the criminal or rebel.

With the onset of the 90s, a new category of hero took centre stage, eroding the popularity of the angry young man. This new hero was represented by none other than Shah Rukh Khan, who would come to be known as King Khan. Beginning his career in 1992, Khan's body was noticeably different from previous heroes—he was hairless, had no moustache and did not have a toned muscular body. He initially took on roles in which he was the troubled anti-hero with a dark past, but he eventually adopted the image he would come to be known for—a charming, wealthy and sensitive lover who shared crackling chemistry not only with his female co-stars but his male ones as well! Remember his warm friendships with men in his many films?

Most of you must have watched *Dilwale Dulhania Le Jayenge* (1995), which sealed Khan's reputation as the ultimate romantic hero. In the film, he plays the role of Raj, a London-based character who is determined to win the hand of his sweetheart, Simran. In order to do so, he must win her heart and also gain permission to marry her from her stern Punjabi father. But her father, Baldev Singh, has other plans for his daughter. He wants to marry her to a true son of Punjab—someone who is tough, rugged and macho. He accepts Raj as a sort of lovable clown more suited to the company of the ladies in his family, but never in his wildest dreams does he think of Raj as a suitable husband for his daughter. It is no surprise then that he is furious when he discovers his daughter is in love with Raj. In the final act of the film, Raj is brutally beaten by Simran's fiancé (chosen by her father) and his friends. Raj is passive while beaten, until his assaulters attack his father. It is only then that he fights back, demonstrating an uncontrollable rage, reminding us of the Shah Rukh Khan from *Darr* and *Baazigar* (1993)—a film persona he had abandoned for characters who were more romantic. Film historian Ravi Vasudevan offers an interesting analysis of this scene. He believes that this is the moment when Raj, the boy-hero with soft and 'feminine' looks, regains his 'masculinity' by defending the honour of his bloodline—thus demonstrating his obedience to the basic rule of patriarchy. As you all know, in the end Baldev sets his struggling daughter free, thereby allowing her to catch the train that is taking away Raj.

If you compare a classic Bachchan film from the 70s with a Shah Rukh Khan film from the 90s, you are bound to notice many differences between the two leading men. The working-class body of Bachchan in the 70s was traditionally masculine—he was sunburnt, unshaven, his knotted shirt revealing chest hair. Khan, who often played the upper-class Hindu man in his most popular films in the 90s, had a softer, more feminine body. The arrival of globalisation and the opening up of the Indian market in the 90s greatly influenced this shift. There was a rejection of the working-class physique associated with masculinity made popular not just by Bachchan, but in the 1980s by the likes of Anil Kapoor and Jackie Shroff. In a way, the 90s was when heroes like Shah Rukh Khan and Aamir Khan, who were smooth-skinned and almost as pretty as their heroines, made their mark.

At the turn of the century, however, this form of hero was gradually replaced by the muscular hero. Make no mistake, this was not a return to the masculinity of the Amitabh era. No, the hardened working-class look was replaced by a gym-toned, carefully sculpted body that reflected the polish and privilege of the affluent global Indian. The 'fitness' of this body was centred on appearance and, more specifically, male beauty. John Abraham is an ideal example of this version of a globalised masculinity.

By the 2000s, the hero's body in Indian cinema increasingly conformed to European standards of male beauty. Previously, the heroine's body needed to carry all the sex appeal, but we now see in many blockbusters that the hero's body is as much of a box-office commodity as that of the heroine's.

Take the example of Shah Rukh Khan. In the 90s he had successfully played the charming, affluent lover in film after film. But even he eventually had to adapt his body to the new culture of male beauty and worked hard to get a six-pack for his 2007 film, *Om Shanti Om*. There is a scene in the film where he dances shirtless—sweat dripping from his glistening, sculpted torso—and one is reminded of the typical, half-clad female dancer of Hindi cinema who is surrounded by dozens of lecherous men. Only this time the dancer is male! And he is an object of desire for both male and female eyes; an object carefully prepared for the global market.

> ***Points to discuss:***
> 1. Can you think of any recent films that defy gender stereotypes? How do they do so?
> 2. List a few examples of new kinds of male protagonists. What distinguishes them from male characters you've seen before.
> 3. Who is your favourite film hero? What are the qualities that you like about him?

13.5 IMPRINTS OF MASCULINITY

The following account by our contributor, R.S., is a frank yet poignant account of his experiences in school, college and in later life. You will notice that this account echoes some of the ideas expressed in Krishna Kumar's 'Growing Up Male' from Unit 2 on socialisation. Reflecting on his experiences, the author sees that what he thought to be 'normal' male behaviour was in fact violent and indifferent to other people's feelings. After several years of working as an engineer, he decided to quit his job and go back to his studies. During this period he describes how he embraced domesticity while his wife worked and supported him. He learnt not only to cook and clean but to also think of what it means to be a woman and a housewife. He learnt that masculinity was not a natural, unchanging trait; though society's definition of masculinity was usually learnt the hard way, it could also be unlearnt.

❖ ❖ ❖

When I was about nine years old, I transferred from a girls' convent school to a boys' mission school in Secunderabad. I had till then studied in a class of about 25 girls with four or five boys. I was probably sent to this school because it was close to home. My first hour at the mission school was traumatic; I was in a class of about 45 boys, all from poor backgrounds, some in rags or walking barefoot. We were sitting on stools in front of small tables and everybody was shouting at the top of their voices. The boy next to me shifted his stool and my thigh was pinched between my stool and his, taking off a bit of skin. I howled with my convent English, 'My leg is jammed!' That was it—the whole class erupted, 'Leg jam, leg jam!' That was my name for the next few months. My friends formed around that name, and they found out other queer things about me, like the fact that I was learning to play the flute. They knew I cried easily, as I did when asked by my tutor to sing the words of songs I tried

to learn. These friends lived near where I did, and we would walk the two to three kilometres back home every day. They would torture me—reducing me to tears every evening for the next five years. Then, in tenth standard, I made new friends outside of school and moved away. But those five years of constant torture made sure I suppressed my desire to cry— something I only relearned 45 years later! Instead, I built a wall of sarcasm and distance, never forging a very close relationship with any of the boys I knew.

There was a recent public-service advertisement by a women's magazine with the tag line 'start with the boys',[1] which showed different situations involving the masculine socialisation of crying boys by family and friends. The film ends with an absolutely shocking sequence: an expressionless man twisting the arm of a woman who turns her face to the camera to reveal her black eye where he has struck her. The final lines are: 'We have taught our boys not to cry. It's time we teach them not to make girls cry. Start with the boys.'

I have never hit a girl, even as a joke.

When I went to my engineering college hostel at the age of seventeen, we 'freshers' were ragged with ritual severity for the first six months of the first year; we were verbally, physically and sexually humiliated (not assaulted). In our second year, we were the 'seniors'. A young fresher who was ragged complained to his brother who was a day scholar in his final year. The brother shouted at the raggers, and that was it! That night, we stood the fresher on the terrace and had all the other freshers as audience to watch as 30 to 40 of us slapped the boy continuously for an hour because he complained! The boy went to the hospital with a fever the next day, and we masked our anxiety with solicitous messages when we visited him. I felt no remorse till a friend asked me (and to this day continues to ask me), 'Who will he complain to about being ragged if not his brother?'

I wonder what this episode did to me. Did it teach me to be more masculine? What was the gender of the boy who complained? Was he not 'man' enough? The violence of masculinity need not be channelled only against women—it will perform its socialising function even if directed at men. What had happened to me, the little 'leg jam' boy who had known what it is to cry or not be masculine enough?

A year later, in 1973, a senior in our hostel (who was in his second year) was caught trying to have sex with a first-year boy. The fresher didn't report any violence. He only said that the senior had asked him for a favour, which he had refused. But it later came out that this senior had tried to do the same with others. A complaint was submitted to the principal. This otherwise gentle soul came to the hostel and gathered all the hostel dwellers in front of the entrance in a large circle surrounding him. He had the 'offender' brought to him, sat him on the ground, personally shaved his head and paraded him before all the inmates. The punishment was meted out by a person who had a doctorate in architecture! The 'offender' was calm and accepted his punishment without complaint.

I remember many of us felt sorry for the senior despite jeering at him. Everybody had experienced the immense sexual pressures of adolescence. Many of us had found an outlet for such pressures through sex workers, or through more lonely pursuits, while others formed relationships (some emotional, others explicitly physical) with other boys. Yet here was this barbaric ritual which ensured the dominance of the masculine heterosexual norm. It was almost as if there was too much

fluidity, too many permitted deviances and a line had to be drawn.

As far as I know, most of us have settled into comfortable heterosexual lives (and now have children and grandchildren of our own). Our memory of those times is reduced to an inexpressible fondness for friends who shared the secrets of that growth into adult masculinity as we traversed queer paths to arrive at 'normalcy'.

By the time I became an engineer, I was a cigarette-puffing, hard-drinking, outspoken, smirking, cocksure fellow of 22. A few explorations and eight years later, I found success with a girl I was fond of and we got married. Through all of this, I was at heart a softy and a bit dissatisfied with my chosen profession. Our marriage was based on a mutual promise—we would support each other through any change of profession without complaint. Our luck was that we didn't have children—otherwise the story would have been different! 20 years later, depressed and disillusioned with the end of the line that was visible to me, I switched tracks to become a political scientist. In order to achieve this, I had to register for an MA and then a PhD in the subject. Since I was already older than permitted, I did the one by correspondence and the second part-time.

While I did this, I relied on my wife's promise. She supported me, and I ran the house while I studied. It was a strange experience. The house embraced me with a strange love. I paid attention to detail—cleaning, cutting vegetables, cooking and washing. Nobody at home, I would sometimes wander off to the crowded streets of General Bazaar in Secunderabad to look at the colourful shops. I found that, like me, there were many women who came to cheer themselves up amidst the riot of merchandise. Sometimes I would look out of my kitchen window on a bright day and exchange smiles with my neighbour—a housewife who was also working in the kitchen. I wonder what we shared! Was it a kind of femininity that arose from a shared experience of housework?

Points to discuss:

1. The 'ragging' incidents described in the account link to prevailing ideas about masculinity like 'a real man is tough and aggressive!' Do you think a less aggressive masculinity would reduce ragging and other kinds of violent behaviour?

2. Expressions of sexuality are closely regulated in our society. In the account, a man expressing homosexual desires is violently punished. Do you think his punishment was justified? Think about the discussion in Unit 11 about the gender spectrum.

3. The account ends with the author describing a less common experience of a man maintaining a home and studying. He cooks, does the washing and cleans the house. Can you think of men in your family or among your friends who have chosen careers or lifestyles that challenge male stereotypes? Even examples from everyday life that blur gender distinctions would be interesting to discuss.

NOTE

1. You can watch Vogue India's #StartWithTheBoys advertisement here: https://www.youtube.com/watch?v=0Nj99epLFqg.

Just Relationships:
Being Together as Equals

14.1 MARY KOM AND ONLER

You may have heard the famous lines, 'If you love someone, set them free. If they come back, they are yours. If they don't, they never were.' This quotation packs so many lessons about how to love, how to be a friend and how to care for somebody without taking control of their lives. All of us long to find someone who lights up our days and stands by us through the darkest moments. But, more than anything else, bonds of friendship or love must allow for each person to be themselves and to feel comfortable pursuing their goals, dreams and passions. A love that ties one down with obligations, watches and controls one's every move—can we really call that love? Unfortunately, violence and the desire to dominate frequently wear the mask of love. This has been discussed in Unit 7 on sexual harassment. Too often films reinforce the idea that even if a girl rejects a boy's advances, if he continues to pursue her then she will eventually break down and succumb to his 'love'.

Reality, however, is not so pretty. Do you know that sometimes girls stop going to school or college just to avoid being teased on the way? If girls fell in love with those who stalked or teased them, then they would not take such a drastic step and risk ruining their education.

An episode of the popular television programme *Satyamev Jayate* dealt with how cinema shapes our idea of wooing a woman—how heroes often manhandle the heroine or treat her like she is an object. One popular item song has a woman admit: 'I am a piece of tandoori chicken.' In *Satyamev Jayate*, however, three leading Bollywood actresses—Kangana Ranaut, Deepika Padukone and Parineeti Chopra—drew on their own experiences to speak of how traumatic it can be to be stalked or treated so roughly against one's will. All of them were crystal clear about one thing: they would not accept an abusive relationship. For them, no definitely means no![1]

Women routinely have to deal with unwanted attention from men. All in the name of 'love'. When a woman turns down a man's offer of love, things can turn ugly. Very often the man refuses to accept the fact that she is not interested, or that she has a right to say no, however much it might hurt him. He then stalks her, badgers her with persistent text messages and phone calls. Some men even retaliate by posting false or malicious comments on social-networking sites, thereby shattering the woman's privacy and damaging her peace of mind.

As you read this, a thought might cross your mind: How is it possible to hurt somebody you love? You may wonder: Is it at all possible to find relationships between men and women that are based on trust, warmth, friendship and mutual respect? Hold on to that thought! In this unit you will read stories about relationships that may not match the conventional model of 'love' but are nonetheless sweet and inspiring in their own way. One such relationship is between the famous Indian boxer, Mary Kom, and her husband, K. Onler Kom. Onler supports Mary by managing their domestic responsibilities so that she can focus on her demanding career. In section 14.2 you will read the heartbreaking story of Laxmi, the victim of an 'acid attack' by a jilted suitor. Her story has a silver lining; she found a partner who loves and respects her for her courage and spirit. Her story also tells us that not all men are brutal and controlling like her attacker, and that there are men who condemn violence and believe that a true and fulfilling relationship is possible only when there is *equality* and consent.

A Boxer's Love Story

Who does not know Mary Kom today? Her list of achievements is long and impressive and includes winning silver once and gold six times at the World Amateur Boxing Championship. The world of professional boxing is traditionally considered a man's domain, but Mary Kom defied all odds to become one of the most successful boxers in women's boxing. And her husband, K. Onler Kom, has been by her side throughout this incredible journey.

There is a popular saying: 'Behind every successful man is a woman.' But what if a relationship is the opposite of this—one where behind every successful woman is a man?

In 2000, Mary Kom was travelling by train from Manipur to Bangalore to attend the Indian Amateur Boxing Federation's national coaching camp. Unfortunately for her, she lost her wallet and someone stole her suitcase with her passport while she was asleep. It was difficult to endure such a setback because her family had little money and they had gone to great lengths to procure a passport. At the time, she felt so low and frustrated that she contemplated ending her life. Fortunately for her, Onler—who was also from Manipur and was the president of the Northeast student body in Delhi—came to know of Mary's troubles and offered to help her.

'I first met Mary at the Nehru Stadium in Delhi,' Onler recalled. 'I saw this girl; she had short hair and a lot of gumption. I knew she wanted to become a boxer against all odds. We were a student community from the Northeast. I told her if she needed anything, starting from financial help to home-cooked food, she could tell me. She once came home to eat. We became friends.' Onler helped her to get a new passport. This was the beginning of a long partnership based on trust and sharing.

'My life was an unending series of tours and training sessions,' Mary said. 'I had little time to socialise. On Sundays, when I had a little free time, Onler and I would meet, and we'd eat a home-cooked meal with friends and relatives. It was very de-stressing for me. We shared a language and background, which helped me relax in Onler's company. He was closely following my career and wanted to help me reach as far as I could.'

A few years later, Onler realised he was in love with Mary. He was already Mary's best friend and yet found it difficult to say what was in his heart. Mary would later joke that he proposed to her over the phone without actually saying anything. It took all his courage to finally say, 'I think you should understand what I'm trying to say even if I don't speak the words out loud.'

While Mary really liked Onler, marriage was a different game altogether. Mary was passionate about boxing; she and her family had sacrificed a lot to help her pursue her passion. She was in her early twenties. After years of struggle, her career was just beginning to take off. She had a busy schedule of tours and training. It was hard for her to think beyond boxing. How would marriage fit into her life?

Despite her doubts, Mary realised that Onler was her soulmate. He had not wooed her with roses but he understood her ambition and her love of boxing. They married in 2004.

'I had my own destiny, but when I came to know her it changed,' said Onler. 'It's not that she is very beautiful or that she is famous. I married her for her simplicity and her willingness to be a successful sportswoman.' Since then he has been by his wife's side, helping her raise their three children while she earned gold medals and the title of champion.

'Onler knew from the beginning that ours would be an unusual marriage,' Mary said, speaking about Onler's role in her life. 'A wife who is absent for most of the year cannot run the home. In our society, the woman runs the house, even if she is a career woman. The kitchen is her domain; she is the one who shops for vegetables and groceries. In our case, Onler runs the house and fulfils social obligations, like visiting ailing relatives or attending weddings and funerals. He tackled problems by himself, like when essential commodities—gas or baby formula—became unavailable. Onler had to cope with all of this on his own. The mobile phone is a crucial thread that keeps us going through our long-distance marriage. When I get lonely or miss home, he speaks loving, encouraging words to me. When I cry, he consoles me. When I need to talk, I know I can say what I want to, holding nothing back.'

Points to discuss:

1. In Unit 2 on socialisation you read about the pressures women and men face to fit into feminine and masculine roles. Can you point out how Mary and Onler break away from such stereotypes?
2. Now that you have read about Mary Kom and Onler, discuss how depictions of romantic relationships in popular films vary from their relationship.
3. Discuss how communication and mutual respect play an important role in Mary and Onler's relationship.

14.2 ROMANCE IN SOUTH-INDIAN CINEMA

While it is true that there are refreshing new trends in Indian cinema, a majority of the films continue to present the hero as a macho man and the heroine as a pretty young thing (sometimes shortened to PYT). This can have major consequences as cinema is known to influence society's attitudes.

Many of you might wonder why we need to take cinema seriously or analyse films so carefully. You might ask, 'Aren't our films unrealistic anyway? We know that they don't depict reality, so why not just watch them for fun?' The truth is that films require our critical attention because they are so popular and have such a wide reach. We all have our favourite heroes and heroines whom we love, admire and even imitate. Consciously or unconsciously, they become our role models. And our role models can have a sizeable impact on how we behave, how we dress, the attitudes we adopt, etc. So, let us carefully examine the portrayal of heroes, heroines and romance in certain films from the last decade.

Most male and female characters in films reinforce traditional roles that society assigns to men and women. Men are usually depicted as strong and courageous, providing for their family and serving honourably as heads of the family. Women, meanwhile, are depicted as carers tending to the family. They play a supportive role. Singaraju Ramadevi describes the kinds of relationships found in films below.

The Typology of Romance in Indian Films

- **One-sided Romance:** This needs no explaining—you find this in 90% of films. The hero follows the heroine, teases and harasses her and does not give up until she says yes.
- **Blackmail Romance:** The hero (and sometimes the heroine) threatens to commit suicide if the object of their affection does not return their love. Many films depict this as a sign of true love.
- **Gratitude Romance:** Many a time, the heroine is rescued by the macho hero from harassers and rapists. She is so grateful that she falls in love with him immediately.

All in all, it seems as if we only have forced romance in most films. The girl and the boy rarely meet and spend time getting to know each other and their tastes and views before falling in love. There is very little respect and desire for an equal relationship.

Points to discuss:

1. Can you think of examples from films that fall into the categories of romance discussed above?
2. Are there other categories that could be added to the table?
3. Are there movies that depict relationships described as 'romance' or romance based on equality? Please share them with your classmates.

14.3 LOVE AND ACID DON'T MIX

In 2005, Laxmi was 16 years old and living in Delhi. She was shopping in a busy marketplace when a man threw acid on her face and arms. Laxmi had earlier turned down a marriage proposal from this man, who was twice her age. Angry and humiliated, this man plotted a terrible revenge on the girl he claimed to 'love'!

Since the attack, Laxmi has undergone seven surgeries. The attack left her physically and emotionally scarred.

However, through all the pain, Laxmi has become active in anti-acid campaigns. She has filed Public Interest Litigations in the Supreme Court which seek changes in the law[2] and has asked the government to take steps to restrict the sale of acid. During the course of her activism, she met the Kanpur-based social activist, Alok Dixit, who ran a campaign on social media against acid attacks called 'Spot of Shame'. Alok was moved by Laxmi's spirit.

'When she came to us,' he said, 'she was bold and smart. Unlike the other girls, who shy away from society and usually move about with covered faces, Laxmi moved freely with an open face. I saw a fighter in her and gradually we fell in love.'

When Alok was 28 and Laxmi 26, they worked together on a campaign that they hoped would eradicate acid attacks in India. Recollecting this episode in her life, Laxmi said, 'Someone asked me the question: what if the attacker still offered to marry me? I said, he has changed my face, but he has failed to change my mind.' She added: 'Afterwards I never wanted to find love. I mean there was no hope in any case because of the scars.' But after meeting Alok, all that changed and she said she learned to love again: 'I couldn't have found anyone better. He understood the kind of pain I was in. He understood what I was going through.'

For Alok, Laxmi was beautiful just the way she was. The couple decided to live together, but they did not want to get married. Alok said, 'We are not going to follow norms that society approves of. We will prove that our love does not need a name. Our love is about understanding and support.' Laxmi and Alok together ran the 'Stop Acid Attacks' campaign.

In 2014, Laxmi won the International Women of Courage award for her campaign against acid attacks on women in India. When she received the award from Michele Obama, the First Lady of America at the time, she delivered a speech in which she recited the following lines in Hindi: 'You haven't thrown acid on my face; you threw it on my dreams / You didn't have love in your heart; you had acid in it.'

Laxmi was also quoted in later interviews as saying: 'You stare at us and gather your children in a hurry, hoping they aren't scared just by looking at us. Why don't you tie a band around your eyes and see how dark it gets? That's how dark our world is. I hope you never have to inhabit it, but I do hope you understand it. Don't give me the strength if you can't, but don't try and break my confidence. I've just learnt to move on.'[3]

Don't you feel Laxmi's story teaches us the value of consent? Women like Laxmi would not have to endure such hardship if consent was part of our vocabulary and convictions. Remember, as discussed in the *Chai pe ek aur charcha* section from Unit 7 on sexual harassment, in the case of love or sex, as with tea, consent is everything.

The Need to Control

Remember Hermione Granger, the intelligent, curly-haired witch from the Harry Potter series? Often described as 'the brightest witch of her age', she is a brave and steadfast friend to Harry Potter and Ron Weasley at the Hogwarts School of Witchcraft and Wizardry. In the films, the role of Hermione was played by the English actor Emma Watson, who is now a leading actor, model and activist. In a speech delivered at the United Nations Headquarters as a Goodwill Ambassador, Watson spoke of feminism as an ideal which was not about hating men but about committing to creating a place where men and women are entitled to equal rights and respect. Furthermore, she spoke about the need for society to move away from gender stereotypes, arguing that, 'If men don't have to be aggressive in order to be accepted, women won't feel compelled to be submissive. If men don't have to control, women won't have to be controlled.' Towards the end of her speech, she called upon society to 'perceive gender on a spectrum instead of two sets of opposing ideals', because doing so would empower men and women to be who they want to be, and to be 'freer'.[4]

> **Points to discuss:**
>
> 1. Emma Watson believes that men are as much imprisoned by gender stereotypes as women are. What do you think she means?
> 2. Try to provide examples of how men are imprisoned by gender stereotypes.
> 3. Emma Watson is an international film star. Do you know of any film stars in India who have spoken up against gender discrimination?

14.4 LOVE LETTERS

This unit explores relationships that may be deemed unconventional. However, they push us to think beyond our narrow understandings of family, domesticity and friendship. For those of us depressed by our daily quota of violence against women in newspapers and on television, these come as a breath of fresh air. They demonstrate how a true partnership can change our lives and the lives of those around us—making the world a much better place! Some of these accounts are from our past, some set in more contemporary times. Together they point to new futures.

Love Letters Like No Other

We begin with a set of unique love letters written by Savitribai Phule (1831–97) to her husband Jotiba Phule (1827–90). They are renowned for taking up the cause of widows, setting up schools for girls in Maharashtra, and fighting against caste discrimination. In addition, Jotiba was a writer and a thinker while Savitribai was a poet and Maharashtra's first female teacher. These letters are translated by Sunil Sardar, who writes that they 'are a testament to the emotional support Savitri provided to Jotiba, her revolutionary husband. Their dream of a new and liberated society—free from the chains of ignorance, bigotry, deprivation and hunger—was the strong thread that bound the couple together, fusing their private and public life into one. When … dominant Maharashtrian society was ranged against Phule's radicalism, perhaps it was the love—and joyous dedication—of his life companion that emotionally sustained Phule in his struggle.... Savitribai and Jotiba emerge in these letters as equal and able companions.' You will glean more about this famous couple and their inspiring relationship from the letters.

❖ ❖ ❖

October 1856
The Embodiment of Truth,
My Lord, Jotiba,
Savitri salutes you!

… As we were talking one day, my brother said, 'You and your husband have rightly been excommunicated because both of you serve the untouchables (mahars and mangs). The untouchables are fallen people and by helping them you are bringing a bad name to our family. That is why I tell you to behave according to the customs of our caste and obey the dictates of the brahmins.' Mother was very disturbed by this brash talk. Though my brother is a good soul, he is extremely narrow-minded and did not hesitate to bitterly criticise and reproach us. Mother did not reprimand him but tried instead to bring him to his senses by saying, 'God has given you a beautiful tongue; it is not good to misuse it so.' I defended our social work and tried to dispel his misgivings. I said, 'Brother, your mind is narrow, and the brahmins' teaching has made it worse. Animals like goats and cows are not untouchable for you. You lovingly touch them. . . . But you consider mahars and mangs, who are as human as you and I, untouchables. Can you give me any reason for this? When the brahmins perform their religious duties in their *madi* clothes, they consider you also impure and untouchable . . . they don't treat you differently from the mahars.'

When my brother heard this, he turned red in the face, but he asked me, 'Why do you teach those mahars and mangs? People abuse you because you teach the untouchables. I cannot bear it when people abuse you and create trouble for you for doing that. I cannot tolerate such insults.' I said . . . 'Learning and knowledge are glorious. One who acquires learning loses his lower status and acquires a higher one. My husband is a god-like man. He is beyond comparison in this world, nobody can equal him. He thinks the untouchables must learn and attain freedom. He confronts the brahmins and fights them in order to teach the untouchables because he believes they are human beings like others and they should live like dignified humans . . . I too teach them for the same reason. Yes, we teach girls, women, mangs, mahars. The brahmins are upset because they think this will create problems for them. That is why they oppose

us and chant the mantra that it is against our religion. They revile and castigate us and poison the minds of even good people like you . . . Let me tell you that my husband does not merely invoke God's name and go on pilgrimages like you. He is actually doing God's own work. And I assist him in that. I enjoy doing this work. I get immeasurable pleasure by doing such service. Moreover, it shows the heights and horizons to which a human being can reach out.'

My mother and brother were listening to me intently. My brother finally came round, repented for what he had said and asked for forgiveness. Mother said, 'Savitri, your tongue must be speaking God's own words . . .'

With humble regards,
Yours,
Savitri

❖ ❖ ❖

29 August 1868
Naigaon, Peda Khandala
Satara
The Embodiment of Truth, My Lord,
Jotiba,
Savitri salutes you!

I received your letter. We are fine here. I will come by the fifth of next month. Do not worry on this count. Meanwhile, a strange thing happened here. The story goes like this. One Ganesh, a brahmin, used to go around villages, fortune telling and performing religious rites. This was his bread and butter. Ganesh and a teenage girl named Sharja, who is from the mahar community, fell in love. She was six months pregnant when people came to know about the affair. The enraged people caught them and paraded them through the village, threatening to bump them off.

I came to know about their murderous plan. I rushed to the spot and scared them away, pointing out the grave consequences of murder under British law. They changed their minds.

Sadubhau angrily said that the wily brahmin and the untouchable girl should leave the village. Both victims agreed to do this. The couple fell at my feet and started crying. Somehow I consoled and pacified them. Now I am sending both of them to you. What else to write?

Yours,
Savitri

❖ ❖ ❖

20 April 1877
Otur, Junnar
The Embodiment of Truth, My Lord,
Jotiba,
Savitri salutes you!

The year 1876 has gone, but the famine has not—it stays in most horrendous forms here. The people are dying. The animals are dying, falling to the ground. There is severe scarcity of food. No fodder for the animals. The people are forced to leave their villages.... Barren land is cracked everywhere.... The people crying for food and water are falling to the ground to die. Some are eating poisonous fruits and drinking their own urine to quench their thirst. They cry for food and drink, and then they die.

Our Satyashodhak[5] volunteers have formed committees to provide food and other life-saving material relief to people. They have formed relief squads.... It would be better if you come from Satara to Otur and then go to Ahmednagar. . . . You have started the

benevolent and welfare work for the poor and the needy. I also want to carry my share of the responsibility. I assure you I will always help you. I wish the godly work will be helped by more people.

I do not want to write more.

Yours,
Savitri

14.5 MOTHERS, FATHERS AND FAMILY

Some kinds of love are highly idealised, such as a mother's love. A mother must be the picture of selflessness and sacrifice. She is happy only when she is looking after the needs of her family—washing, cleaning, cooking and feeding. Remember the countless advertisements for washing powder? They often began with a young, active child (almost always a son), strolling back home. He has had hours of outdoor play and his clothes are now muddy and filthy. His mother greets him at the doorway—despite the state of his clothes and her mock exasperation, her eyes are full of love, joy and pride. No worries!

All she has to do is soak his clothes in a bucket filled with water, brand-name washing powder and love. Abracadabra! Her son's clothes are clean and bright again. We know he will get them dirty in no time at all, but that does not matter because his mother will smilingly take care of the laundry!

Except, as we learnt in Unit 4 on housework, it does matter; mothering involves hard labour that is invisible and often unappreciated. So sacred is the idea of mother as caretaker that to consider her work for her family as labour would be unthinkable. In Unit 4, the poem 'Vantillu' by Vimala shows how such idealisation can be unfair to women by dismissing their needs and aspirations as unnecessary or unimportant.

Thankfully, in many families and communities, sons do help their mothers. They share the burden of housework, shop for groceries and fetch medicine when necessary. 'Madiga Badeyya' a story by Gogu Shyamala, the noted dalit writer from Telangana, captures such a relationship. In the story, Badeyya's mother, Ellamma, must go into a forest every day to gather *tangedu* leaves. One day, as her landlord passes by, she removes her *chappals* to follow the strict caste rules of her village and a dog runs away with one of them. Unable to retrieve her *chappal*, she walks barefooted until pierced by a thorn. Badeyya is upset when he discovers what happened. He is outraged by the unjust custom which led to his mother hurting herself. He cannot bear to think about her walking in pain to the forest the next day. When the family goes to sleep that night, Badeyya quietly slips out with his father's leather-making tools. He stays awake the entire night making a pair of slippers for his mother. When he gifts them to her the next morning, she is so happy that she goes

around telling everyone in the village: 'Look, my youngest son has made these slippers for me!' It is interesting to note that although Badeyya is the darling of the village because he is the only child who goes to school, in class the teacher and the other children ignore him. There is no recognition of his humane personality, intelligence or skills. A school is an important place where there should be just relationships too.

The Problem That Has No Name...

In Unit 10 you read about the American feminist writer Betty Friedan and her book, *The Feminine Mystique*, which went on to influence women's movements across the world. In that unit we looked at how the idealised 'happy housewife' image of American women was rooted in the specific history and politics of the USA in the post-war period. But the phenomenal influence of the book can be traced back to her study of how this image was marketed to many women as the best thing that could happen to them. The reality, Friedan revealed, was that middle-class housewives in affluent, suburban American homes felt unhappy even though they apparently had every material comfort in the world! Friedan identified this problem as the continuous pressure on women to fit into the feminine role of 'mother' or 'wife' without getting a chance to realise their potential as human beings. She called it 'the problem that has no name' because it was invisible and could not even be acknowledged as a problem.

A lot of advertisements sell products which cash in on traditional images of the wife or the mother. But this was not the case for an advertisement for Havells cables and wires. Their advertisement shows a working-class mother making *chapattis* in a makeshift hovel that is the family's home. While she cooks, she tugs on a rope tied to a cloth cradle to rock her baby to sleep. Her older son sits next to her and tries to study, but he finds it difficult to concentrate. He cannot ignore his mother's struggles—the way she burns her fingers every time she takes a *chapatti* out of the fire. He puts his book down, searches a construction site, picks up a length of cable and makes a pair of tongs for his mother to use without scorching herself. The advertisement ends with the mother looking at her son lovingly while using the tongs.

Don't you wish there were more such advertisements?

'Marriages are made in heaven.' Or so they say. Yet you only need to take one look at matrimonial ads to realise marriages require a lot of work and have plenty of terms and conditions which need to be met. The bride must be fair and beautiful, the groom tall, handsome and earning a respectable amount of income. Castes must match, which often leads to matrimonial ads declaring: 'Wanted: brahmin boy', or 'Wanted: nair girl', etc. It goes without saying that all these ads are for first-time marriage only. In the Indian context, a second marriage—especially for a woman—still remains largely unacceptable. However, the winds of change are blowing! More women now believe that life does not necessarily come to a standstill if their marriage ends. Go through the matrimonial section in a newspaper and, every once in a while, you will come across an ad for a second marriage.

Tanishq Jewellers released an advertisement which captured this changing trend: the bride is not marrying for the first time and has a daughter, but the bridegroom welcomes her and her daughter as his new family.

Fathers

People always talk about a mother's duties and responsibilities. Let us stop for a moment and talk about fathers.

Many people still hold onto the notion that there are fixed differences between men and women. This belief greatly influences our idea of the family. A father must earn to support his family and protect them from danger. He must be strong and powerful. A mother, on the other hand, must nurture her family. She must cook for her husband and children, clean and bathe her children and send them to school and take care of them in health and sickness. She must be soft, sweet and sacrificing.

Despite such notions, fixed gender roles have been and continue to be challenged by the behaviour and experiences of people in different communities. Are you aware of the ground-breaking research conducted by the renowned anthropologist Margaret Mead (1901–78)? Her studies show that concepts of masculinity and femininity vary across cultures. Mead's field research among certain tribes in New Guinea, Samoa and Bali indicated that the gender norms in these tribes did not match with those that were more popularly held by Western societies.

For example, at the time of her research, what the Tchambuli tribe (now known as the Chambri people) in New Guinea regarded as masculine would have been viewed as feminine in Western societies. Similarly, among the Arapesh of New Guinea, both men and women take responsibility for child rearing.

More recently, an extraordinary report titled State of the World's Fathers showed that men and women are born with an innate and equal capacity to care for others, including young children.[8] However, this ability in men is repressed by social norms of masculinity which discourage them from acting as carers. The report collected information from thirty countries across five continents to conclude that, 'Increasing numbers of fathers around the world are actively involved with their children: feeding them, changing diapers, staying home with sick children, and bringing their sons and daughters to school.' Importantly, the report implied that involved and caring fatherhood helps men break out of the stifling constraints imposed by conventional cultural ideas of what it is to be a man. The report quoted men from all corners of the world testifying that finding a place in their heart to love and nurture their children has helped them become better human beings—less violent, less prone to risk-taking, physically and mentally healthier and more emotionally fulfilled.

Yusuf, a 43-year-old Turkish man, is quoted in the report as saying: 'I started to see and feel: "Something is about to change." Then my child started to talk a lot to me. A lot. And he noticed I was listening. Now, I try to show my son the love, attention and care that I lacked from my own father.'[9]

Queen and Her Gang of Friends

Even today, a woman is often defined in relation to a man—as a mother or a daughter or a wife. So much so that she herself may forget that she is an individual in her own right. Thankfully, women (and men) are sometimes lucky enough to enter a relationship that does not set up any boundaries but allows them to grow and have their own space. Have you ever come across a story or film that shows such a relationship?

One such film is *Queen* (2014), directed by Vikas Bahl, which received the Best Hindi Film award at the National Film Awards. Kangana Ranaut won the Best Actress Award for her performance as Rani, a character refreshingly different from typical Bollywood heroine roles.

Rani is a girl from a middle-class, conservative Punjabi household in Delhi, who dreams of a fairy-tale marriage to her fiancé, Vijay. However, just two days before the marriage, Vijay dumps her. She is heartbroken but makes an extraordinary decision; she plans to go on her honeymoon to Paris all by herself. Her parents let her go, hoping the trip will help her recover. In Paris she finds a place very different from the world she is so used to. Imagine a lone Indian girl who has never travelled before in a strange foreign city! In a typical Bollywood film, she would be overwhelmed by the city and its strange customs, frightened and lost until some Prince Charming swooped in to protect her. They would sing a few songs and she would finally settle down and marry him.

But this is not Rani's fate. She makes silly mistakes, encounters difficulties and nearly gets mugged, but she does not let any of this dampen her spirits. Instead, she finds and makes friends with some extraordinary individuals who are unlike anyone she has ever met before.

In Paris, Rani meets Vijayalakshmi, a free-spirited French-Indian. Vijayalakshmi teaches her how to let her hair down, enjoy life and just be happy. In Amsterdam, she shares a room in a cheap hostel with a Japanese student, a black Frenchman and a Russian artist. Like a 'good Indian girl', she is so terrified by the idea of having to share a room with strange men that she decides not to sleep in the room but outside. When she is woken up by the black Frenchman, she screams in absolute terror till he manages to calm her down and explain that, if she wants, the men will move out of the room for the night so that she can sleep in peace. Here again is another important life lesson she learns: Never judge a person by the colour of their skin. Friendships are based on trust and ***mutual respect*** and a willingness to accept difference. Rani slowly finds out that her roommates may look and act very different, but that they are still gentle and caring human beings worthy of dignity. So begins her friendship with this diverse group.

Points to discuss:

Queen follows the journey of a girl discovering who she is while making friends with others who are considered to be outside the conventional boundaries of her society. Watch the film and then discuss the following:

1. Try to come up with a list of words that captures the spirit of friendship shown in *Queen*. An example of one might be, 'freedom'.
2. Can you think of a friendship (from films, books or life) that is similar to what Rani shares with her friends? What makes this friendship so unique?

14.6 FURTHER READING

Just and fair relationships extend beyond family. You have already read about the shared ideals and passion for social justice that bound Jotiba Phule and Savitribai together. What follows now is the inspiring story of Rosa Parks (1913–2005), who fought to end racial discrimination in America. Like Martin Luther King, Jr (1929–68), she too dreamt of a world where people were not divided on the basis of the colour of their skin.

Rosa Parks the Braveheart

Rosa Parks was born Rosa Louise McCauley. She was raised on her grandparents' farm in Alabama, a state in the racially divided American South. Growing up, she was exposed to the realities of segregation. For instance, she had to walk to school because the elementary school bus system did not allow black students to ride the bus. She later attended the Alabama State Teachers' College, but due to her grandmother and mother suffering from illnesses, she was forced to drop out and care for them. At 19, she met Raymond Parks, who worked for the local office of the National Association for the Advancement of Coloured People (NAACP). They married in 1932, and after much encouragement from Raymond, she went on to earn her High School diploma. Rosa joined Raymond in the NAACP, serving as the chapter's Secretary and Youth Leader, though she also worked elsewhere to help make ends meet.

She and Raymond lived in Montgomery, Alabama. At the time, the city had introduced a number of laws which ensured bus passengers were segregated by race. 'Coloured' sections were at the back of the bus, and 'White' sections at the front. Black people could not sit in the same row as white people, and were forced to give up their seats if there were not enough seats available for white people.

On 1 December 1955, after a long day at work, Rosa caught a bus back home. She sat in one of the middle rows. When the white section filled up, the bus conductor ordered her and three other black people to move to the back. The other three did as instructed, but she did not. She was determined not to give up her seat to a white man, and was determined to find out what rights she possessed as a human being. She was arrested and fined $14.

Her arrest, and trial, sparked one of the largest boycotts in American history—over 17,000 black people in Montgomery walked to work or travelled by carpool instead of taking the bus.

The boycott was ended on 21 December 1956 when the Supreme Court ruled that segregation on city buses was unconstitutional. Parks became a national hero. It was the beginning of a mass movement of nonviolent social change, culminating in the Civil Rights Act of 1964 and the Voting Rights Act of 1965.

People like Rosa Parks fought at great personal risk for a new world where women and men could live with dignity and without discrimination. It is for us to take the struggle forward in our own surroundings, neighbourhoods and social worlds.

> **Points to discuss:**
> 1. What does Rosa Parks's life tell you about discrimination and equality?
> 2. Look around you. Is there anything that you can identify as 'discrimination'? What steps do you believe are necessary to counter this discrimination? Do you believe we can take the steps necessary to make a difference?

NOTES

1. Visit the following weblink to watch the episode of *Satyamev Jayate* where they speak about 'When Masculinity Harms Men': http://www.satyamevjayate.in/when-masculinity-harms-men.aspx.

2. Until 2013, there was no specific provision in place in the Indian Penal Code for acid attacks. However, the Justice Varma Commission constituted by the Central Government observed that acid attacks clearly sought to destroy a woman's identity and therefore possessed a specific gender dimension in India. They recommended that acid attacks should not come under offences affecting the human body but should be treated as a separate offence which took into account the long-term and permanent psychological and physical damage committed against the victim. Accordingly, in the 2013 (Criminal Law) Amendment, S 326 A and

326 B were inserted specifically to penalise acid attacks. For further information, visit the following weblink: https://himachal.nic.in/WriteReadData/l892s/240_l892s/1500444109.pdf.

3. Read Laxmi's story here: https://www.hindustantimes.com/india/don-t-stare-at-me-i-am-human-too-acid-attack-survivor-laxmi/story-I5U4wL8wSBmvNqRREMcQOK.html.

4. Watch Emma Watson deliver her speech at the UN here: https://www.youtube.com/watch?v=gkjW9PZBRfk.

5. The Satyashodhak Samaj (the Truth Seekers' Society) was set up by Jotiba Phule in 1873 to fight for the rights of women and all members of the shudra and dalit castes. Phule and Savitribai believed in the importance of education for these people. The Samaj played a very significant role in powerfully questioning and challenging existing social inequalities of the time, and provides inspiration for present-day struggles too. Those who are interested in learning more can refer to G. P. Deshpande's *Selected Writings of Jotirao Phule* (2012).

6. Watch the Havells' advertisement here: https://www.youtube.com/watch?v=CQ8144h068M.

7. Watch the Tanishq wedding advertisement here: https://www.youtube.com/watch?v=P76E6b7SQs8.

8. Read the most recent report by State of the World's Fathers here: https://sowf.men-care.org/.

9. Read an article on the report by State of the World's Fathers here: https://www.thehindu.com/opinion/columns/Harsh_Mander/harsh-mander-on-howmuch-fathers-matter/article7460405.ece.

Our Bodies, Our Health

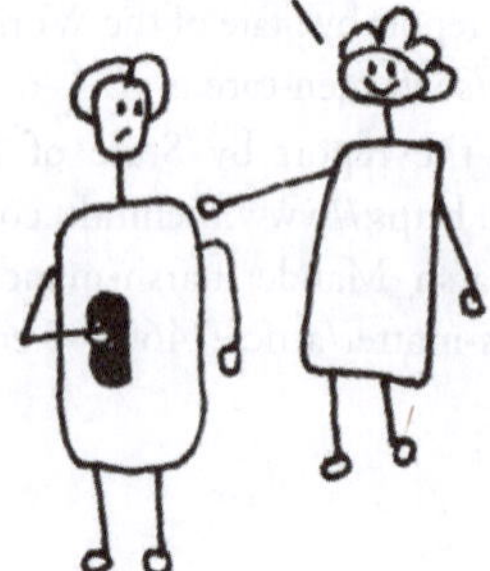

15.1 BODY PARTS: WHAT THEY ARE, WHAT THEY DO…

Our bodies are constantly changing as we grow older: one phase of rapid change is between the ages of 12 and 20, which is known as *puberty*. There are lots of questions—often of an intimate and personal nature—that we want the answers to. Some of us have family or friends with whom we can discuss these matters. Sometimes, we get our information through television, films or books. You might find the following sections from TARSHI's *The Blue Book* (1999) useful.[1]

You learn about your body from an early age, but that knowledge is limited. No one tells you as much about your sexual organs as they do about your nose, eyes or stomach, for example. Knowing the right names of sexual organs is the first step to understanding more about how they function.

Men

The male genital organ is called the *penis*. The outer layer of skin covering the penis is the foreskin. When a penis is erect, the foreskin moves back so that the tip of the penis or the glans is exposed. The foreskin is attached to the underside of the glans and should not be pulled back with force. People of some communities remove the foreskin during childhood—this is called circumcision. This is a matter of preference and custom. When a penis is circumcised, the glans is fully exposed all the time. The penis is usually slightly curved towards the tip. Also, the penis is not absolutely straight. It may slant towards the left or right. Penile size cannot be increased by exercise, massage or medicine. Penile size is not important for sexual satisfaction—it is technique that matters. To maintain genital hygiene:

- Wash your genitals daily with water. No soap, antiseptic, deodorants, etc. required.

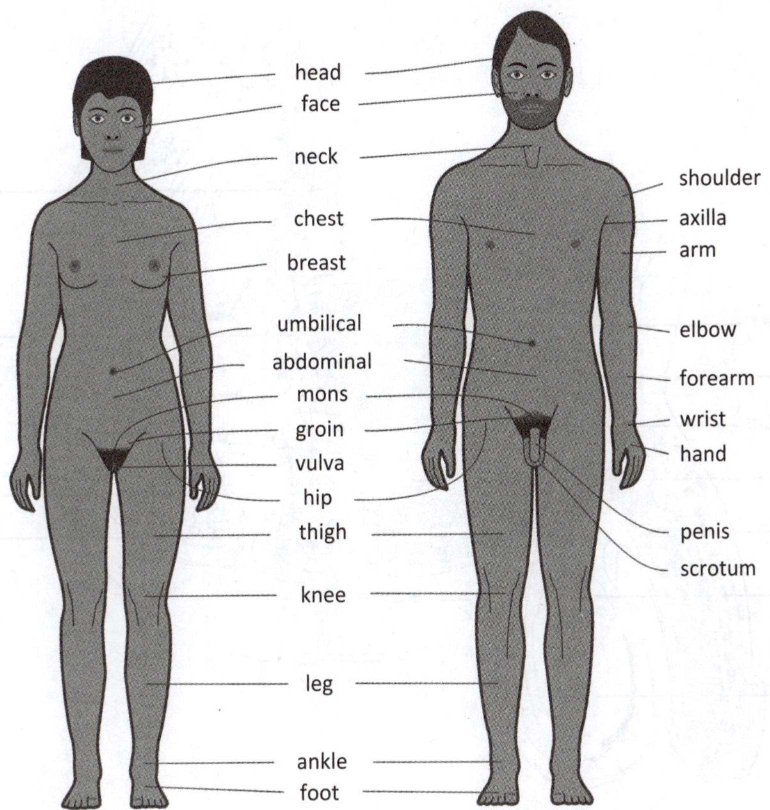

- Dirt might accumulate as a sticky substance, called smegma, under the foreskin. Gently pull your foreskin back and wash the tip of the penis. It will be easier to do this when you do not have an erection.
- While washing after defecating, wash in a motion away from the penis, that is, front to back, to avoid the risk of infection.
- Change your underwear regularly (at least once a day), and avoid underwear made from synthetic material.
- Wash your underwear carefully to make sure no detergent remains. Dry underwear in the sun. Sunlight is an excellent disinfectant.

- Avoid waxing or using razors, bleach, hair removers or other chemicals near the penis or testes because the skin around your genitals is very sensitive. If at all you need to, you can carefully trim your pubic hair with a pair of clean scissors.

When a man is sexually excited, his penis becomes hard and 'stands up'. This is known as an erection or a 'hard-on' and occurs because of increased blood flow to the penis. Erections sometimes occur spontaneously, without any sexual stimulus. Many men have morning erections and erections while they sleep. This is perfectly natural and normal. It does not mean they are 'oversexed'.

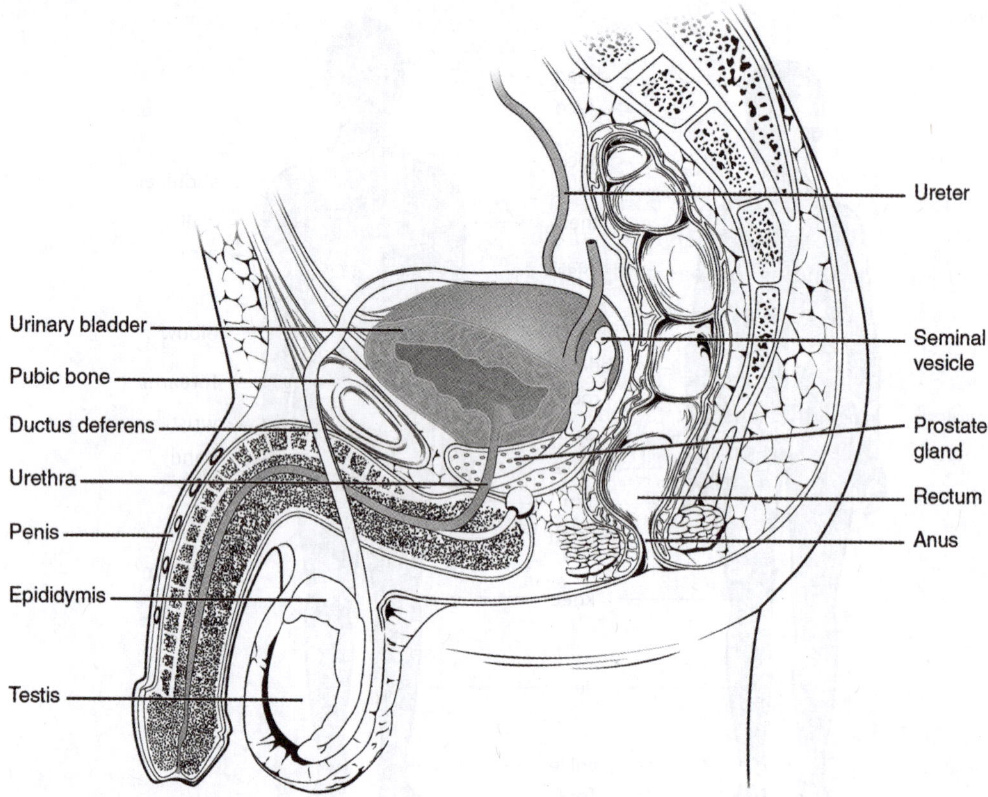

Below the penis are two **testicles** which may not be of equal size. This is where **sperm** is produced. Semen or 'cum' is the sticky whitish substance that comes out of the penis. It is continuously formed in the body and contains sperm along with other substances. A few drops of clear, sticky fluid are secreted from the tip of the penis soon after it becomes erect. This is 'precum' or pre-ejaculatory fluid. Pre-cum also contains some amount of sperm (actually, thousands of sperm) so it can also cause pregnancy. The quality and quantity of semen varies from person to person, and for the same person from time to time. Semen is not made up of blood as many people believe.

Sometimes semen comes out of the body at night, during sleep. This is called nocturnal emission, night fall or wet dreams. A nocturnal emission is not necessarily accompanied by sexual feelings or sexual dreams. They begin to happen around puberty and some boys get quite embarrassed or frightened by this. A nocturnal emission is a normal occurrence and does not lead to any weakness or loss of semen, because semen is produced continuously. Semen cannot be stored in the body at the rate at which it is produced. While urinating, you might find that a few drops of a whitish fluid come out just before the urine does. Both the semen and the urine come out from the same tube and opening and so if semen is present in the tube, it naturally comes out before the urine does.

Very tight underwear and jeans may damage sperm production as the temperature in the testes increases due to tight clothing.

Women

Women's chests are different from men's. This is because women have ***breasts*** that are made up primarily of fatty tissue. This fatty tissue contains a milk-duct system which is activated when a child is born. Breasts may be round, conical, upright, sagging, soft or firm depending on age and fitness. The variation in size and shape depends on genetics. The tips of breasts are called ***nipples***. They are darker in colour than breasts and are highly sensitive to touch and temperature. The dark circular area around each nipple is called the areola. Sometimes when the nipples are touched or stimulated, they become hard and seem to stand out. This is called nipple erection. This happens to both men and women.

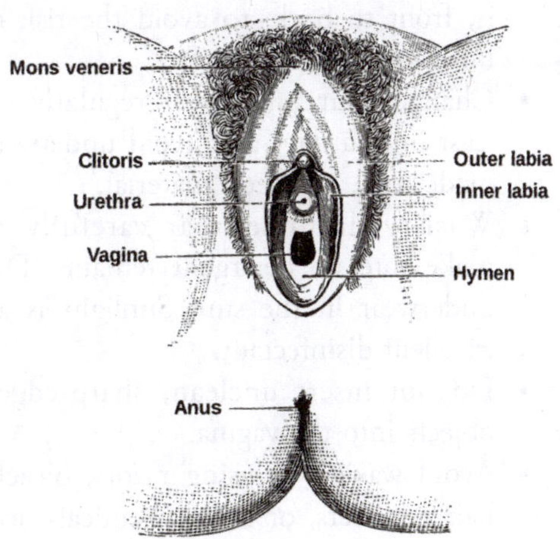

Do you know . . . ?

- Breast size cannot be increased except by surgical means.
- Breasts are not equal in size. There is usually a slight difference in size between both breasts.
- The shape and size of breasts change with age.
- The size of your breasts has no bearing on your interest in sex or your ability to receive or give sexual pleasure.
- Breasts are sensitive and respond well to gentle stimulation. Rough handling and squeezing may lead to severe pain.
- Unusual discharge from or lumps within breasts require immediate medical attention.

The outer lips, inner lips, ***clitoris*** and ***vagina*** may differ in size, shape and colour from woman to woman. All these structures are part of what is called the ***vulva***. The clitoris is a tiny structure (about the size of a small pea) above the urinary opening, hidden within the folds of the inner lips where they join. It is extremely sensitive to touch and when stimulated gently becomes firmer and slightly larger (like a nipple erection).

The vaginal passage is elastic and muscular. It stretches during delivery to allow the baby to come out. The vagina is bathed with secretions produced by the body to keep it clean and healthy. It is normal for these parts of the body to exude a distinctive smell. When a woman is aroused, the amount of vaginal lubrication increases and she feels wet.

The ***hymen*** is a delicate tissue in the vaginal passage. It has openings that let menstrual blood pass through it. Sometimes, when the body is jolted like when you run or jump, this tissue may break. A few girls are born without a hymen. The hymen can be ruptured through physical activity as well as through sexual intercourse. To maintain genital hygiene:

- Wash your genitals daily with water. No soap, antiseptic, vaginal deodorants, etc., required.
- While washing after defaecating, wash in a motion away from the vagina, that

is, front to back, to avoid the risk of infection.

- Change your underwear regularly (at least once a day) and avoid underwear made from synthetic material.
- Wash your underwear carefully to make sure no detergent remains. Dry underwear in the sun. Sunlight is an excellent disinfectant.
- Do not insert unclean, sharp-edged objects into the vagina.
- Avoid waxing or using razors, bleach, hair removers, or other chemicals near or in the vulva because the skin around your genitals is very sensitive. If at all you need to, you can carefully trim the pubic hair with a clean pair of scissors.

How Menstruation Occurs

In most women, an ovary releases one egg or ovum every *menstrual cycle* (the time between two consecutive *periods*). Also, during every cycle the womb (uterus) prepares itself to receive a fertilised egg by thickening the lining of its walls. This process is illustrated below. If fertilisation has taken place (sperm meets ovum), then the thickened lining is required to nurture the growing baby. If it has not happened, then there is no further need of the lining and the body sheds it so that it comes out through the vagina as bits of lining, blood, clots and mucus. This usually takes about two to eight days. Menstruation is regulated by the hormonal system, which in turn may affect energy levels and moods. That is why sometimes before and during periods, some women may experience mood changes, pain and tiredness.

The Menstrual Cycle

Menstruation, menses, or periods is a part of the female reproductive cycle. You may have heard that a woman is 'ill' or is 'dirty' because she is having her periods. This is not true. In fact, it is a sign that her body is functioning healthily and well. Some girls and women may have pain and cramps before and during periods, some women may experience mood changes, pain and tiredness.

What To Use During Periods

The menstrual blood that flows out totals up to only a couple of tablespoons. However, because it flows out of the body, it needs to be absorbed by something for reasons of hygiene and convenience. Most women use either pads or tampons to absorb the blood.

Pads may be made of different materials. The ones that are available in the market are in the form of an absorbent cotton pad encased in a synthetic material. They may be beltless, in which case you have to take off the

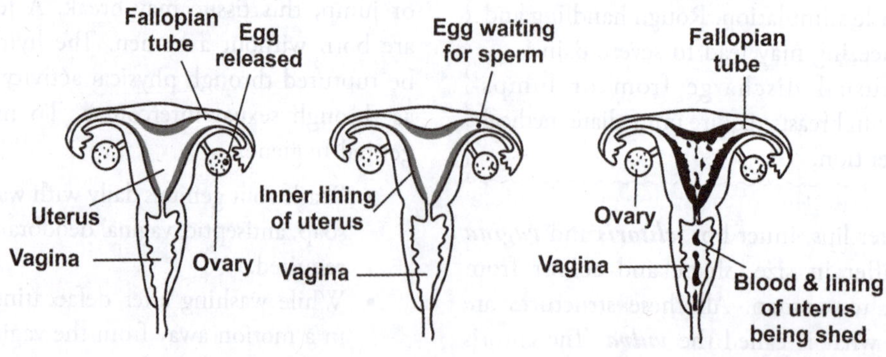

adhesive strip and stick the pad on to your panties. They may also come with a thin belt, in which case the ends of the napkin are kept in place by the belt. Sanitary napkins come in a range of prices. If ready-made napkins do not suit your budget or cause an allergic reaction, you can make them at home. To maintain menstrual hygiene:

- Always use a clean sanitary towel or tampon to absorb the blood.
- Sanitary towels or tampons need to be changed frequently (at least every four to six hours) in order to prevent bad odour or infections.
- If you are using a cloth which is to be reused, it should be washed thoroughly and disinfected by drying in the sun. In fact, re-usable pads made of cloth are more environment friendly than ready-made sanitary napkins that are for a one-time use.
- Many women nowadays also opt for menstrual cups made of silicone or latex. They are relatively cheap (because they are re-usable) and are an eco-friendly option. Each time the cup fills up, or every five to six hours, remove the cup, empty it out and clean it with warm water before re-inserting it again. Make sure that you clean your hands with soap thoroughly before and after you do this.
- Maintain hygiene during your periods. There is no reason why you should not bathe, wash your hair, etc.

Period Pain

Sometimes some of you may feel pain or heaviness in the breasts, lower abdomen, lower back and thighs before or during your periods. It might help to use a hot water bag on the abdomen or gently massage the lower abdomen to ease the blood flow.

Gentle exercise like walking and continuing with daily activities is helpful in preventing muscles from becoming constricted and cramped. In case of extreme pain, excessive flow of blood or irregular dates (cycles), consult a gynaecologist in order to avoid complications.

Do you know . . . ?

- Menstruation usually begins in women between the ages of 9 to 16 and stops for women between the ages of 45 to 55.
- Menstrual cycles usually fall within a range of 21 to 35 days, the average being 28 days long. Sometimes a woman's cycle may become irregular as her periods may be delayed or occur earlier than expected because of illness, mental tension, etc.
- Irregularities in the menstrual cycle are quite common amongst young girls who have just begun to menstruate.
- A missed period is usually one of the first signs of pregnancy in sexually active women.
- Due to regular loss of blood, women need to supplement their diets in order to protect themselves from the harmful effects of nutritional deficiencies.
- If you want to engage in penetrative sex during your periods, always use a condom to avoid infection as well as pregnancy. There is no single day when the chance of pregnancy is zero percent.
- Sometimes, either due to sports, functions or trips, some women try to delay or hasten their periods through self-medication. Such steps should be avoided as they may harm the body and its natural rhythms. If you need to take any medicine to delay or hasten periods, consult a gynaecologist.

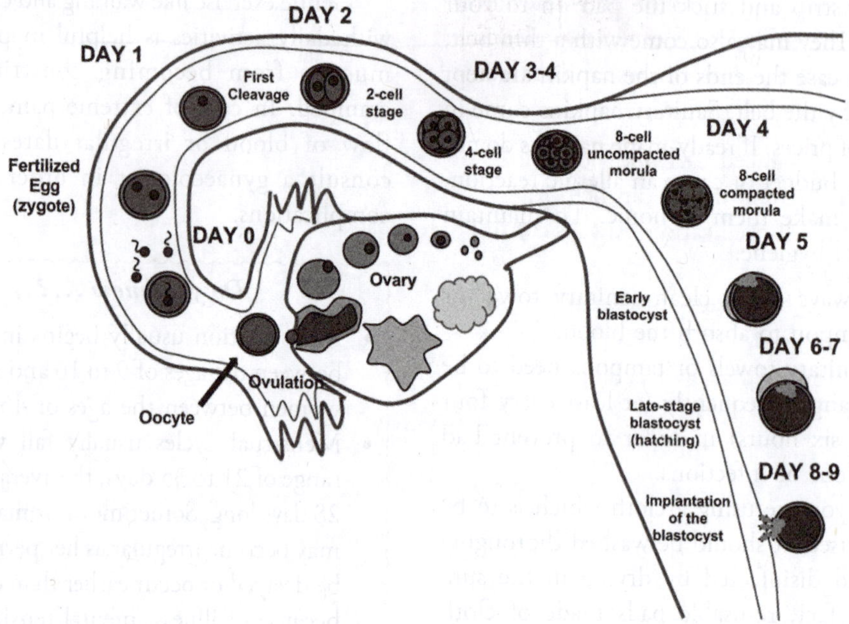

15.2 MAKING BABIES

All it takes for a baby to be made or conception to occur is for a single sperm to meet the ovum. A man's semen contains millions of sperm. The lifespan of a sperm is 72 hours. When a man ejaculates in or near the vagina, the sperm in his semen travel through the vaginal passage to enter the uterus or 'womb', and from here they move to the fallopian tubes. It is in the fallopian tubes that the sperm meets the ovum (ovaries release one ovum every month) to form a fertilised egg. The egg, after fertilisation, moves into the uterus where it implants itself into the uterine lining which the body prepares afresh every month. The egg grows in the uterus for nine months after which it emerges into the world as a newborn baby. Pregnancy begins at conception and lasts until delivery. The most common sign of pregnancy is a missed period.

Pregnancy can happen any time the sperm enters the vulva or is inside the vagina.

Remember that the pre-ejaculate (pre-cum) also has sperm. Ejaculation near the vagina can also lead to pregnancy. The only way to check if you are pregnant is to do a pregnancy test (at home with a home-pregnancy kit available at a pharmacy or in a lab). Pregnancy is usually a very special period in a couple's life.

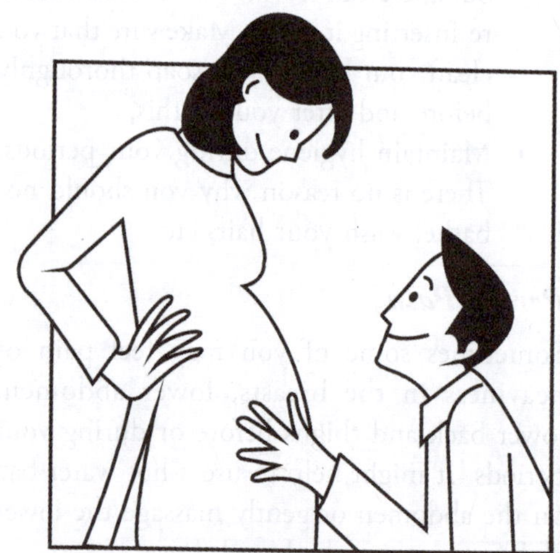

The first few months of pregnancy may be difficult, with some women experiencing morning sickness, tiredness and extreme emotional states. If pregnant, you need to:

- Eat a balanced diet and not smoke or drink alcohol if you can help it.
- Avoid self-medication. Always consult a doctor.
- Report bleeding or spotting to your gynaecologist.
- Go for regular gynaecological check-ups.
- Take your immunisation shots.
- Do not have intercourse if it is painful or uncomfortable.

A sexually active couple can use various methods to prevent conception if they do not want a child. These methods are called *contraceptives*—meaning 'against conception'. Using contraceptives that are safe and reliable are a sign of responsibility and concern for yourself and your partner. A mix of methods is more reliable than using one method alone.

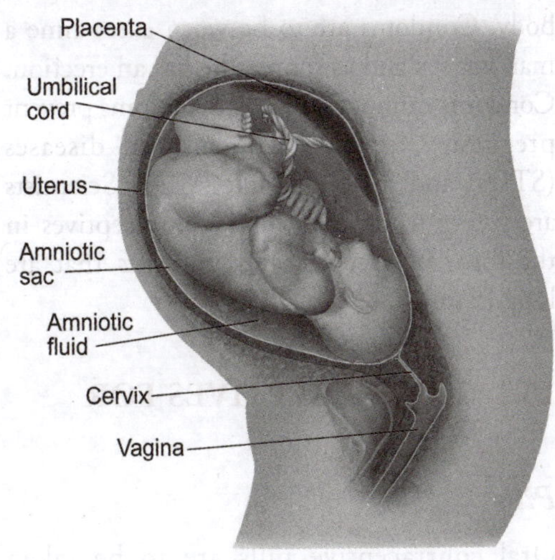

Some methods are discussed in the sections which follow.

15.3 CONTRACEPTIVE FOR MEN

Condoms

A condom is a thin latex sheath to be worn on the penis to prevent semen and pre-ejaculate from coming into contact with a partner's

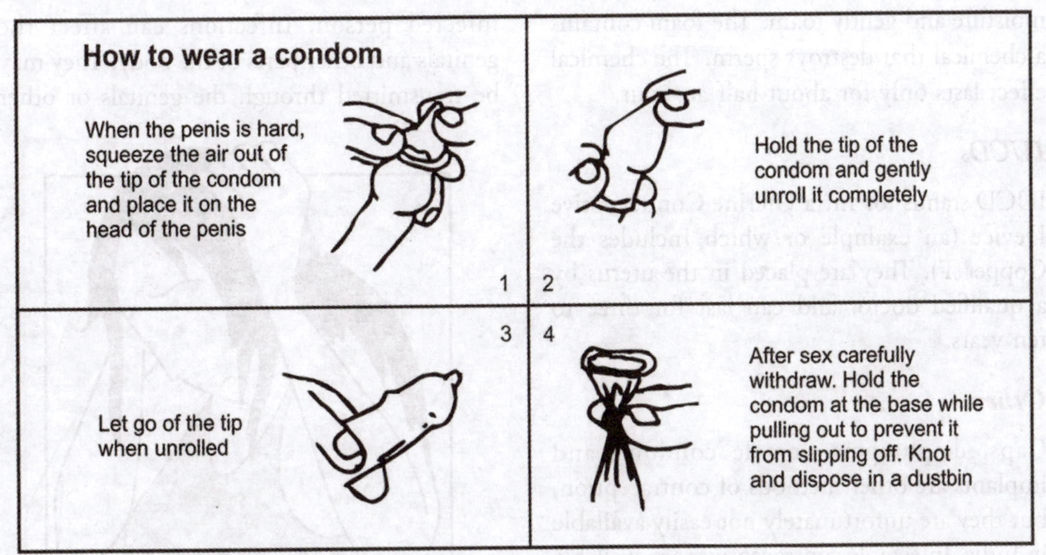

body. Condoms are to be worn every time a man has sex and as soon as he has an erection. Condoms cannot be reused. Condoms prevent pregnancy, sexually transmitted diseases (STDs) and infections like AIDS. Scientists are trying to develop male contraceptives in the form of vaccines and implants that are long-lasting.

15.4 CONTRACEPTIVES FOR WOMEN

Pills

Oral contraceptive pills are to be taken regularly even if a woman is not having sex every day. These pills are available in the market but should be taken only after consulting a gynaecologist as they may not suit some women. Pills are a very reliable form of contraception.

Pessaries

Pessaries are tablets that are inserted into the vaginal opening 10 to 15 minutes before intercourse. Once inserted, they absorb moisture and gently foam. The foam contains a chemical that destroys sperm. The chemical effect lasts only for about half an hour.

IUCDs

IUCD stands for Intra Uterine Contraceptive Device (an example of which includes the Copper T). They are placed in the uterus by a qualified doctor and can last for three to ten years.

Others

Caps, diaphragms, female condoms and implants are other methods of contraception, but they are unfortunately not easily available in India. Injectable contraceptives are available but are controversial due to their side effects. It is advisable to consult a qualified doctor before deciding which contraceptive to use, as some are known to cause side effects.

Sometimes, despite taking precautions, a woman may find herself pregnant without being equipped or prepared for it. In such a situation she has to decide whether to continue the pregnancy or terminate it. This may be a difficult and painful decision to take. If she decides to terminate the pregnancy, she can have an abortion or a Medical Termination of Pregnancy (MTP). MTP is legal in India as long as it is within the first 12 weeks (or, in certain exceptional cases, within the first 20 weeks), and should only be performed by a qualified doctor. If it is done within the first three months then the risk involved is relatively low. The risk increases considerably if done in the fourth or fifth months. It can even be life-threatening.

15.5 DANGEROUS STUFF

Infections can occur because of certain habits, medication, lack of hygiene or sex with an infected person. Infections can affect the genitals and other parts of the body. They may be transmitted through the genitals or other

organs through sexual acts. Some infections that affect the genitals may have nothing to do with sex; they also happen to people who are not sexually active. However, these infections may have symptoms that are similar to those caused by Sexually Transmitted Infections (STIs). The older term for these infections was STDs, meaning Sexually Transmitted Diseases.

The most common signs and symptoms of infections are: a burning sensation while urinating (different from the slight burning if you do not drink enough water); itchiness, redness or a rash in the genital area (or mouth, if you practise oral sex); genital sores; an unusual discharge from the genitals; a foul smell from the genitals.

STIs are usually spread from one person to another through sexual activity. Some STIs have signs and symptoms, but some have no external signs. Some are easily curable if caught at an early stage, some can cause complications later on in life and some can be fatal.

HIV infection is the most dangerous of these as it can be life-threatening. HIV stands for Human Immunodeficiency Virus. It can lead to AIDS, which is the incurable Acquired Immune Deficiency Syndrome. This means that the body's immunity is compromised and weakens till it can no longer fight infections, even minor ones. The person who develops AIDS is prey to and may fall ill from infections and may finally die because the body simply cannot recover.

HIV is present in the body fluids of an infected person; blood and sexual body fluids—semen and vaginal secretions—have the highest concentration of the virus. Certain 'safer sex' activities lower the risk of exchanging infected blood or sexual body fluids (which is the most likely way to spread HIV).

Here are the various ways by which people may be infected with HIV: by blood

transfusion and sharing equipment that allows the transfer of HIV-infected blood (injection needles, etc.); by engaging in unprotected sex—oral, anal or vaginal; and potentially by being born to an HIV-positive woman.

There are no external signs that indicate whether a person is infected with HIV or not. The only way of detecting HIV infection is through a specific blood test. Before taking the test, one must attend 'pre-test counselling' during which information about HIV, the test, the results and their implications are provided and discussed.

After the test, one must attend 'post-test counselling' which focuses on how to deal with the test results, negative or positive. A negative result means that the person is not infected. To remain uninfected, people need to follow some basic precautionary measures. To stay HIV-uninfected:

- Use only blood screened for HIV
- Use disposable needles and syringes
- If sexually active, use 'safer sex' techniques

HIV is not transmitted by hugging, kissing or touching, or by sharing clothes, food, toilets or work spaces. It is not transmitted by mosquito or insect bites either. Anyone can become infected depending on what they do, not who they are. Discriminating against someone on the basis of their HIV status is wrong. People who are HIV positive (infected) need to take good care of themselves in terms of diet, medication, rest and stress control. Emotional and social support are crucial.

15.6 FOUL PLAY!

There are many ways of relating to someone sexually. Some things feel good whereas other things do not. For example, certain forms of contact might make you feel good while others might make you feel dirty, horrible, disgusted, angry or upset. It is for each person to decide what feels good and what does not. Sexual harassment can take many forms: visual, verbal, physical, psychological. Examples include the following forms of behaviour: touching someone without their permission or patting or brushing against someone; leering; indecently exposing genitals or 'flashing' someone without their consent; making inappropriate or malicious sexual jokes, comments, stories or posters; physically assaulting someone; demanding sexual favours or placing someone under increasing pressure to grant sexual favours (this pressure may be explicit or implicit).

Sexual abuse is considered to include any exploitative sexual activity, whether or not it includes physical contact, between you and another person who, by virtue of his or her power over you—due to age, strength, position or relationship—uses you to meet his or her sexual and emotional needs. In very simple terms, this refers to any sexual activity that you do not want.

Some people think that unwanted sexual activity is abuse only when there is physical violence involved. This is not true. Threats, blackmail and the possibility of violence are as frightening as actual physical violence. Just

because someone may not have reacted the way one imagines they should have, it does not mean that 'they wanted to be raped' or that they were 'not really abused'. No matter what a person does (before, during and after), if that person does not want sex, it is abuse and not the assaulted person's fault.

Anyone can be vulnerable to sexual abuse. Both girls as well as boys are at risk. Sexual abuse takes many forms and does not necessarily involve direct physical contact. A sexual act involving forced intercourse is rape. Another term that you have come across is 'sexual harassment'. This is any unwanted attention or action of a sexual nature as mentioned earlier. When someone is sexually abused by a relative it is incestuous abuse.

Studies have shown that most sexual abuse is committed by someone known to the person who was abused, such as, for example, a friend, relative or neighbour. No one 'asks for it'. The fake logic of sexual abuse being motivated by provocative clothing or behaviour is often used by abusers to wash their hands clean of what they have done.

The person who has been abused is not at fault. Abuse involves a serious betrayal of trust and may affect a person's self-esteem and mental and physical health.

Unfortunately, sexual abuse is quite common and many people have experienced it in some form or the other. If it has happened to you, remember that it is not your fault; it is the abuser who did wrong, not you. It does not have to scar you for life; seek help if you are overwhelmed by negative feelings. If you are currently in a situation that you feel might be abusive, speak to someone you trust, try getting out of the situation if you can, try not to be alone with the abuser.

Someone who has been abused needs your support and reassurance, and respect for their wishes and privacy. If you know someone who

is an abuser, do not protect them—they are a danger to other people.

NOTE

1. TARSHI stands for Talking About Reproductive and Sexual Health Issues. Visit the following weblink to read more, or even the entire book: http://www.tarshi.net/downloads/blue-book.pdf. There is an updated version of this book with additional information that is available for purchase at https://zubaanbooks.com/shop/the-blue-book-what-you-want-to-know-about-yourself/.

Bibliography

UNIT 1

Guha, Phulrenu, et al. *Towards Equality: Report on the Status of Women in India*. New Delhi: GOI, Ministry of Education and Social Welfare, 1974. Print.

Levtov Ruti, Nikki van der Gaag, Margaret Greene, Michael Kaufman and Gary Barker. *State of the World's Fathers: A MenCare Advocacy Publication*. Washington, DC: Promundo, Rutgers, Save the Children, Sonke Gender Justice, and the MenEngage Alliance. 2015. Web. 26 February 2019. <https://sowf.s3.amazonaws.com/wp-content/uploads/2015/06/08181421/State-of-the-Worlds-Fathers_23June2015.pdf>.

UNIT 2

'Complan Khata Kya Hain HD–Hindi.' *YouTube*, uploaded by Kraft Heinz India. 28 October 2014. Web. 29 April 2021. <https://www.youtube.com/watch?v=zRmvw1ry8IY>.

UNIT 3

Lukose, Ritty A. *Liberalization's Children: Gender, Youth and Consumer Citizenship in Globalizing India*. New Delhi: Orient BlackSwan, 2010. 59–70. Print.

UNIT 4

'Care Work and Care Jobs for the Future of Decent Work.' *International Labour Organization*. n.d. Web. 22 October 2019. <https://www.ilo.org/global/publications/books/WCMS_633135/lang--en/index.htm>.

Choudhary, Natasha, Asuthosh Tripathy and Beena George. *Women's Economic Contribution through their Unpaid Household Work: The Case of India*. n.d. Web. 15 September 2019. <https://healthbridge.ca/images/uploads/library/India_summary_report_final.pdf>.

'ILO: Women Do 4 Times More Unpaid Care Work Than Men in Asia and the Pacific.' *International Labour Organization*. 27 June 2018. Web. 22 October 2019. <https://www.ilo.org/asia/media-centre/news/WCMS_633284/lang--en/index.htm>.

'India: National Domestic Workers Movement (NDWM).' *International Domestic Workers Federation*. 2 October 2014. Web. 22 October 2019. <https://idwfed.org/en/affiliates/asia-pacific/national-domestic-workers-movement>.

'National Policy on Domestic Workers.' *Press Information Bureau, Government of India, Ministry of Labour & Employment*. 7 January 2019. Web. 29 April 2021. <https://pib.gov.in/Pressreleaseshare.aspx?PRID=1564261>.

UNIT 5

John, Mary E. *Sex Ratios and Gender Biased Sex Selection: History, Debates and Future Directions*. UN Women. 2014. Web. 26 February 2019. <https://docplayer.net/82489280-Sex-ratios-and-gender-biased-sex-selection.html>.

Sen, Amartya. 'More than 100 Million Women are Missing.' *The New York Review of Books*, 37.20 (1990). 20 December 1990. Web. 29 April 2021. <https://www.nybooks.com/articles/1990/12/20/more-than-100-million-women-are-missing/>.

UNIT 6

Biswas, Soutik. 'Why are India's Media Under Fire?' *BBC News*. 12 January 2012. Web. 26 February 2019. <https://www.bbc.com/news/world-asia-india-16524711>.

Kaushik, Martand. 'Missing the Story: Lessons for Indian Journalism from Dalit Mobilisation Online.' *The Caravan*. 1 March 2016. Web. 29 April 2021. <https://caravanmagazine.in/perspectives/missing-the-story-lessons-indian-journalism-dalit-mobilisation-online>.

Muthyam, Kotur, ed. *Nenu Chindula Yellammanu: Chindu Bhagavatham Atma Katha*. Hyderabad: Drusti Publications, 2006. Print.

Naqvi, Tahira. 'The Beguiling Ismat Chugtai, Through Her Own Words.' *The Wire*. 14 August 2015. Web. 29 April 2021. <https://thewire.in/books/the-beguiling-ismat-chugtai-through-her-own-words>.

Satyanarayana, K, and Susie Tharu, eds. *Steel Nibs are Sprouting: New Dalit Writing from South India. Dossier II: Kannada and Telugu*. New Delhi: HarperCollins, 2013. Print.

Tharu, Susie, and K. Lalita, eds. *Women Writing in India: 600 BC to the Present*. Volume 1. New Delhi: OUP, 1991. Print.

UNIT 7

'A "Conversation" Between a Daughter and a Mother.' *Anveshi Research Centre for Women's Studies*. 7 January 2014. Web. 29 April 2021. <http://www.anveshi.org.in/a-conversation-between-a-daughter-and-a-mother/>.

'Action Hero #87' *Blank Noise Action Heroes*. 8 April 2013. Web. 26 February 2019. <http://actionheroes.blanknoise.org/search/label/everything%20I%20want%20to%20say%20to%20my%20harasser>.

'Chai pe ek aur charcha.' *YouTube*, uploaded by Turquoise Tales. 13 December 2015. Web. 26 February 2019. <https://www.youtube.com/watch?v=OTmu62peWw0>.

'Criminal Law (Amendment) Act, 2013.' *National Portal of India*. 22 June 2017. Web. 29 April 2021. <https://www.india.gov.in/criminal-law-amendment-act-2013>

'Handbook on Sexual Harassment of Women at Workplace (Prevention, Prohibition and Redressal) Act, 2013.' *Ministry of Women & Child Development, GOI*. 23 June 2016. Web. 29 April 2021. <https://wcd.nic.in/act/sexual-harassment-women-workplace-preventionprohibition-and-redressal-act-2013>.

'I Never Ask For It.' *Blank Noise*. n.d. Web. 26 February 2019. Web. <http://www.blanknoise.org/ineveraskforit/vision>.

UNIT 8

Choudhary, Natasha, Ashutosh Tripathy and Beena George. 'Women's Economic Contribution through Their Unpaid Household Work: The Case of India.' *HealthBridge*. n.d. Web. 26 February 2019. <https://healthbridge.ca/images/uploads/library/India_summary_report_final.pdf>.

Das, Priyanjana Roy. 'Shanti Devi, India's Only Female Truck Mechanic, Fixes Tyres and Breaks Stereotypes.' *101 India*. n.d. Web. 29 April 2021. <https://www.101india.com/people/shanti-devi-indias-only-female-truck-mechanic-fixes-tyres-and-breaks-stereotypes>.

Dundoo, Sangeetha Devi. 'The History Teller.' *The Hindu*. 2 August 2012. Web. 26 February 2019. <https://www.thehindu.com/features/friday-review/history-and-culture/the-history-teller/article3716916.ece>.

Lahiri, Tripti. 'By the Numbers: Where Indian Women Work.' *The Wall Street Journal*. 14 November 2012. Web. 26 February 2019. <https://blogs.wsj.com/indiarealtime/2012/11/14/by-the-numbers-where-indian-women-work/>.

Lal, Amrith. 'What Munnar Rebellion Says About Kerala's Women Labour.' *The Indian Express*. 18 September 2015. Web. 29 April 2021. <https://indianexpress.com/article/explained/what-munnar-rebellion-says-about-keralas-women-labour/>.

Mallick, Aditi. 'Will Telangana get its First Woman Bus Driver? Meet the Woman for the Job.' *The News Minute*. 5 March 2017. Web. 29 April 2021. <https://www.thenewsminute.com/article/will-telangana-get-its-first-woman-bus-driver-meet-woman-job-58153>.

'Maternity, Paternity at Work.' *International Labour Organization*. n.d. Web. <https://www.ilo.org/wcmsp5/groups/public/---dgreports/---gender/documents/briefingnote/wcms_410183.pdf>

Nair, Supriya. 'Meet Mumbai's Women Firefighters.' *Live Mint*. 6 October 2017. Web. 26 February 2019. <https://www.livemint.com/Leisure/az0tX79tGcvJtiTXL8rhiP/Meet-Mumbais-women-firefighters.html>.

'National Sample Survey Office (NSSO).' *Ministry of Statistics and Programme Implementation, GOI*. 26 February 2019. Web. 29 April 2021. <http://mospi.nic.in/NSSOa>.

'Office of the Registrar General & Census Commissioner, India.' *Ministry of Home Affairs, GOI*. n.d. Web. 26 February 2019. <http://censusindia.gov.in>.

Singh, T. Lalith. 'Ramulamma Makes a Comeback.' *The Hindu*. 1 March 2015. Web. 26 February 2019. <https://www.thehindu.com/news/national/andhra-pradesh/ramulamma-makes-a-comeback/article6947683.ece>.

Subramanian, Lakshmi. 'With Scissors and Razors, in a Man's World.' *The Week*. 7 March 2016. Web. 29 April 2021. <https://www.theweek.in/webworld/features/society/with-scissors-and-razors-in-a-man-world.html>.

Thomas, Suresh P. 'They Sat Down For Their Rights.' *Fountain Ink*. 5 May 2015. Web. 26 February 2019. <https://fountainink.in/reportage/they-sat-down-for-their-rights>.

UNIT 9

Agnes, Flavia. *My Story . . . Our Story of Rebuilding Broken Lives*. 3rd ed. Mumbai: Majlis, 1990. Print.

Golder, Sakti, et al. 'Measurement of Domestic Violence in NFHS Surveys and Some Evidence.' *Oxfam India*. n.d. Web. 29 April 2021. <https://www.oxfamindia.org/sites/default/files/2018-10/WP-Measurement-of-Domestic-Violence-in-National-Family-Health-Survey-surveys-and-Some-Evidence-EN.pdf>.

Invoking Justice. Dir. Deepa Dhanraj. Prod. Women Make Movies, 2011. Film.

Mill, John Stuart. 'The Subjection of Women.' *Early Modern Texts*. n.d. Web. 26 February 2019. <http://www.earlymoderntexts.com/assets/pdfs/mill1869.pdf>.

'National Family Health Survey, India.' *International Institute for Population Sciences*. 31 December 2018. Web. 26 February 2019. <http://rchiips.org/nfhs/>.

'Reworking Gender Relations, Redefining Politics: Nellore Village Women against Arrack.' *Economic and Political Weekly* 28.3–4 (Jan 1993): 87–90. Print.

UNIT 10

K. Lalita, et al. 'Chityala Ailamma.' *'We Were Making History . . .' Life Stories of Women in the Telangana People's Struggle*. New Delhi: Kali for Women, 1989. Print.

Kesavan, C. *Jeevitha Samaram*. (Mal.) Kottayam: D. C. Books, 2010. Print.

Khastagiri, Soudamini. 'Striloker Paricchad' in *Bamabhodini Patrika*. 97.8 (1872): 148–52. Print.

Srilata, K., ed. *The Other Half of the Coconut: Women Writing Self-Respect History, An Anthology of Self-Respect Literature (1928–1936)*. New Delhi: Kali for Women, 2003. Print.

Tharu, Susie and K. Satyanarayana, ed. 'C. K. Janu.' *No Alphabet in Sight: New Dalit Writing from South India, Dossier I: Tamil and Malayalam*. New Delhi: Penguin, 2011. Print.

UNIT 11

Banerjee, Manabi. 'Transgenderism: "Society Can Be Cruel."' *The Guardian*. 14 July 2009. Web. 9 October 2019. <https://www.theguardian.com/world/2009/jul/14/india-gender>.

Bhan, Gautam. 'For All that We May Become: On the Section 377 Verdict.' *The Hindu*. 7 September 2018. Web. 9 October 2019. <https://www.thehindu.com/opinion/lead/for-all-that-we-may-become/article24885398.ece>.

Biswas, Soutik. 'India's First Transgender College Principal.' 27 May 2015. *BBC News*. Web. 9 October 2019. <https://www.bbc.com/news/world-asia-india-32895375>.

'Definitions.' *United Nations Human Rights*. n.d. Web. 19 April 2019. <https://www.unfe.org/definitions>.

Fausto-Sterling, Anne. *Myths of Gender*. Rev ed. Perseus Books (HarperCollins), 1992. Print.

Liang, Lawrence. 'Vocabulary of Justice and Being.' *The Hindu*. 6 February 2016. Web. 9 October 2019. <https://www.thehindu.com/opinion/lead/the-lgbtqi-movement-and-the-supreme-courts-role/article8199176.ece>.

Masci, David, et al. 'Same-Sex Marriage Around the World.' *Pew Research Center*. 17 May 2019. Web. 29 April 2021. <https://www.pewforum.org/fact-sheet/gay-marriage-around-the-world/>

Menon, Nivedita. *Seeing like a Feminist*. New Delhi: Zubaan Books, 2012. Print.

'N. Bengal Needs Someone Who Can Harness Talents: Pinki.' *The Statesman*. 21 August 2013. Web. 9 October 2019. <https://www.thestatesman.com/bengal/n-bengal-needs-someone-who-can-harness-talents-pinki-11319.html/amp>.

'Semenya "Must Not Be Humiliated".' *BBC Sport Athletics*. 11 September 2009. Web. 9 October 2019. <http://news.bbc.co.uk/sport2/hi/athletics/8250469.stm>.

'Writ Petition.' *Orinam.net*. n.d. Web. 9 October 2019. <http://orinam.net/377/wp-content/uploads/2016/06/Johar-UoI-2016.pdf>.

UNIT 12

Kaufman, Michael. 'Working With Men and Boys to Challenge Sexism and End Men's Violence.' *XYOnline*. n.d. Web. 21 29 April 2021. <http://xyonline.net/sites/xyonline.net/files/Kaufman%2C%20Working%20with%20men%20and%20boys.pdf>.

UNIT 13

Kapur, Ratna. 'Rape and the Crisis of Indian Masculinity.' *The Hindu*. 19 December 2012. Web. 14 October 2019. <https://www.thehindu.com/opinion/op-ed/rape-and-the-crisis-of-indian-masculinity/article4214267.ece>.

Lahiri, Manojit. 'Rajesh Khanna: Exit the King of Romance.' *News18*. 12 July 2012. Web. 14 October 2019. <https://www.news18.com/news/india/rajesh-khanna-exit-the-king-of-romance-489077.html>.

Srivastava, Sanjay. 'Taking the Aggression out of Masculinity.' *The Hindu*. 3 January 2013. Web. 14 October 2019. <https://www.thehindu.com/opinion/op-ed/taking-the-aggression-out-of-masculinity/article4266007.ece>.

Tanvir, Kuhu. 'Snapshots of Bollywood Masculinity in the Age of Hindutva.' *University of Pittsburgh Special Affects*. 1 May 2014. Web. 29 April 2021. <https://www.fsgso.pitt.edu/2014/05/snapshots-of-bollywood-masculinity-in-the-age-of-hindutva/>.

Vasudevan, Ravi. *The Melodramatic Public: Film Form and Spectatorship in Indian Cinema*. Ranikhet: Permanent Black, 2010. Print.

UNIT 14

'Alok Dixit.' *Wikipedia*. June 2012. Web. 14 October 2019. <https://en.wikipedia.org/wiki/Alok_Dixit>.

Baweja, Harinder. 'Don't Stare at Me, I Am Human Too: Acid-attack Survivor Laxmi.' *Hindustan Times*. 20 July 2013. Web. 14 October 2019. <https://www.hindustantimes.com/india/don-t-stare-at-me-i-am-human-too-acid-attack-survivor-laxmi/story-I5U4wL8wSBmvNqRREMcQOK.html>.

Bilkis, Maria. 'Mary Kom, Husband, Disclose Their Love Story.' 9 December 2013. Web. 14 October 2019. <https://timesofindia.indiatimes.com/sports/off-the-field/Mary-Kom-

husband-disclose-their-love-story/articleshow/27101229.cms>.

Green, Matt. *Biography Series: Martin Luther King Jr. and Rosa Parks.* Google Play: 2014. eBook.

'Love-letters Like No Other.' *Lokayat.* 10 January 2019. Web. 14 October 2019. <http://lokayat.org.in/love-letters-like-no-other/>.

Mander, Harsh. 'Involved Fatherhood.' *The Hindu.* 25 July 2015. Web. 14 October 2019. <https://www.thehindu.com/opinion/columns/Harsh_Mander/harsh-mander-on-how-much-fathers-matter/article7460405.ece>.

Mani, Ranjan Braj, and Pamela Sardar, eds. *A Forgotten Liberator: The Life and Struggle of Savitribai Phule.* Trans. Sunil Sardar. New Delhi, Mountain Peak: 2008. 39–47. Print.

UNIT 15

'The Blue Book: What You Want to Know about Yourself.' TARSHI. n.d. Web. 29 April 2021. <https://www.tarshi.net/downloads/blue-book.pdf>.